Religions of the World

Expressions of Faith and Pathways to the Divine

Edited by F.C. La Spina

James Madison University

 cognella® | ACADEMIC PUBLISHING

Bassim Hamadeh, CEO and Publisher
Kassie Graves, Director of Acquisitions and Sales
Jamie Giganti, Senior Managing Editor
Jess Estrella, Senior Graphic Designer
Carrie Montoya, Manager, Revisions and Author Care
Natalie Lakosil, Licensing Manager
Kaela Martin and Christian Berk, Associate Editors
Kat Ragudos, Interior Designer

Cover image copyright © Depositphotos/A7880S.

Printed in the United States of America

ISBN: 978-1-5165-1177-8 (pb) / 978-1-5165-1178-5 (br)

 cognella® | ACADEMIC PUBLISHING

Dedication

Chris and Mike were brothers, with Mike being two years older than Chris. The two brothers were very close, grew up in western Virginia, graduated from Virginia Tech, married childhood sweethearts and together ran a 500 acre farm. They built their houses 75 yards from each other and were solid partners as well as brothers.

In between their two houses was a ravine that separated their land. One day, Chris was cultivating some land with his tractor and got a little careless. He accidentally plowed into the levy of a dam that bordered the property, and a day's worth of water came gushing out, in effect forming a river between his property and his brother's. Chris really didn't know what to do. He was pondering the situation when his brother came out to survey what had happened and was overcome with anger. When he saw his brother, he said, "How could you have been so careless? Don't you know this water will draw every mosquito between here and West Virginia?"

"Mike, it was an accident!" Chris replied, to which Mike said, "Accidents are caused by stupid people," and he stormed off into his house.

In most cases, anger will dissipate over time, but not with Mike. As the days went on, his anger intensified. In fact, he refused to acknowledge his brother. He was trying to think of a way to blot the river, as well as his brother, out of his life. All of a sudden it came to him: he would build a fence! A fence which would allow no light in and act as a barrier between himself and his brother.

At that very moment, the doorbell rang. It was a carpenter, with a toolbelt slung over his shoulder. He said, "I'm looking for work—do you think you might have some?"

Mike, with eyes wide open, said, "This is your lucky day!" and he brought the carpenter in the back to explain the project. "Remember," he said, "I want the boards to butt up next to each other so no light will come through."

The carpenter went to take some measurements and then came back. Upon reaching Mike, he said, "How much are you willing to pay?"

Mike said, "A thousand dollars."

The carpenter replied, "I'll tell you what. I'll do it for $500, but you have to agree to leave for three days. And when you come back, I will have built exactly what you need." So Mike paid him half the money up front.

Table of Contents

Introduction   vi

1   **Native American Religions**   2
    by Kenneth Melo
    Chapter review questions

2   **African Traditional Religions**   26
    by Mutombo Nkulu-N'Sengha;
    ed. Miguel A. De La Torre
    Chapter review questions

3   **Studying Hinduism in Practice**   44
    by Hillary Rodrigues
    Chapter review questions

4   **Buddhism and Jainism**   54
    by Eugene F. Gorski
    Chapter review questions

5   **Sikh Dharam**   74
    by Pashaura Singh
    Chapter review questions

6   **Background to Daoism**   94
    Background to Daoism by Livia Kohn
    Chapter review questions

7   **Chinese Philosophy III: Confucianism**   110
    by Ray Billington
    Chapter review questions

8   **What is Shinto?**   126
    by Inoue Nobutaka
    Chapter review questions
    Overview of Shinto History

9   **Zoroaster and His Teachings**   136
    by Mary Boyce
    Chapter review questions

10   **Reform, Orthodox, and Conservative Judaisms, Zionism**   146
    Judaism, the Basics
    by Jacob Neusner
    Chapter review questions

11   **Christianity and the Divine**   160
    by James Adair
    Chapter review questions

12   **Islam and God**   180
    by Oliver Leaman
    Chapter review questions

Figuring he was now $500 to the good, Mike took his family to the city for the weekend, staying at a hotel, going to a show, and taking them out to dinner. On Sunday evening they headed back, Mike all excited about seeing his new fence.

Mike drove into his driveway, went around back, and that's when it hit him. Instead of a fence, there was a bridge spanning the stream, linking his property to his brother's. And I don't mean any bridge—this bridge could have been on the cover of *Virginia Living* magazine, as it featured benches and shrubs. It was truly a crafted work of art.

Now remember that, even though the bridge was beautiful, Mike wanted a fence. He was livid. He clasped his hands into a fist and was ready to hit something, but then he saw his brother coming across the bridge. Chris exclaimed, "Mike, here I thought you were mad! All the time you were planning to build a bridge to join our houses together!" And he hugged his brother. Mike, overcome and feeling reflective, hugged his brother back. Mike said, "This bridge is truly what we needed." Chris, by the way, paid the other half of the fee.

Now the carpenter was packing up his tools when Chris and Mike said, "Hey, don't leave! We're having a party tonight on the bridge in your honor! We're inviting the whole neighborhood, get you a lot of business!" The carpenter shook his head and said, "No, gotta move on—too many other bridges yet to build."

The above story is adapted from "The Sower's Seeds" by Fr. Brian Cavanaugh, T.O.R. It is told in the Franciscan tradition, and legend has it that if a Franciscan story isn't true, it should be! I've told it many times and am dedicating this book to the premise of the story: It is only through building bridges between those of other faiths that we can truly achieve understanding and harmony.

F.C. La Spina, MTS
Editor

Introduction

It seems that ever since man has walked the earth—which is in itself sometimes a religious question—people have been influenced by what may be referred to as the divine. We have imagined something greater than ourselves, and almost everyone has speculated on what happens to us upon our death. The funny thing is that no one has any real clue about that speculation.

The word religion comes from the Latin word *religio*, which refers to the fear or awe one feels in the presence of the divine—a spirit or god. It is interesting to note that in Roman Catholicism, one of the gifts of the Holy Spirit (based on Paul's writings) is fear or awe of the Lord.

That definition of religion being as it may, religion has come to mean—most likely due to practicality—a standard of organized beliefs that stem from a certain faith tradition. For the most part, and this is very much in general, for a religion to call itself a religion, it has to have three things: A Creed, A Code, and A Cult. Let me elaborate on this point.

First of all, a **creed**: A religion has to have a set of beliefs or it simply cannot be considered a religion. The one which comes to mind most easily is the Nicene Creed, which originated roughly 1800 years ago and is used by the majority of mainline Christian Churches. It is repeated by many denominations each week and serves to reaffirm what Christians believe as a people. Similarly, Islam has the Shahada, which affirms their belief in Allah as well as the prophet Muhammed. Without a creed, a religion could not stand for or represent anything. Therefore, it is an essential element in a tradition being referred to as a religion. Think of it this way: How could someone be persuaded to become part of a religion if there were no answer to the question of what was believed? The Creed serves as sort of a launching pad for a religion.

Second, a **code**: Religion is generally associated with how one lives his or her life. It has been said that all of the major religions have some version of the Golden Rule—which originates in Matthew's gospel—as part of their moral code. People are considered religious not just because of how devout they are in services or rituals, but how they live out their lives as well. With a belief system comes a way of living out that belief system.

Third, a **cult**: A religion, for the most part, has to have some kind of ritual associated with it, whether it be celebration of sacraments in Christianity, the Amrit ceremony in Sikhism, or the Bar Mitzvah in Judaism. Some sort of ceremony must be part of religiosity. This can be elaborate—such as the Greek Orthodox mass—or very simple, like a Friends meeting in which people sit in silence for sometimes an hour. Ritual has to have some part in religion because it is all part of divination, which will be discussed later.

All of the above raises the question of what religion has done for the world and why mankind has sought it so vehemently, sometimes to a violent end.

There are some other characteristics religions hold in common which have given them impact and influence on the world. First of all, they usually, but not always, deal with an unseen world—i.e. demons, spirits, or ancestors. One need only look at the Judeo-Christian belief in the afterlife to see this. Second, religions usually have a way of communing with the unseen world through ritual—this is sometimes called divination. Third, generally there is a system of scripture and hierarchy of priests and temples in which to worship. Fourth, most religions have some statement about the hereafter: either reincarnation or, as in Christianity, resurrection. Fifth, they have a moral code (see above), and sixth, they have attracted a following.

Let me mention something about the above: it seems that for a religion to take hold, it has to have staying power or longevity. This characteristic of surviving through adversity and still being around for centuries seems to give religions their credibility. This is also probably why religions that are new undergo great persecution. All one need do is look at the book of Acts in the Christian scriptures. Judaism had been around for 2000 years and was therefore accepted. Christianity, called "The Way," became the new scapegoat.

When we look at a religion, we have to look at various issues and answer some basic questions. What culture did the religion emerge from? As we know, traditions are influenced by the environment in which they grow. Judaism came out of a culture in which mercy and forgiveness were considered to be for the weak. Therefore, the Hebrew scriptures contain much about punitive, violent action against the violator. Also, was there a founder? What contributed to the discovery? For instance, Muhammed received the revelation of the Quoran during a time in which Saudi Arabia was in the midst of polytheism.

We also have to ask ourselves, are there texts from which to base our belief in this religion? How has the religion progressed, and in some instances changed, over time?

In just the same way that religion has caused as much good as destruction in our world, it still remains the most pervasive phenomenon of culture. It seems to be the basis for what people will live for, stand for, and even die for—and they will defend their beliefs and challenge anyone who won't allow their traditions or, in some cases, who think differently. In this regard, it is truly, as Paul Tillich said, the ultimate concern. Unfortunately, some religious differences are so great that people resort to violence and even go to war.

This collection, however, while being realistic, will take the high road when talking about religion and religious differences. We will try and examine the benefits and good that various religious traditions have given to the world.

Earliest Theories on the Origin of Religion

Someone once said that there are two types of people—those who have an abundant faith and those who have none. This theory can apply to how one considers the beginning of religion. Some believe that religion is nothing more than a crutch that man made up to help him through the pitfalls of life, providing hope. Others, namely Karl Marx, felt that religion was an opiate by which to control the masses. Still others feel that religion was created to justify behavior—i.e., killing a people in the name of faith. Those who have a grounded belief generally feel that their religion has been revealed by the actions or words of a chosen person. For people of the Book—Jews, Christians, and Muslims—this is in the persons of Abraham, Jesus, and Muhammed. For Buddhists (literally "the awakened ones") it is in the teachings of Siddhartha Gautama. For Hindus, it is not so much a revelation as it is an understanding of how the universe works. It is safe to say that those who have an impact on religion embrace it with passion, not from a lukewarm posture.

Different Forms of Religion

Base Religions

For the most part, the terms *base* or *basic religions* refer to those religions that are indigenous to a region or area and cannot be traced back to a founder or revealer. Simply put, the belief is that the people have just always done these things for as long as people can remember. One could put "The Lottery" by Shirley Jackson in this category.

This category embraces beliefs such as animism (everything has a spirit), totemism (a symbolic allegiance to an animal by a tribe), polytheism (belief in many gods), and henotheism (belief in the possibility of many gods). Because of the loose structure and lack of defined revelation in these basic religions, one can see how religions such as Christianity and Islam made inroads and took hold. Saudi Arabia at the time of Muhammed was strewn with polytheistic beliefs, and Christianity was born out of pagan emperor worship.

Religions from India

Hinduism, Jainism, Buddhism, and Sikhism all hail from India and are similar in that they seek escape from this world either in one life or in several—or hundreds of—lives. Each believes in many gods (except for Sikhism, which takes its God from Islam), but the primary goal is release, either by actions, meditation, or a prayerful life. This is one fundamental difference between eastern religious thought and its western counterpart—reincarnation verses resurrection.

Religions from the Far East

With regard to China and Japan, the three pervasive faith traditions are Taoism, Confucianism, and Shinto. Each has a belief in many gods, as well as ancestor veneration, honor of nature, and honor of country (Shinto).

Religions of the Middle East

Sometimes referred to as the cradle of civilization, the Middle East has produced the religious traditions that have affected the world the most taken as a whole. Zoroastrianism, Judaism, Christianity, Islam, and Baha'i all stem from this region. All believe that people have only one life and are judged in accordance with it. And all believe in one Supreme Creator God—in essence, the God of Abraham. Christianity and Islam alone make up roughly 60% of the world's population.

Religion: A Force for Good and Peace or Evil and Violence?

Religion and violence at first glance seem oxymoronic. But the fact is that more people have been killed in the name of religion than for anything else. However, we have to distinguish between religious acts which serve as punishment for those people believed to be evil; violent acts which are, in and of themselves, religious; and clashes between religious communities/traditions. We need only to look to New England and the witch trials, which somehow justified violence. Nazi Germany, at least partly, justified the Holocaust by calling Jews "Christ killers." In this respect, the violence seems to be the result of finding a scapegoat.

When religious communities exhibit violent behavior toward one another, it usually is the result of one of two things: either a group has threatened another group by believing differently or political agendas are masked by religion. Examples of this would be the violence in Northern Ireland in the 1980s, which resulted in people going on hunger strikes. The surface reason in Belfast might have been Catholicism against Protestantism, but the underlying root cause was clearly Irish freedom from British rule. The Crusades of the Middle Ages were ostensibly to retrieve the Holy Land from Islam, but the cause was as political as it was religious.

At times there is backlash—If Hindus defile a mosque by killing a pig in it, Muslims may come back and sacrifice a cow in a Hindu Temple. At this point it becomes difficult to find religion in any of these actions as foolish pride and personal agendas take over. As someone wise once said, religion can bring out the noblest traits of humanity but can also motivate and justify the most twisted and depraved among us. For this reason we must look at becoming a pluralistic society when it comes to belief—it is the only way as a people we will survive. This text contains material that lends itself to this belief.

The Need for Religion Today—Yes or No?

Society is beginning to ask itself: do we really need religion today? Another less severe way to put it is to ask whether or not religion has a place in modern life.

Paul Tillich (1886–1965), a German theologian, gave the world many definitions for which he became well known—defining religion as the "Ultimate Concern," the "ground of being" when discussing God, and "the new being" when discussing Christ. But while definitions help, they fall short when it comes to religion becoming part of who a person has become. For instance, do we attend a house of worship because we are told to through a set of rules set up to be a hierarchy, or have we truly made it our ultimate reason for living? Do we attend halfheartedly—on Christian and Jewish high holy days—or has worship taken a front seat in our everyday existence? Is God truly a ground of being for us or something that we reach out to when we have a need? Do we practice a religion in order to "get to heaven," which is in and of itself self-serving? The final question is, can religion get us out of our egocentricity into a state of other-centeredness—which was a characteristic of those through which the major religions were revealed?

We have seen the decline of some organized religions ("I don't get anything out of it") and the emergence of some others. The so-called "megachurches" have begun to make themselves known, drawing upwards of 30,000 people. These churches are for the most part non-denominational Christian, but they offer an intangible to the masses—they all feel good when they leave. People literally fight to get into these places, partly because of the message and partly for their entertainment factor. This should not come as a surprise: our movie industry has never been bigger and the Super Bowl is watched by half of humanity.

One factor that seems to have had an effect on the faith of people, and ultimately their involvement in religion, is the retreat experience. Regardless of the faith or denomination within that faith, whether it be the Vision Quest of Native Americans or the Cursillo experience of Christians, a voluntary time away with one's faith tradition can serve as a spark to get people thinking seriously and more deeply about what they believe. Theologians have begun to call this the "leap of faith," which causes people to fully embrace what they have been a part of—totally on their own volition.

Still others have said religion is needed for the morality it teaches. Every major faith discussed in this text has some version of the Golden Rule (Matthew 6), and, in some more than others, the body is seen as the temple of the Holy, which leads to living a moral, chaste, and monogamous life. Could these values exist without religion in their corner? Maybe, but religion gives mankind a basis from which to start and from which to refer back.

Why Study Religion?

This fundamental question leads to another question: Why don't we leave the study of religion to religious communities? After all, that's where it belongs! While that argument may hold some weight with some, it doesn't provide for objectivity. A person teaching a faith that he or she is part of in a religious setting by definition cannot be objective. He or she is simply expounding and proselytizing. On the other hand, when religion is approached as an academic study or discipline, it makes no difference what faith tradition the researcher is—it is merely an objective study.

To fully understand, appreciate, and gain insight, a person studying religion has to be without bias. In our American society—which is roughly 50% Christian—it is almost impossible to be objective when learning about a faith that is foreign to us. However, as searchers for the facts, we must strive to be empirical and remain completely objective. There is a huge difference between a study of religion and a religious study.

Religion has been seen by some to be a projection of human needs—i.e., a primitive community needs rain to grow crops, so they submit to the god of rain, which they either created or has been handed down to them; human sacrifice is committed to appease a god that a community fears; a person is designated a "sin eater" to symbolically take away the sins of a person who has died. Each of these situations speaks to a need met through a religious statement or practice. Greek and Roman mythology exhibit this perfectly as well—Atlas holds up the world and Neptune commands the sea.

Ludwig Feuerbach (1804–1872) said that religions were essentially projections of the wishes and needs of humanity. According to Feuerbach, people tend to see themselves as helpless and dependent when faced with the challenges of life. They therefore seek to overcome their problems through imagining a power of goodness who can help them. Put another way, humanity is not created in the image of God, but God is created in the image of idealized humanity. He believed that people seek in heaven what they cannot find on earth. Thus, religion is reduced to a form of wishing. Feuerbach further believed that when people become knowledgeable or powerful, religion is replaced by technology and politics.

Obviously, the above author is coming from an atheistic standpoint, but he does make some interesting points. For instance, is religion still viable when it is reduced to merely asking for what we want? Isn't that the same as believing in one giant benefactor who gives us everything? For the Christian, Jesus accepted the cross even though he could have run away, which proves that this faith—which is based on his teaching—has nothing to do with selfishness and everything to do with selflessness. In the case of many, even when it comes to religion, the question that remains is, "How can I get what I want?"

The famous author Karl Marx stated, "Man makes religion, religion does not make man ... it is the sigh of the oppressed creature, the heart of a heartless world ... it is the opium of the people." Marx was trying to say that religion offers hope and can be used as manipulation, or opium, if you will. This is seen most vividly in some cult situations in which people are asked to give everything they own for a great reward—either monetary or a place in heaven. To be sure, religion has been used for unscrupulous reasons and will continue to be as long as people seek escape.

Theories abound calling religion a crutch for people who can't stand on their own two feet and saying that when one matures he or she can face the world without God or religion (Sigmund Freud). However, people of religious faith are not all in it for self-serving reasons. Countless millions sacrifice much of their lives for the benefit of mankind and not for any personal after-death benefit. They are simply living a religious life and following a moral code. Their philosophy is that whatever happens after this life is up to God. I call that more of a realistic faith than a self-serving one.

There needs to be something said at this point regarding two concepts: religion and martyrdom and religion and being self-serving. First, martyrdom seems to be an integral part of many religions—to be a martyr is to be, in effect, a witness to the faith by what a person says and does. In the Roman Catholic baptismal rite, parents and godparents are asked to be an example to the child being baptized through the witness of their faith "by what they say and do" (Roman Canon Baptismal Rite). However, the term "martyr" has come to mean someone who actually dies for his or her faith and, by so doing, becomes an eternal witness inspiring others.

Some witnesses die for questionable causes and even seek suicide as a way of becoming a martyr. Others decide to take unwilling others with them; a case in point would be the suicide bombings of 9-11. The true sincere martyr, however, faces the adversary without fear and accepts death if that's what it takes to advance the cause. The martyr does not include other unwilling people in the action. From the Christian perspective, Jesus was a true martyr—going to Jerusalem in the midst of Passover and turning over the Temple tables— and faced both the Roman government and the Jewish religious hierarchy. Mahatma Gandhi exhibited martyrdom behavior when he stood up to Great Britain in a non-violent protest and was killed by an assassin's bullet. Martin Luther King, who fashioned his actions off of Gandhi, was martyred during the Civil Rights Movement. What was unique about these three individuals was that they didn't back down, but in fact embraced their roles as martyrs.

The second, and polar opposite, view of religiosity is being self-serving. We live in a society today that is strewn with two things—comfort and speed. We communicate at the touch of a button, and we seek to avoid struggle. And we like what we like. I would submit that this is why people will "shop" for a good preacher or seek a house of worship that fulfills their needs. To a great extent, religion competes with other facets of our society, and much of it is based on entertainment. The obligation card works for fewer and fewer these days, and people will seek a "product" that serves them the best. As harsh as that sounds, it is a function of today's society. The question all people have to ask themselves is: are you one who seeks to serve for the benefit of mankind (the extreme among us becoming martyrs) or do you wish to be served?

Religious Response

Religious affiliations can be sources of both comfort and conflict. Religion in its purest form can provide people with meaning and consolation in difficult times of life. I can recall being summoned to the hospital at 3:00 a.m. for the wife of a man dying of liver failure. She only wanted to know if, when he died, he would be with God.

However, with the new globalization making our world smaller than ever before, there has arisen an urgency to understand others' beliefs. For many people around the world, religion is the central aspect of meaning in their lives. Religious experience may inspire courage and charity, but may also breed hatred and violence toward others. In general, the latter is caused by people behaving in their own self interest or trying to shape the divine to suit their own purposes.

Although we look at a religion as a way to communicate with a divine being or the supernatural, Buddhism qualifies as a religion and has neither of these characteristics. Perhaps we could substitute the term "sacred" for "divine" when speaking about being in a religious presence. In this one example, we can see how difficult a religious response can truly be.

Basic Religious Thought

Mythology

When we use the terms *myth* or *mythology*, we immediately think of a falsehood. But one should be careful to note that there is a huge difference between fact and truth, and many myths, while lacking in the facts, possess a great deal of truth. For instance, in the story of Pandora's Box, it makes very little difference whether or not there was a real Pandora or if she even had a box. What is important is the truth the story tells us—that the temptation of being curious can have serious consequences. The same can be said of the Garden of Eden story in Genesis 2. It makes very little difference if one believes in an actual Adam and Eve and an actual Garden; what is important is the question, faced with the same choice and temptation as the two of them, what would we have done? It has been said that a well structured myth contains more truth than factual evidence. Many pieces of religious literature—Judeo-Christian scriptures and Shinto writings, among others—have within them learning points disguised in myth.

Magic

Many non-religious people, and that is not said in a disparaging way, tend to equate magic with religion. After all, you ask for something and—Presto!—you get it. If people reduce religion to merely asking for things and expecting something in return, they truly have crossed over into what might be termed magic. This is not to say that petition prayer has no place in religion; after all, many people practice only this type of prayer. The problem enters when one either gets what they want, or they leave or turn away from the religion. It is clearly a form of manipulation, and that is the root of magic.

Religion, on the other hand, is about asking for guidance and strength to somehow find within ourselves the solution—on our own merit. Clearly, we are a results-oriented people: if something happens that we like, God loves us. However, if the opposite happens, we doubt his love or even at times his existence. One thing that should be remembered is that in the three Abrahamic religions (the People of the Book), at no time does the deity in question say things would be easy or that life would not contain struggles. The rule of thumb is that if one is looking for a quick fix, one is most likely on the magic bandwagon.

So why, one might ask himself, is anyone religious? If we don't necessarily get what we want (Jesus did not run from the cross, but he certainly did not want it), why be religious? There seem to be various reasons why people seek a religion or to lead a religious life. First, religion provides a moral compass for a certain lifestyle. Second, it states a belief, something on which people can rely. And third, there is a certain ritual component that puts people some way in contact with the eternal. Notice that the truly religious person does not expect anything from the deity. Unlike magic, a religious person does his or her best and worships the deity merely because that deity exists in one's mind and heart. A truly religious person is not self-centered but other-centered. Instead of "If I do this and this will I get to heaven," the religious person might ask, "How can I make this world a better place by practicing my religion?"

Divination

The practice of divination is very much a part of many religious traditions, as it deals with predicting the future and therefore carries with it many "shaman"-like qualities. In ancient Rome, a *haruspex* would read the entrails of animals to see what the future held. Even in the Hebrew Scriptures, prophets were called on to choose the king through sacred dice, a form of divination. As the word "priest" has evolved, the word now describes in many faith traditions an intermediary between the human and divine, and not a soothsayer or clairvoyant.

Rites of Passage

Key parts of many religious and even secular societies are rituals or rites of passage. Generally, these rites deal with the main parts of a person's life—birth, puberty, marriage, and death. Societies use these times to mark transition from one stage to the next, and in so doing see the faith tradition permeate through the entire life of the individual.

At birth, Judaism celebrates being one with the covenant by having each male circumcised on his eighth day. Females join the covenant through their fathers. At its very root, this symbolizes complete faith in God, as it is defilement of a body part. Today, this ritual has turned into a secular procedure, which some believe protects the child from disease. In the more ritualistic Christian churches, babies are baptized with water, following the command of Jesus. In some more primitive cultures, a rite of passage might be an ordeal of some kind. For instance, in some Native American tribes, young males who are going through puberty are encouraged to go on a Vision Quest, which might show their ability to withstand physical and emotional hardship for a three- or four-day period.

It is worth pointing out here that rites or rituals of passage usually involve critical points in a person's life and, correspondingly, these crisis points are when religion is sought out. Some rites of passage, for instance getting a driver's license, are a passage but secular in nature. Depending on the severity of the faith, religious passage rites take on different weight for different people or different societies.

Taboos

In some societies, certain actions are to be avoided in order to be faithful to the religious tradition. One of the most familiar taboos is the avoidance of pork by the Muslim or Jewish person. This taboo, although taken seriously, is actually based on dietary law and for health reasons. In some cultures, touching a dead person is considered unclean, as is associating with women who are in their menstrual cycle. Some ultra-Orthodox Hasidic Jews consider it taboo to even touch a woman other than one's wife. While this is not necessarily considered a taboo, the Roman Catholic Church used to forbid its members to eat meat on Friday in observance of Jesus's death. Still other cultures see twins as taboo, while at the same time some see them as a blessing.

Sacrifice

One of the oldest expressions of religious ritual is that of the sacrifice. We see in Leviticus that the Hebrews offered sacrifices of different animals depending on the severity of their offenses. While animals are a common form of sacrifice, grains and milk products have often been used. These sacrifices are for the precise reason to appease the gods. At times, there has been what is called a "shared sacrifice," in which some commodity is left for the gods and the rest is consumed by the person who made the offering.

Ancestor Worship

Most religious services wind up in one way or the other at a grave or final resting place. A Christian may have what is called an internment service; a Jewish person may have Kaddish prayers prayed over his or her grave. We put flowers on a tomb for one reason—to honor those who have gone before us. Probably the most common element among religions is the tradition of reverence for family members who have passed away. Native Americans believe that people really don't die, but that their spirits live on through the people they touched. On Sunday afternoons, people visit the graves of family who have gone before them.

Symbolism

The last introductory item I wish to deal with is the use of symbols in religion. When you think about religion—almost every type of religion—you think of symbolism. Perhaps this is because symbols evoke thoughts of what the religion means. For instance, the cross was an instrument of execution in ancient Rome and other countries. However, many Christians wear crosses around their necks and even have the symbol hanging up in their homes. The symbol has been transformed from just a method of killing to a symbol of hope for those who believe in the resurrected Jesus. In Buddhism, the symbol of the wheel with eight spokes around it becomes a symbol for the eight-fold path to Nirvana. In Sikhism, the Khanda is the symbol of complete Sikh belief and implies that the sword does not have to be an instrument of violence.

Symbols permeate our culture; from stop and yield signs to the American flag, it isn't merely the object itself, but the symbolism behind it. For instance, to a child, the American flag may conjure up the fourth of July, swimming, and a picnic, while to a veteran of war it may evoke an entirely different image and meaning. Religion is the same way, affecting people in different ways—for some a religious symbol is merely a signpost, while to others it touches the very fabric of their being.

As we embark on this collection of religious studies, let us remember that for the most part religion has provided a moral compass for much of the world, given people a ritualistic way of celebrating, and helped to join the human and the divine in cultures. Also, I am deeply indebted to the Hopfe and Woodward text *Religions of the World* (Pearson), which is the textbook I used for the previous five years to teach World Religions.

1 Native American Religions

Kenneth Mello

Introduction

This chapter seeks to examine Native American religions as adaptive, flexible, culturally-localized traditions which have shaped native responses to historical and cultural changes across a broad spectrum of both time and space. One of the first things we should realize is that the term 'religion' is elusive in terms of its definition (see Introduction and Chapter 1 How to study religion in the modern world). What might be considered religion or religious activity within one group, community, or culture would not have the same consideration among other groups. Rather than looking for 'truth' in the study of religion, then, we should be looking for an objective understanding of how a tradition or faith might function, from the inside, according to its followers. This chapter will examine Native American religions as not just sets of beliefs, but calls to action and agency, based on long-held cultural values and experiences.

Historically, Native American religions (it is relevant to note here that there is no term that connotes the concept of 'religion' in any Native American language, as it was not and is not understood as a concept separate from daily life) have not fared well in competition with mainstream, Western religious traditions. They have been seen as polytheistic, paganistic, and sometimes as 'devil worship'. Yet these understandings reveal little more than a misunderstanding and misconception of how religious and spiritual activity functioned and was understood within native communities.

What does it mean to say that Native Americans have a unique way of looking at the world? Vine Deloria Jr., probably the pre-eminent scholar in the study of Native American religions, has noted that there are two types of philosophies which orient human societies: there are those types of people who orient their lives around the 'idea of history', and there are those who orient their lives around 'the idea of nature'. This chapter will attempt to clarify these terms, and then examine the ways in which such a localized, culturally contextualized relationship with place has shaped native agency right up to the present.

> If we believe that religion has a presence in human societies in any fundamental
> sense, then we can no longer speak of universal religions in the customary manner.
> Rather we must be prepared to confront religion and religious activities in new and
> novel ways.
>
> (Deloria, 2003: 64)

Western religious traditions, such as Christianity and Judaism, are understood to be linear in their orientation—they place all of human history on an established timeline, and trace important events, including creation, back to that timeline in order to make sense out of them. Native American religious traditions, on the other hand, are understood to be spatial in their orientation—they place greatest emphasis on the places where things have happened, and tend to devalue the need to define events and activities according to a specific timeline. We need to begin to understand exactly how these concepts of linear and spatial function to both define traditions and shape the ways in which peoples view the world and their place in it. This will be critical to understanding Native American religions and how they have functioned to define groups of people and their understanding of the larger questions of life.

The first goal of this chapter, then, is to begin to unravel what exactly Native American religions were and are about—how they function within communities and cultures, how they are similar to and different from other types of religions, what is distinctly unique about them, and how they continue to adapt, change, and function within the lives of contemporary native peoples today.

Linear and Circular Orientations

Although somewhat simplistic, one of the best ways to see what is unique about the philosophical underpinnings of Native American religions is in comparison to other 'types' of religions. The common markers of distinction which have been drawn have been between religious systems which are linear, historical and temporal in nature, and those which are local, contextual, and spatially oriented around a relationship with a defined physical place.

Linear traditions typically focus on time, and assume that time proceeds in a logical, linear fashion. As such, people and institutions are judged according to their progress over time, an idea which traces its origins back to various realms of both science and philosophy, including Enlightenment environmentalism and Darwinism. In its application to religion, such a philosophical orientation leads to traditions which place near absolute value on both time and human history, but which tend to devalue or denigrate the role and value of the natural world, and the places where events occur. The 'divine plan' is thus worked out through a series of historical events, which can be neatly plotted along a linear timeline, each one progressing from the event before it. In such a view, revelation is historical, and the present is focused on cementing and transmitting dogma.

Oppositionally, spatial traditions, like those of Native Americans, are those in which advocates see a unique value and power in the natural world, and orient themselves and their cultures to it. Spatial traditions typically look to experience, rather than dogma, and are religious systems that are triggered by long-standing relationships with places, typically among small cultural groups within defined geographical areas. They are local in context, do not purport to have any type of universal, historical message, and see revelation as a continuous process occurring in the world around them to which the individual and group must both attune themselves.

> In circular philosophy, all things are related and involved in the broad scope of Indian life. As part of their life ways, the indigenous peoples of the Americas have studied the Earth, observed the heavenly bodies and contemplated the stars of the universe. The Mayans recorded a calendar based on the number of new moons in a year. The Lakota completed an astronomy about the heavenly bodies, and the Muscogee Creeks incorporated the stars and galaxies into their ethos of the universe . . . Native peoples looked for the constants in life as a part of the universe. They understood life to occur in cycles and those powers of nature formed definite patterns that occurred, repeating themselves.
>
> (Fixico, 2003: 42–43)

As an example of these two ways of seeing the world and placing the human in it, let us think about the variety of creation narratives which exist. The Biblical creation is understood by many to be a true, historical event—the beginning event of a linear time sequence in which the divine plan is to be worked out. The natural world is seen as corrupted, and man is given authority to rule both animals and nature in whatever way suits his needs and desires. This monogenetic creation narrative then lays out a series of historical events, each linked in linear progression, in which what is important is human beings and their events, and what is not is nature and everything else.

Native American creation narratives are typically not concerned with pinning down, in terms of time, the beginnings of anything, but rather tend to be more concerned with explaining how a given group of people have come to inhabit the place that they do, and what their relationship with this place is meant to look like. These traditions view all of creation as good, as having their own roles and functions, which are often separate from human needs and desires, and locate the human within the larger web of natural systems, not outside of it. They are flexible and adaptive to both cultural and historical changes, and thus resistant to strict dogma. They also typically blur the lines between past, present, and future, and instead use experiences and lessons from the past, applied to contemporary situations, with an eye on the future, to shape actions and ideas.

Native American Religions and Western Colonialism

In both missionization and the various Native American responses to it, native people employed agency and their spiritual and cultural flexibility to respond to colonialism and to survive it. History is not simply victors and victims, but rather action and reaction, and native people fell back on their spiritual beliefs and values in order to know how to respond to their changing world, both pre- and post-contact.

Missionization

Almost from the moment of contact, Europeans began the effort to force Native Americans to give up their own religious traditions and beliefs and to adopt European models (particularly Christianity) instead. Many of the early explorers of the 'New World' were accompanied by religious missionaries, and missionization quickly became part of the larger process of 'civilizing the Indians' which would drive much of the activity focused towards Native Americans in the early days of European and American colonization.

> Prior to contact Native people had their own cultural and religious systems that sustained their physical and spiritual well-being for centuries. However, with the arrival of European colonizers came the suppression and prohibition of traditional Native religious practices. In an attempt to 'civilize' the Indians the colonizers sought to undermine traditional ways of worship. Europeans challenged the authority of religious leaders and banned Native worship, penalizing and/or jailing those who continued their traditional ways.
>
> (Vernon, 1999: 76)

It was these early missionaries who began to negatively label Native American religious traditions as childish, simplistic, and primitive (these were the kinder labels) or pagan, demonic, and devil worship (these were some of the harsher labels). These ideologies would frame the ways in which average Euro-American colonists and settlers would view Native Americans, and would lead to missionization and Americanization moving from the realm of ideology to national policy. Missionaries often blurred the lines between messages of faith and messages of colonization and acculturation, and typically sought to achieve conversion through the larger process of forced cultural change. They actively worked to promote religious, economic, political and social change in Native American communities, and often bought into the ideology of cultural and religious superiority which drove colonization as a whole.

Luckily, a great deal of primary source material remains from these missionaries (journals, diaries, church writings, etc.) which allows us a view into what missionaries were thinking and saying about Native American traditions, and how natives were responding to this effort to wipe out their traditions and replace them with new ones. Many native people accepted missionization, but we want to look closer at the reasons why, for they are varied, and sometimes have little to do with actual beliefs or acceptance of faith. In fact, historically, it is safe to say that missionization failed in its efforts to provide complete conversion and the elimination of Native American religious systems. Despite their flexibility and willingness to incorporate some of this 'new religion' into their already well-established traditions, most Native Americans were unwilling to accept a singular, abstract deity, but rather sought to incorporate this new god into the gods they already accepted in the world around them. Many Native Americans also actively resisted the 'global truth' of Christianity when it did not make sense in comparison to their own cultural beliefs, thus enacting agency in choosing the parts they liked, and rejecting the parts they didn't, rather than wholeheartedly rejecting one for another. This would be typical of native responses to religious change from the contact period to the present.

> The question that the so-called world religions have not satisfactorily resolved is whether or not religious experience can be distilled from its original cultural context and become an abstract principle that is applicable to all peoples in different places and at different times. The persistent emergence of religious movements and the zeal with which they are pursued would seem to suggest that cultural context, time and place are the major elements of revelation and the content is illusory. If not illusory, it is subject to so many cultural qualifications that it is not suitable for transmission to other societies without doing severe damage to both the message of revelation and the society which receives it.
>
> (Deloria, 2003: 65)

Prophecy and Prophetic Movements

Prophecy has always played an important role within Native American spiritual communities, and has served, historically, as one of the ways in which native people responded and adapted to colonialism and the changes that came with it. In times of great social, political, and economic distress, great prophets have often arisen within native communities to try to help their people to reorient themselves, to overcome hardship, and to move forward and survive, blending new ideas and established cultural traditions. Prophets performed similar functions long before contact, as both social critics and as harbingers of great social and cultural change. Within many native communities and traditions there are narratives in which prophets foretell the coming of Europeans, the great social and cultural changes that would be forthcoming, and the potential end of the world.

> Full-fledged prophetic movements almost never occurred in the initial encounter
> between Native Americans and Europeans. Rather, they emerged after several gen-
> erations of either direct or indirect contact. They emerged most often within the
> kind of unequal and exploitative relations that characterized full-fledged colonial-
> ism . . . they not only reacted and rebelled against colonialism, they also innovated
> tradition and initiated new ways of life within the world created by contact.
>
> (Martin, 1991: 683–4)

Some prophetic movements have also been associated with times of warfare. The Pueblo Revolt of 1680 is associated with the great Pueblo prophet Popé, who foresaw the defeat of the Spanish by the Pueblo peoples. During the American Revolution, great prophets such as the Shawnee Prophet, Pontiac, and Handsome Lake also rose to prominence among their peoples in times of great social distress. But the majority of religious prophets in native communities functioned as arbiters of social activity and change, and offered a way for communities to respond to great social, political and spiritual changes, within a cultural framework that would make sense within their communities.

Prophets incorporated traditional ideals, while also borrowing freely from both other native groups and from non-natives. This often led to the creation of new dances, new songs, and new stories meant to repre-sent the transforming reality of a given place and time. Prophets, in their criticism, attacked specific social and cultural practices within their own communities, and tended to focus on practices that endangered the community rather than just the individual. The things they attacked, such as alcohol use, changes in family structure and kinship relations, and the incorporation of Christian ideals, were not seen as inherently bad in and of themselves, but rather specifically in terms of their negative threats and consequences to the com-munity. Prophecy should thus be understood as an internal system which had existed long before contact with Europeans, focused on reorienting a people within a changing historical and cultural framework.

In almost all these revolts, the critique of colonialism began at home with self-critique. This self-critique brought to consciousness major ways in which the people had collaborated with colonial forces . . . the internal struggle, which sometimes became civil war, demonstrated once again that transformative movements were movements in which Native Americans reclaimed their power to shape their own future as they saw fit, in accord with their understandings of power. For participants in these movements, history was understood not from the perspective of passive victims confronting a monolithic and inevitable invasion. Rather, they affirmed that their situation was partly their responsibility by asserting that their situation resulted from the action of *traitors within*, traitors who had neglected tradition. . . .

(Martin, 1991: 686–88)

Ceremonialism and Ritual Activity

Despite the changes wrought by colonialism, Native American religious systems survived, partly because of their ability to adapt and change as conditions changed and opportunities arose. New, pan-Indian religious movements, such as the Ghost Dance, arose during the nineteenth century, and centuries-old traditions, such as the Potlatch in the Pacific Northwest and the Sun Dance on the Plains, changed dramatically in response to significant cultural changes. The common link between them, however, is the fact that in each instance, native communities sought to assert and maintain cultural uniqueness, both in how they interpreted change, and how they applied these ideas to their own traditions to make them relevant to the specific time and place they were practised. Once again, we see agency being very strongly asserted from within Native American religious traditions.

The Ghost Dance Movement

Probably the most well known religious movement among Native Americans in the nineteenth and twentieth centuries has been the Ghost Dance movement. Started in Nevada in the late 1800s and stemming from a series of spiritual visions received by the Paiute Jack Wilson (Wovoka), the Ghost Dance became a nation-wide movement which connected Native Americans across the country around common issues of poverty, destitution, despair, and hopelessness. This spiritual movement was able to offer varied people hope in times of great despair, despite their cultural differences, and functioned as a catalyst for many future changes in the relationships between Native Americans and the larger political entities which were overseeing them during this period.

The Ghost Dance also brought severe rebuke, however, from missionaries, from Indian agents, and from the government as a whole, who all greatly feared a spiritual movement which was banding Native Americans together and causing them to question their current conditions and call for drastic changes. Ultimately, this conflict over the Ghost Dance led to the greatest single massacre of unarmed Native Americans in US history—that of Wounded Knee (South Dakota) in 1890, where hundreds of Native Americans were gunned down, left to die in the snow, and buried in unmarked mass graves. This landmark event signalled the determination of the government to subdue Native American religious activities and identity, to the point of being willing to kill people to make it happen.

Where we see native agency in the Ghost Dance movement is in the ways in which different groups interpreted the message of the prophet Wovoka. Rather than a static, generalized message meant to fit all people and all situations, the message was reshaped, moulded, and changed by communities to fit their own needs and situations. What was considered a peaceful spiritual endeavor by the Paiute was interpreted as a call to activism and resistance by the Lakota. Much like with missionization and the ideals of Christianity, the message had to make sense, within a given cultural and spiritual framework, or it would be rejected. Native people sometimes syncretized cultural ideals, elements of Christianity, and new ideas from pan-Indian movements like the Ghost Dance to come up with whole new, locally and culturally specific religious movements, through which they responded to their current situations and made decisions about their futures.

> References to the Great Father, Jesus and the Bible attest to the influence of Christian missionaries. The presence of Christian syncretisms in Ghost Dance rituals suggests that the Kiowa adopted concepts from Christianity that accommodated their needs. Belief or disbelief in Christianity was founded in the Kiowa notion of *dwdw*, or power, which has remained intact since the collapse of the horse and buffalo culture. Kiowa individuals merely chose the religion they felt was most powerful.
>
> (Kracht, 1992: 463)

Potlatch and Sun Dance

The Potlatch is a ceremonial complex distinct to the Pacific Northwest, Western Canada and Alaska. Originally, it served a variety of functions in different communities: as an initiation ritual, used to mark important life events such as the birth of a child, or marriage; as a validation of social status within a community; or as reverence and awareness of supernatural power in the world. However, with the influx of European trade goods like blankets and copper items, the ceremony changed and evolved into a means of maintaining and observing social hierarchy, community values, and a sense of cultural identity. The Potlatch, or 'give away' ceremony as it is sometimes called, became a way to balance wealth within the community, by ensuring a more even distribution of material items, but also became a way for people to validate their status within the society through gifting and exchange.

> The ability of the potlatch to serve as the key link between the 'thought of' and the 'lived in' socio-cultural order explains its centrality in nineteenth-century Tlingit life, as well as its survival into the present, despite years of criticism from missionaries and government officials and significant changes in the native culture and society.
>
> (Kan, 1986: 207)

The Potlatch has economic, social, legal and spiritual dimensions, and as such, offers a good example of the lack of separation between what is 'sacred' and what is 'profane' within Native American communities. With the influx of new materials in the region, such as the Hudson Bay blanket, and the removal of groups from specific geographical areas, Potlatch served as a logical response mechanism through which to filter new cultural situations and economic realities. It synchronized social reality with cosmology and spiritual beliefs, and also allowed these native communities to participate in two economies at once: the capitalistic economy being forced on them by outsiders, and the traditional spiritual economy of exchange (through the development of items like the Button Blanket). Native people were able to act out and express their spiritual ideals and cultural values through the incorporation of new social structures, political ideals, and material objects.

In the late nineteenth and the early twentieth century, Potlatching was outlawed and, in some cases, actually made illegal, as part of the effort to subdue Native American religious activity and force conversions to Christianity and acceptance of the process of Americanization and Westernization. Despite these efforts, however, the Potlatch continued to be practised, in a more clandestine fashion, and continues to function within Native American communities in these areas today. The Potlatch continues to include important ceremonial feasts, the exchange of gifts and commodities, and revolves around their concepts of cultural balance and identity.

The Sun Dance, typically practised in the Great Plains region of the United States, but sometimes seen to have extended into other areas and communities as well, has always been one of the most controversial Native American ceremonial activities. Typically involving the ritual piercing of practitioners as part of their ritual offering, missionaries, Indian agents, and outsiders have held the ritual up as a prime example of Native American paganism and savagism, and have misunderstood the ceremony to be some sort of horrific ritual to the Sun or Sun-god.

Yet the Sun Dance is in fact a highly ritualized, deeply ceremonial, community-based activity, meant to cement the relationship between the individual and the Creator, but also meant to ensure the health, safety, and continuity of the entire community by the individual giving of their own flesh for the sake of others. From the preparation of the location to the choosing of the Sun Dance pole to the actual ceremony itself (which sometimes lasts as long as four days) the Sun Dance stands out as a distinct example of American Indian spiritual activity, which was often community-based or -oriented and which was often directed at healing, health, and maintenance of a people and a way of life.

Because of the impact that colonialism has had on native communities on the Plains, the Sun Dance has undergone various changes over time. There are many varieties of the ceremony, some considered to be more 'traditional' than others, some of which have incorporated elements of Christianity and other beliefs, and some of which bear little resemblance to their historical predecessors. Again, I would suggest that we read this as cultural and spiritual flexibility, and as a tool that works both to help a community and a religious complex survive, and to make spiritual activity make sense in a specific time and place. To fall into arguments over what is and isn't 'traditional' is in part to miss the point. Tradition is what people *do*, now, in the contemporary, not what they *did* in some distant, ill-defined past. Plains people have maintained and grown their traditions in large part because of their cultural tenacity and ability to adapt their beliefs and values to current experiences rather than abstract dogmas, and native people will continue to do so into the distant future. This, again, is part of that larger process of spiritual agency and strength.

Environmentalism and Religious Freedom

As we have noted, Native American religions are place-based, and inasmuch, their maintenance and continuity requires continued access to important, spiritual places at specific times of the year. This relationship to place has led to the stereotype of Native Americans as 'simpler' people, and has brought them sometimes undue and unwanted attention from groups like the environmental movement, for whom native people and their traditions have become almost mascots. It has also caused significant legal issues, particularly around the issue of religious freedom, access to places and religious materials, and the control and use of native remains. Native religions have resisted simplification of their conceptions of the world, and have actively sought to maintain their social and cultural distinctness, despite such external intrusions.

The Environmental Indian

The stereotypes of the 'environmental Indian' or the 'Indian as natural man' have plagued Native Americans since the time of earliest contact, and continue to be employed by various outside entities such as the modern environmental movement, the Boy Scouts of America, and the New Age movement. Today, people are encouraged to treat the world as the Indians did, to walk on the earth like the Indians, and to be more nativistic in their overall orientation to the natural world. Is such a thing possible? In our contemporary, materialistic society, how can we connect with the world around us, and does it make sense to try to mimic another culture, and really, another religious system, in order to develop or maintain such a relationship? Despite efforts to do so, is it possible to mimic another culture from within one's own?

> What we have here is a native cosmology that is so fundamentally different from ours as to make even comparison very difficult. To suggest that we might adopt such an Indian world view is preposterous ... surely we deluded ourselves when we imagined that the Indian could teach us his peculiar land ethic; we did not understand that it is not just a land ethic but a comprehensive way of life. Anyway, as far as the Indian is concerned, it isn't he who does the teaching, but rather the land ... We are not presently in a position to understand culture and humaneness in discourse with the land—or with the Indian for that matter. Both, unfortunately, are inarticulate in the world as we presently define it.
>
> (Martin, 1981: 250–51)

Traditional native relationships with place are based on close observation of both nature and natural phenomena. Native people, in spending generation after generation in the same place, developed a deep knowledge—what we might call a scientific knowledge—of the world around them, and attuned themselves to this world. They recognize that all things exist on their own terms, and that there are webs of interaction and power in the world, with which the human must align himself. Native Americans thus managed their environments accordingly, and through this specialized environmental knowledge, developed ceremonial activities directed toward maintaining relationships with powerful, non-human persons all around them. If we understand that the word culture, in its root form, means basically 'to inhabit and care for a place' we begin to see the inherent connection between the development of a culture and the place in which that culture develops. No culture develops in a vacuum, and therefore, in inhabiting a place and cultivating it for a long period of time, Native Americans were, and continue to be, developing cultural practices which would be actualized through the body (through actions) into specific places. Sound ecological ideals converted into religious terms and ritual became the physical representation of social values, creating kinship with place.

With this in mind, is this notion of the environmental Indian a valid one? Native Americans certainly had, and continue to have, specialized ecological and environmental knowledge and philosophies, but these are not inherent racial, social, or cultural traits. Instead, they represent hundreds if not thousands of years of relationships with specific places, and may only seem foreign to most of us because most Americans, as fairly new residents of the 'New World', lack this length of relationship with and experience of place. Native Americans are active in environmentalism and ecological movements today, but perhaps for very different reasons than most Americans, and likely for reasons which are much more religious and spiritual in nature than the average.

FIGURE 1.1 The Black Hills

Devil's Tower in the Black Hills region of Wyoming. Sioux tribe members continue to fight the US government over the rights to this picturesque region more than a century after the discovery of gold forced the Sioux tribes to give up the Black Hills and enter reservations. Courtesy Getty Images.

Religious Freedom

The First Amendment to the United States Constitution notes that, 'Congress shall make no law respecting an establishment of religion, or prohibiting the free exercise thereof'. If this is the case, and we take this text on its face value, why is religious freedom such an important issue for Native Americans today? The reasoning lies in the wording of the amendment, and how it has been understood through the development of American policy towards American Indians and their religious activities and identities. In this case, 'free exercise' has been interpreted to protect beliefs, but not actions. What is clear is that the First Amendment has been understood to make a clear distinction between a religious belief and a religious activity, which is troubling for Native American religious followers, who don't make such a distinction, and whose traditions are less focused on maintaining a text or set of religious dogma, and more focused on the continued performance of religious ceremonies and activities in both daily life and according to ritual cycles. In as much, native religions have come into direct conflict with environmental groups, who wish to maintain the sanctity of natural places for very different reasons, and who fail to understand native religious ideologies or needs, or, more likely, simply choose to ignore those needs for the sake of others that are considered more valid or pressing.

Historically, the battle over religious freedom was fought between Native Americans and agents of the government, including missionaries, Indian agents, and educators. After centuries of oppression, many native religious activities 'went underground' as a protective mechanism, and therefore seem to have disappeared to the general public. Yet they are still active and vibrant within communities, but also now held very secretively, away from the public eye.

> The list of indigenous practices prohibited by federal regulations promulgated in 1883, 1892, and again in 1904 included: 1) all dances and 'any similar feast', 2) all plural and polygamous marriages and those not 'solemnized' by an appointed judge, 3) all practices of medicine men and the prevention of Indian children from attending religious schools, 4) the destruction, injury, taking or carrying away of any personal property without reference to its value, particularly in the case of the death of an Indian, 5) immorality, particularly the exchange of gifts between families when negotiating marriages, 6) intoxication, and 7) the failure to 'adopt habits of industry, or to engage in civilized pursuits or employments'.
>
> (Gooding, 1996: 161, taken from 'Rules for Indian Courts', 1892)

Various legal battles are underway today in America to clarify this issue, and also to get the US government to recognize that Native American religions are just as valid as other religions, and deserve equal protection under the law. Most of these legal battles centre around access to and use of specific places on the natural landscape—so-called sacred spaces, which are critical to the maintenance and function of native religious traditions. Places such as Devil's Tower in Wyoming, the Medicine Wheel in the Bighorn Mountains and Mount Graham in Arizona have become hotbeds for arguments about religious freedom, and what it really means to practise religion in America today.

One of the other significant contemporary religious freedom issues Native Americans are dealing with is the issue of repatriation. With the passage of the Native American Graves Protection and Repatriation Act (NAGPRA) in 1990, a door was opened to discuss the history of the collection of all things materially Indian, the pilfering of graves, and the violation of ceremonial activities and sites by geologists, anthropologists, grave robbers, and collectors of all kinds. NAGPRA has opened the door for tribes to attempt to re-obtain important ceremonial, cultural, and individual material goods which have long been lost to them, housed in universities, museums, and private collections throughout the United States and the world.

Yet this law has also created new challenges to tribes. How do they go about 'proving' that things belong to them without invalidating the sanctity of their spiritual activities and beliefs? How do they handle these powerful and sacred items in an appropriate and respectful manner, and what is to become of these things once they are repatriated? This has created very different, and sometimes conflicting, ideas both within native communities and between them in terms of whether such powerful items should be repatriated, what to do with them if they are, and how to address their original loss to outsiders. It has also created great tension between tribes and the institutions which are currently in possession of these materials, including some of the largest and most important museums in the country, as these organizations do not wish to give up these artifacts, and have actively fought to prevent tribes from repatriating ceremonial and cultural artifacts, out of fear of those artifacts being lost or destroyed.

Native American Religions in the Contemporary Context

This section focuses on two important developments in Native American spiritual traditions today—the development of new, more globalized religious movements such as the Native American Church, and the subsequent rise of movements intent on spiritually appropriating Native American religious ideas, including the New Age movement and 'hobbyism'. Ironically, the spiritual appropriators are often operating on the assumption that Native Americans have disappeared, or are at least no longer culturally 'authentic', and therefore their religious traditions are up for grabs, while new, pan-Indian religious movements suggest exactly the opposite—that Native Americans are still alive and well, and still actively engaging their spiritual lives and practising cultural and spiritual agency in the contemporary world.

Spiritual Appropriations

Native American religions are facing a relatively new challenge in the contemporary period—the appropriation of their spiritual systems, practices, and beliefs by outsiders, particularly non-native individuals and groups functioning as part of the modern New Age movement. This is an ironic twist, considering that not a century ago, native traditions were outlawed in the United States, and seen as Paganism by most Americans. The New Age movement is a relatively new movement on the American religious scene, and has been interested in culling ideas from a wide variety of religious systems and beliefs in order to create an individually-centred religious system which is acceptable to those who feel lost or disenfranchised by mainstream religious systems (see Chapter 12 on Spirituality and Chapter 13 on New Age religion). The New Age movement has often framed Native Americans as somewhat 'mythical and magical' and many within the movement have sought to profit from native rituals, ceremonies and knowledge through the selling of books, hosting of workshops, and the sale of religious ceremonial participation, which is particularly distasteful to Native Americans today. Their basis for doing so is the idea that contemporary natives are 'corrupted', and they challenge notions of native religions being culturally affiliated and not open to anyone.

America has always been more about individual rights than responsibilities, and many, though not all, New Agers have expressed this 'right' in their appropriation of all things native.

> Commercial exploitation of Native American spiritual traditions has permeated the New Age movement since its emergence in the 1980s. Euro-Americans professing to be medicine people have profited from publications and workshops. Mass quantities of products promoted as 'Native American sacred objects' have been successfully sold by white entrepreneurs to a largely non-Indian market . . . New Age interest in Native American cultures appears more concerned with exoticized images and romanticized rituals revolving around a distorted view of Native American spirituality than with the indigenous people themselves and the very real (and often ugly) socio-economic and political problems they face as colonized peoples.
>
> (Aldred, 2000: 329–333)

Hobbyism has become another way in which native spiritual practices are being appropriated by those outside the cultural bounds of the traditions. Hobbyists are those people who 'play Indian' on the weekend, dressing up in what they consider to be 'authentic' Indian garb and performing a wide variety of generic 'Indian' ceremonies. These groups typically have no connection with actual native communities, and have actively bought into the stereotype of mimicking natives to 'get back to nature'. 'Indian clubs' have become very popular in Europe, and are beginning to infiltrate America as well, as non-natives take to wearing Indian garb, practising Indian ceremonies, and imitating Indian cultural and social activities, typically in weekend gatherings at clandestine locations.

Yet this type of 'religious borrowing' has been actively resisted by many American Indians, who see such spiritual appropriation as simply another step in the long history of cultural loss and assault. This has led to some outright conflicts between individuals, tribes, and New Age groups, and raises important arguments about what religion really is, who has control over it and rights to it, and what to make of those who take freely from other traditions and cultures without actively participating in or contributing to them.

The Native American Church

One of the ways in which Native American religiosity is playing out in the contemporary world is through the proliferation of the Native American Church (NAC), sometimes also called the Peyote Church or Peyote Religion, both within communities and across community bounds in a larger, pan-Indian context. The NAC is built around traditional religious values and activities, such as the use of purification and the sweat lodge, as well as healing and community-building, but has also incorporated elements of Christianity into its rituals, making it a more syncretic faith, and signalling a more common adaptation among native people today—the joining of faith ideas into new religious ideologies and movements.

Religious use of peyote, a hallucinogenic cactus, is said to have begun in indigenous communities in Mexico thousands of years ago. Through both travel and trade, peyote made its way into various Native American communities, where it was incorporated into religious ceremonies and rituals. The Native American Church, as an established movement, is said to have started around 1890, and incorporated significant Christian elements. It is still very actively practised in native communities across the United States, and is said to be the largest religion practised by Native Americans today.

The NAC recognizes two roads to contemporary native life. The first road is known as the 'profane road'. It is wide and paved, but also full of temptation and trouble. It is easy for an individual to go down this road, but it is rarely fulfilling. The second road is the Peyote Road. Visualize it as being narrow, unpaved, and weaving back and forth through the natural world, rather than straight over it. It is a journey that one must, at its core, make alone, and the journey is often challenging, and uphill. It is peyote that will help the individual crest that hill, and then begin moving downhill, which will be much easier.

FIGURE 1.2 Peyote ceremony Navaho Indians at Peyote Ceremony in Hogan, near Pinyon, holding a special ceremony for a sick boy. Time & Life Pictures/ Getty Images.

Summary

- Native American religions are adaptive, flexible, culturally localized traditions that are based more on experience than dogma, and more 'spatial' than 'linear'.
- Linear traditions are those focused on time and its linear progression, focused on the working out of the 'divine plan' at the expense of the natural world, spatial traditions are those which arise from a relationship with a specific geographical location, and which orient themselves around that relationship. Place is more important than time.
- Missionization functioned as part of the larger process of colonialism in the United States.
- Missionaries saw native religions as childish, archaic, simplistic paganism.
- Native Americans practised agency in their relationships with missionaries, accepting parts of their religions, but rejecting others, based on their ability to correlate them with the beliefs they already had.
- Prophets and prophetic movements function as social critique, evaluating changes that occur, and devising new responses based on the syncretism of old and new ideas.
- The Ghost Dance movement, probably the best known Native American religious movement, was adapted by each group that practised it, in order to make it culturally relevant.
- Changes in the Potlatch ceremony were a logical response that allowed natives in the Pacific Northwest to participate in the market economy while also maintaining cultural and spiritual traditions.
- Native Americans have been stereotyped as being more 'in touch with nature' when in fact their environmental knowledge has been cultivated over long cultural and spiritual relationships with places.
- Religious freedom is a critical issue for Native Americans, who do not separate religious beliefs from religious actions.
- The issue of repatriation centres around issues related to Native American burial remains, particularly those in museums and collections.
- Participation in the New Age movement and hobbyism are ways that non-natives have appropriated Native American spiritual traditions.
- The Native American Church is one of the largest religious movements among natives today, and shows integration of traditional ideas with Christianity.

Key Terms

agency The exertion of power or influence to promote ideas or desires.

Button Blanket New cultural materials, constructed by Native Americans in the Pacific Northwest, made from Hudson Bay blankets. A good example of the integration of traditional symbols and motifs with an imposed material object.

dogma A settled, authoritative doctrine that is rarely open to change.

Ghost Dance A national religious movement among Native Americans which began in the late nineteenth century and which predicted a return to traditional ideals and values.

hobbyism A movement typified by non-Native Americans who dress and act like 'Indians' and who appropriate native spiritual ideals and rituals.

Indian agents Government agents assigned to oversee Native American reservation communities and impose government ideals and values there.

linear traditions Traditions oriented around the progression of time and the historical value of human events.

missionization The process of attempting, sometimes forcibly, to convert individuals from one religion to another.

monogenetic creation The idea of a single act of creation, out of which all peoples can trace descent.

Native American Church Also known as the Peyote Religion, a contemporary religious movement in Native American communities that syncretizes native and Christian ideals.

New Age movement A self-help spiritual movement often associated with the appropriation of Native American spiritual ideals, sometimes for financial gain.

Pan-Indian A term used to describe ideas, concepts, music, religions, etc., which are not culturally bounded within specific native groups, but rather are more general and universal.

peyote A hallucinogenic cactus plant used in ceremonies by the Native American Church.

Potlatch A ritual complex from the Pacific Northwest focused on exchange, cultural standing, and the maintenance of cultural ideals.

prophecy The act of foretelling future events, but also the act of self-critique and criticism practiced by Native American religious figures.

religious freedom Legal protection from religious persecution, this concept is important for Native Americans because it has legally been interpreted to protect only religious beliefs and not actions.

repatriation The return of material objects and funerary remains, including human remains, to Native Americans from museums, universities and other collections.

ritual piercing Part of the Sun Dance ritual, individuals are pierced on the chest, legs, and/or back with bones and offer their flesh for individual and community health.

sacred spaces Places on the land where religious activity occurs, these are often contested in religious freedom cases in the United States.

spatial traditions Traditions oriented around a long-developed relationship with a geographical location. Religious ideals and values spring up from this relationship with place.

spiritual appropriation The practice of religious traditions by those who are not actually members of that tradition.

Sun Dance A ritual complex typically found in the Great Plains which focuses on ritual piercing and sacrifice to obtain individual and community health.

sweat lodge A Native American domed structure often used for purification rituals, either alone or as part of another ritual complex.

syncretism The blending of ideas from multiple traditions, cultures, etc., to form a new set of beliefs, ideals, etc.

traditional ecological knowledge A term used to describe Native American environmental knowledge, formed over a long time in a particular place.

Wounded Knee The site of a massacre in 1890 associated with followers of the Ghost Dance movement. It is the largest massacre of non-military individuals in US military history.

Wovoka Also known as Jack Wilson, the Paiute prophet whose visions became the foundation of the Ghost Dance movement.

Further Reading

Linear and Circular Orientations

Vine Deloria Jr.: 'Thinking in Time and Space'. In *God is Red: A Native View of Religion*, thirtieth anniversary edition (Golden, CO: Fulcrum Publishing, 2003, pp. 61–75). A critique of Christianity and its linear focus, which also addresses issues of civil religion and its relationship to Native American spatial traditions.

Donald Fixico: 'American Indian Circular Philosophy'. In *The American Indian Mind in a Linear World: American Indian Studies and Traditional Knowledge* (New York: Routledge, 2003, pp. 41–61). An examination of the notion of circularity as it pertains to Native American ideologies and religious systems.

Winona LaDuke: 'What is Sacred?'. In *Recovering the Sacred: The Power of Naming and Claiming* (Cambridge, MA: South End Press, 2005, pp. 11–15). A brief examination of the ways in which the notion of 'sacred' functions in Native American belief systems.

M. Jane Young: '"Pity the Indians of Outer Space": Native American Views of the Space Program'. *Western Folklore* 46, (1987: pp. 269–279). An examination of what is unique about Native American ideology through an examination of ideas about outer space, space exploration, and the continuation of frontier ideology.

Native American Religions and Western Colonialism

Michael D. McNally: 'The Practice of Native American Christianity'. *Church History* 69(4), (2000: pp. 834–859). An attempt to look at the religious actions resulting from Missionization, focusing specifically on Ojibwe hymn singers and their syncretism of Ojibwe and Christian concepts.

Joel W. Martin: 'Before and beyond the Sioux Ghost Dance: Native American Prophetic Movements and the Study of Religion'. *Journal of the American Academy of Religion* 59(4), (1991: pp. 677–701). Looks at the historical function of prophecy in Native American communities, and the ways in which prophets help communities to accept change and integrate new ideas.

Irene S. Vernon: 'The Claiming of Christ: Native American Postcolonial Discourses'. *MELUS* 24(2), (1999: 75–88). Examination of the consequences of Missionization in Native American communities, particularly the notion of syncretism and how Christian ideals have been adapted to fit native realities.

Elizabeth Vibert: '"The Natives Were Strong to Live": Reinterpreting Early Nineteenth-Century Prophetic Movements in the Columbia Plateau'. *Ethnohistory*, 42(2), (1995: pp. 197–229). An examination of the role and function of prophecy on the Columbia Plateau, particularly focusing on the existence of prophetic movements before contact with Europeans.

Ceremonialism and Ritual Activity

Arthur Amiotte: 'The Lakota Sun Dance: Historical and Contemporary Perspectives'. In Raymond DeMaille and Douglas Parks (eds), *Sioux Indian Religion: Tradition and Innovation* (Norman, OK: University of Oklahoma Press, 1987, pp. 75–89). An examination of the history and function of the Lakota Sun Dance, as well as some of the contemporary changes which have occurred within the complex.

Raymond Bucko: 'The Contemporary Lakota Sweat Lodge'. In *The Lakota Ritual of the Sweat Lodge: History and Contemporary Practice* (Lincoln, NE: University of Nebraska Press, 1998, pp. 59–96). Shows the role and function of the Lakota sweat lodge, both as a stand-alone ritual and as a cleansing ceremony often used before another ceremonial complex.

Thomas Lewis: 'The Contemporary *Yuwipi*'. In Raymond DeMaille and Douglas Parks (eds), *Sioux Indian Religion: Tradition and Innovation* (Norman, OK: University of Oklahoma Press, 1987, pp. 173–187). Examines Yuwipi as it is practised in the contemporary world, and looks at some of the changes which have taken place within it over time.

Sergei Kan: 'The Nineteenth-Century Tlingit Potlatch: A New Perspective'. *American Ethnologist* 13(2), (1986: pp. 191–212). Suggests that Potlatch moves from being a religious complex to being an economic one due to the imposition of capitalism and the subsequent cultural change that occurs.

Benjamin R. Kracht: 'The Kiowa Ghost Dance, 1894–1916: An Unheralded Revitalization Movement'. *Ethnohistory* 39(4), (1992: 452–477). Examination of the Ghost Dance among the Kiowa, its cultural relevance for them, and its continuation beyond the more well known versions of the complex.

Joseph Masco: '"It is a Strict Law That Bids Us Dance": Cosmologies, Colonialism, Death, and Ritual Authority in the Kwakwaka'wakw Potlatch, 1849 to 1922'. *Comparative Studies in Society and History* 37(1), (1995: 41–75). Examines the historical functions of the Potlatch in this native community, and the historical and cultural changes/adaptations which have occurred within the complex over time.

Thomas W. Overholt: 'The Ghost Dance of 1890 and the Nature of the Prophetic Process'. *Ethnohistory* 21(1), (1974: pp. 37–63). Looks at the ways in which the message of the Ghost Dance was transmitted through middle men, and subsequently adapted to fit the needs and cultural values of different communities.

William K. Powers: *'Sun Dance' in Oglala Religion* (Lincoln, NE: University of Nebraska Press, 1975, pp. 95–100). A brief overview of the process of the Sun Dance, including some of the ritual activities leading up to the dance itself.

William Powers: *Selected Readings from Yuwipi: Vision and Experience in Oglala Ritual* (Lincoln, NE: University of Nebraska Press, 1982, pp. 38–72). An extremely detailed explanation of the Yuwipi ritual, its processes, and its function in native communities.

James R. Walker: *Selected Readings from Lakota Belief and Ritual* (Lincoln, NE: University of Nebraska Press, 1980, pp. 176–191). A collection of first-person descriptions and narratives about the meaning and function of the Sioux Sun Dance.

Environmentalism and Religious Freedom

Vine Deloria, Jr.: 'Secularism, Civil Religion and the Religious Freedom of American Indians'. In Devon Mihesuah (ed.) *Repatriation Reader: Who Owns American Indian Remains?* (Lincoln, NE: University of Nebraska Press, 2000, pp. 169–179). A brief overview of the history of the issues of religious freedom, as well as its relevance and impact for Native Americans.

Roger C. Echo-Hawk: 'Ancient History in the New World: Integrating Oral Traditions and the Archaeological Record in Deep Time'. *American Antiquity* 65(2), (2000: pp. 267–290). An attempt to elucidate ways in which Native American oral narratives can be used as 'evidence' in issues of religious freedom, where other written evidence does not exist.

T.J. Ferguson, Roger Anyon and Edmund Ladd: 'Repatriation at the Pueblo of Zuni: Diverse Solutions to Complex Problems'. In Devon Mihesuah (ed.), *Repatriation Reader: Who Owns American Indian Remains?* (Lincoln, NE: University of Nebraska Press, 2000, pp. 239–265). An examination of the issue of repatriation as it applied to a specific repatriation effort undertaken by the Zuni tribe in order to return religious objects to tribal control.

Susan Staiger Gooding: 'At the Boundaries of Religious Identity: Native American Religions and American Legal Culture'. *Numen*, 43(2), Religion, Law and the Construction of Identities, (1996: pp. 157–183). An overview of the American legal system and its dealings with Native American religions.

Ira Jacknis: 'Repatriation as Social Drama: The Kwakiutl Indians of British Columbia, 1922–1980'. In Devon Mihesuah (ed.), *Repatriation Reader: Who Owns American Indian Remains?* (Lincoln, NE: University of Nebraska Press, 2000, pp. 266–281). A historical examination of a lengthy effort by the Kwakiutl tribe to return important artifacts to the tribe, and the result of such repatriation.

Shepard Krech III: 'Reflections on Conservation, Sustainability and Environmentalism in Indigenous North America'. *American Anthropologist* 107(1), (2005: 78–86). An attempt to counter ideas of Native American environmentalism by showing ways in which Native Americans acted counter to environmental ideals at times.

Calvin Martin: 'The American Indian as Miscast Ecologist'. *The History Teacher* 14(2), (1981: 243–252). An examination of the stereotype of the Native American as natural ecologist, and the issues associated with the promulgation of such a stereotype.

Robert S. Michaelsen: 'The Significance of the American Indian Religious Freedom Act of 1978'. *Journal of the American Academy of Religion* 52(1), (1984: pp. 93–115). An examination of the significance, or lack thereof, of the American Indian Religious Freedom Act, and its inability to effect real protections for Native American religious traditions.

Raymond Pierotti and Daniel Wildcat: 'Traditional Ecological Knowledge: The Third Alternative (Commentary)'. *Ecological Applications* 10(5), (2000: pp. 1333–1340). A complex piece which attempts to elucidate ideas about Native American environmental knowledge and the notion of being native to a place.

Native American Religions in the Contemporary Context

Lisa Aldred: 'Plastic Shamans and Astroturf Sun Dances: New Age Commercialization of Native American Spirituality'. *American Indian Quarterly* 24(3), (2000: pp. 329–352). Shows the history of New Age spiritual appropriation, especially as it concerns commercialization and the sale of books, rituals, and ceremonies to non-natives, by non-natives.

Phil Cousineau and Gary Rhine: 'The Peyote Ceremony'. In Huston and Reuben Snake (compiled and eds), *One Nation Under God: The Triumph of the Native American Church* (Santa Fe, NM: Clear Light Publishers, 1996, pp. 77–101). An inside examination of the role of the Peyote ceremony, and more specifically, of the meaning of the different elements of the ritual as a whole.

Rayna Green: 'The Tribe Called Wannabee: Playing Indian in America and Europe'. *Folklore* 99(1), (1988: pp. 30–55). An examination of the history of hobbyism among a variety of groups, both in the United States and Europe.

Emerson Spider Sr.: 'The Native American Church of Jesus Christ'. In Raymond DeMaille and Douglas Parks (eds), *Sioux Indian Religion: Tradition and Innovation* (Norman, OK: University of Oklahoma Press, 1987, pp. 189–209). A description of one faction of the Native American Church that rejects traditional Native American religion and ideals and uses almost wholly Christian ideals to fashion its rituals and ceremonies.

Figure Credits

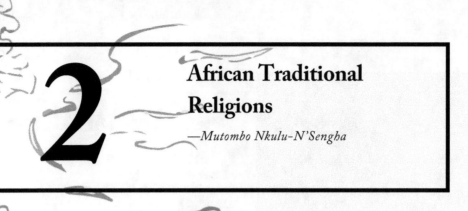

2

African Traditional Religions

—Mutombo Nkulu-N'Sengha

Liberation According to the "Bumuntu Paradigm" of Ancestral Religions

To those who subscribe to the economic, political, and civilizational orthodoxies of our time, African liberation theology may seem obnoxious, fallacious, or even blasphemous. And yet for the masses of Africans crushed by poverty, genocide, dictatorship, neocolonialism, economic exploitation, political oppression, and racism, much of the current "world order" is blasphemous. Over the last five centuries, African interaction with the outside world transformed the continent into a melting pot of different religious, moral, cultural, economic, political, and philosophical structures and worldviews which bequeathed to the people a "cross of humiliation and marginalization" amidst an ambivalent progress of modernity. Indeed, in the global context of geopolitics and market economy, Africa has remained since the fifteenth century poor, weak, and a battlefield of competing powers of domination and domestication.

At the same time it remains a continent of resilience and resistance par excellence, the land of Chaka zulu, "Jeanne d'arc du Congo," Patrice Lumumba, Kwame Nkrumah, Nelson Mandela, Desmond Tutu, or Wangari Maathai. In other words, Africa is a privileged locus of liberation theology. This chapter will articulate the basic tenets of such a liberation theology as it developed for centuries under the guidance of ancestral spirituality which has continued to work in new religions, be it Islam or Christianity. In so doing we shall address the question of "what Africa needs to be liberated from, and how." Traditional Africa referred to oppression with the concept of witchcraft (butshi, ndoki, buloji) which includes evil heart (mucima mubi), evil eye (diso dibi), poisonous tongue or evil speech (ludimi lubi), and greed (mwino). Oppression is thus viewed as that which diminishes the vital force, brings about death, destroys life, destroys peace and harmony, creates chaos, anxiety, and insecurity, and hinders human flourishing. It is the opposite of a harmonious mode of existence.

As a "pursuit of unhappiness," oppression takes a myriad of forms. But for the sake of brevity, we can identify ten major categories of local and global forms of oppression which affect ten major dimensions of African existence: First and foremost we find cultural and racial oppression, which constitute the justification of other forms of oppression, notably economic, political, and religious oppression. To these types of oppression, we shall add gender oppression, biological oppression or "bioterrorism," environmental oppression, and artistic and aesthetic oppression. These forms of oppression are often grounded in the tenth category of epistemic violence or intellectual oppression which includes scientific, philosophical, and theological terrorism. Such intellectual oppression serves to rationalize oppression and to belittle African creative capacity and contribution to world civilization and thus world spiritual and moral values. In so doing it turns dehumanization into humanism and forms of oppression into pacification and liberation.

On the local level, oppression can be summarized into "seven deadly sins" which include the abusive use of divination (mwavi); tribalism; patriarchy, polygamy, and female circumcision; dictatorship; the manipulation of taboos and dietary regulations; the abusive use of the ideology of "divine kingship"; and moral vices in general (more notably greed, selfishness, envy, and libido dominandi). As for foreign forces of oppression, we could identify "ten plagues" that accompany the process of globalization since its inception: 1) "pauperisme anthropologique," 2) racism, 3) economic terrorism and "beggar thy neighbor" trade policies, 4) political terrorism, 5) military terrorism and arms trade folly, 6) cultural and linguistic terrorism, 7) religious, spiritual, and theological terrorism, 8) ecoterrorism, 9) bioterrorism, 10) sexual terrorism. A thorough analysis of such a catalog of oppression is beyond the scope of a succinct chapter such as this. We shall therefore limit ourselves to highlighting a few major categories of oppression in the local and global context.

We shall proceed in two major steps. First, in order to clarify our locus theologicus, we will articulate the basic beliefs of African traditional religions that constitute the foundation of traditional African liberation theology. Here we will focus on two basic notions, *Shakapanga* (the supreme creator or God) and *Bumuntu* (the concept of a virtuous person). The notion of God as creator points to that of an ultimate judge of oppressive behaviors and an ultimate source of legitimacy for liberation struggle and resistance to oppressive rulers. The notion of genuine personhood (*Bumuntu*) establishes the sacredness of human dignity and thus delegitimizes oppression. Second we will analyze local and foreign or global forces of oppression and response of African liberation theology. For the sake of brevity we will focus on political, economic, cultural, intellectual, religious, and gender oppression.

The Basic Tenets of African Liberation Theology

African Traditional Religions and the Foundation of Liberation Theology

African liberation theology is based on the notion of the transcendence which constitutes the foundation of human dignity and the sacredness of the struggle for liberation from all forms of dehumanization. It is in reference to God and religious moral values that a behavior or institution is deemed oppressive or liberatory. Therefore a genuine understanding of the nature of African liberation theology requires a careful understanding of the fundamental beliefs of African traditional religions.

African traditional religions provide meaning of life to almost three hundred million people in Africa and in the Americas. This religious tradition is not a thing of the past but rather a living religion which entered a profound phase of revival with the collapse of colonial empires in the 1950s. African traditional religions originated more than twenty-eight thousand years ago[1] in the Bantu area that spans roughly from Nigeria to South Africa. Since the encounter between Europe and Africa in the fifteenth century, they progressively migrated to Europe and especially to the Americas where they found major centers of development, especially in Brazil, Haiti, Jamaica, Cuba, and the United States, where they are practiced in about ten different ways, including Vodun (prevalent in Haiti and Louisiana), Santería or Lucumi (Cuba), the four types of Afro-Brazilian religions (Candomblé, Macumba, Umbanda, Quimbanda), Kumina (of Jamaica), Shango (of Trinidad and Tobago), and Orisha or Yoruba religion. Some elements of African traditional religions can also be found to a lesser degree in Curanderismo and Espiritismo.

For centuries colonial scholarship denied any moral and spiritual value to African traditional religions. Theories and concepts such as "Deus otiosus," "anamarthesis," animism, ancestor worship, witchcraft, and magic contributed to turning African ancestral spiritual tradition into a religion of error, terror, and horror. We shall not dwell on this issue here; but suffice it to mention that although some of these colonial and racist fantasies still linger today, the process of decolonization of knowledge that began after World War II and intensified with the independence of most African nations in the 1970s and 1980s has led conscientious scholars to progressively acknowledge the spiritual and moral values of African traditional religions. Thus R. Bastide acknowledged that "among the Yoruba and Fon there is an entire civilization of spirituality comparable to that of the wood carvings and bronzes of Benin" (Zahan and Martin, 1983:126). Even Pope John Paul II acknowledged in 1994 that although Africa remains economically poor, "she is endowed with a wealth of cultural values and priceless human qualities which it can offer to the Churches and to humanity as a whole. . . . Africans have a profound religious sense, a sense of the sacred, of the existence of God the

Creator and of a spiritual world. The reality of sin in its individual and social forms is very much present in the consciousness of these peoples, as is also the need for rites of purification and expiation" (Browne, 1996:245).

Broadly speaking, African traditional religions encompass many of the beliefs common to traditional religions found in various regions of our planet, from Native American religions to Shintoism in Japan: the belief in a "Great Spirit," one supreme deity understood as the main source of all existence in the universe; the veneration of the ancestors, the veneration of nature as sacred and home to various spirits; the belief in the afterlife, the belief in communication with the world of the dead; the practice of divination; rituals of initiation, and rites of passage; the belief in goddesses and a greater role for women as priestesses and receptacles of deities; the practice of exorcism and a greater role of religion in the healing process; and a code of ethics based on solidarity, hospitality, harmony, and the notion of "pure heart" (*mucima muyample*). Worship includes incantations, prayers of various kind, purification rituals, libations, sacrifices, dance, trance, and observance of taboos, especially dietary regulations and rules pertaining to sexual behavior and bodily functions. It should be noted however that the goal of religion is ultimately to join the village of the ancestors safely and enjoy a blissful immortality. Hence the centrality of good character in African traditional religion, for as a Yoruba proverb has it, "Good character is the essence of religion" ("Iwa Lesin").

Thus the notion of God as Creator and the notion of Bumuntu as good character constitute the basic theological principles that guide liberation theology within the realm of African traditional religions. They serve as the criterion of distinction between good and evil, between oppression and liberation.

The Notion of God

The African conception of God is well articulated in creation myths, proverbs, praise songs and prayers, incantation formulas, and indeed the names by which the African people refer to God.[2] For the sake of brevity we shall not assess all the studies produced on the subject. Suffice it to mention that God is understood fundamentally as Creator of all life and Supreme Owner and Ruler of the universe; and in this capacity he is called the Ancestor of days (Hilolombi), the Bearer of the universe (Mebee), He who is everywhere and hears and sees everything (Nyi), and Father of all humans and things (Sha-Bantune-Bintu). In many creation myths God is spoken of as the Molder or the Potter who created the first human couple (male and female) by using clay. The Shilluk believe that God used clay of different colors in making men, which explains the diversity of human races. The Dogon explain racial differences by the fact that Amma who created all human beings used the light of the moon for the skin of Europeans and the sun for Africans. Thus contrary to an ingrained prejudice against the so-called tribal religions, Africa has the conception of a universal creator which led to an ethic that values the dignity of every human being and not merely that of the members of one's clan or ethnic group. The motherhood of God, another important point in African religion, constitutes the foundation of an African feminist theology.

Finally, God is referred to as "Vidye kadi katonye" (the blameless God). This belief in divine purity and goodness is enshrined in timeless cosmogonies. In their numerous creation myths, Africans have wrestled with the question of the origin of evil and suffering. The conclusion is that the source of evil is not God but rather the human heart. Because he abhors evil and punishes evildoers, God is not merely the fundamental source of morality but a God who abhors oppression. Africans say that God has long ears and is "the great eye," the Discerner of hearts, who sees both the inside and outside of human beings. As omnipotent, omniscient, pure, and wise, God is fundamentally against oppression and as such he remains the source of legitimacy for all forms of resistance and struggle for liberation.

Bumuntu: The Concept of Human Beingness

The fundamental question before us is "what makes somebody a good human being," a liberated person and a liberator, or an oppressor and an evil man. The African conception of the nature of human beings can be gleaned from African proverbs, creation myths, taboos, moral precepts, marriage and family institutions, kingship, and many other customs and traditions. The African vision of personhood is encompassed in ten key concepts (Muntu, Kintu, Bumuntu, Mucima Muy-ampe, Ludimi luyampe, Bilongwa biyampe, Fadenya, Badenya, Buya, Bubi) and ten key proverbs.

To the critical question of liberation theology, "what is a human being?" Africans respond with one word: *Bumuntu*.[3] The term stems from the lexicon of Bantu languages. A human being is referred to as a *Muntu* in Kiluba language (with *Bantu* for the plural). The concept of *Bumuntu* refers to the essence of being a human. The word *Bumuntu* comes from the Kiluba language, but it is widespread in regions that speak Bantu languages, from some areas of West Africa up to South Africa where *Bumuntu* has different linguistic variants such as *Ubuntu*. *Muntu* is not an ethnic concept but rather a generic term for every human being of any ethnicity, gender, or race. The opposite of a genuine *Muntu* is *Kintu* (a "thing"), a term that is used to refer to a human being without moral content, a person who has lost his *Bumuntu* through immoral conduct. *Bumuntu* is the African vision of a refined gentleperson, a holy person, a saint, a shuntzu, a person of dao, a person of Buddha nature, an embodiment of Brahman, a genuine human being. The man or woman of *Bumuntu* is characterized by self-respect and respect for other human beings. Moreover he/she respects all life in the universe. He/she sees his or her dignity as inscribed in a triple relationship, with the transcendent beings (God, ancestors, spirits), with all other human beings, and with the natural world (flora and fauna). *Bumuntu* is the embodiment of all virtues, especially the virtues of hospitality and solidarity.

While compassion, generosity, solidarity, and hospitality are expected from family members, a genuine *Muntu* is expected to extend these virtues to the global village of the human race; the highest expression of

Bumuntu is found in the treatment of those who cannot be expected to pay back favors: the strangers, children, and the most marginalized segments of society, especially the handicapped, the sick, poor, and beggars. In other words, one is genuinely human only when one honors humanity in every human being. Hence the belief among the Yoruba that prayers and invocations offered in Ile-Ife remain incomplete until prayers are offered for the people of the entire universe (Abimbola, 1990:138); this is why the Meru of Kenya believe that a genuine believer must pray not only for himself or herself but also for the welfare of all humanity, begging God to remove "the trouble of the other lands that I do not know" (Shorter, 1997:197–98).

This attitude of hospitality and solidarity is extended in a special way to the stranger, the poor, the weak, the defenseless, and people with disabilities. Thus the Bulsa treat strangers, orphaned, handicapped people, beggars, and lepers very well because of their belief that their ancestors visit them in these forms, and the Fang people of Gabon believe that an ancestor passes by in the person of a stranger, and therefore a stranger should be given a very kind and warm treatment (Olikenyi, 2001:105). The Fang are not an isolated case. As Moila rightly pointed out, generally in most African communities, it is believed that unexpected guests are the embodiment of ancestors; hence, they are given the ancestors' food (2002:3). Such a hospitality goes beyond simple courtesy. It is viewed as a way of communicating with the ancestors.

Such is the manifestation of *Bumuntu*, or the African understanding of "good character." This vision of *Bumuntu* is well expressed in the wisdom of proverbs. In West Africa, for example, an Akan proverb proclaims the divine origin of humans: "All human beings are children of God, no one is a child of the earth." Hence the centrality of good character on the path of becoming humane as the Yoruba put it explicitly, "Good character, good existence, is the adornment of a human being." Such goodness of character is inconceivable without hospitality and respect for the stranger and people with disabilities. Thus a Luba proverb commands to treat an alien guest with care and respect due to deities, for "your guest is your God." As for those with disabilities another Luba proverb warns: "Do not laugh at a crippled person, God is still creating." And to those proud of their knowledge a Luba proverb reminds them that the only true or worthwhile knowledge is to know how to live in harmony and loving relationship with our fellow human beings. In this African model of society, altruism and appreciation for the community are not viewed as antithetical to self-love, for as an Akan proverb has it, "If you do not let your neighbor have nine, you will not have ten." This vision of the humane mode of being is extended to political power. Thus a Luba proverb reminds the ruler who has a penchant for tyrannical behavior that "power is the people." Likewise in South Africa the tyrant is reminded that "one is a King only as long as he is acknowledged as such by the people." To those who suppress individuality, many proverbs remind them of the uniqueness and dignity of each individual in the eyes of the ancestors. "Human beings," says a Chewa proverb, "are like sand out of which one cannot make a mountain." Likewise the Baluba emphasize the value of individual privacy: "No one can put his arm into another person's heart not even when sharing the same bed."

One of the most striking aspects of this African theological anthropology is the distinction between a real or authentic human being and an empty human being that is regarded as a nonhuman. From West

Africa to South Africa, there is the widespread belief that people of bad character are not truly human. In Nigeria, the Yoruba say: "He/ she is not a person." In South Africa we find the expression "he is not human" or "he is a dead body walking." From an African standpoint a vicious dictator, for instance, is not merely regarded as a "bad ruler." He is viewed as a nonhuman altogether. The same is said about any person whose behavior is oppressive to others. The distinction between a good and a bad human being is well expressed in the *Muntu-Kintu* paradigm of Luba religion. According to Luba anthropology, every human being exists as a pendulum between two categories of being, *Muntu* and *Kintu*. A person of good thought, good speech, and good deeds is a genuine *Muntu*, a person of *Bumuntu*. The person of evil thought, evil speech, and evil deeds loses his humanity and falls into the *Kintu* category of things, as the following table shows:

BUYA (goodness) Mwikadilo Muyampe	*BUBI* (evil) Mwikadilo Mubi
mu-ntu (good human) LIBERATOR	*ki-ntu* (a thing, worthless or evil person) OPPRESSOR
mucima muyampe (good heart)	*mucima mubi* (evil thought)
ludimi luyampe (good speech)	*ludimi lubi* (evil speech)
diso diyampe (good eye)	*diso dibi* (evil eye)
bilongwa biyampe (good deeds)	*bilongwa bibi* (evil actions)

In African society, "the perfect person is the person with a good heart"; that is, one is human who has learned the art of living and promoting the essential harmonies of life. Such a person must have acquired fundamental *Bumuntu* virtues, and the whole traditional process of education in the African family and initiation in school consists of inculcating these virtues. The most important of these virtues are: respect for and protection of life, hospitality, solidarity, compassion, love, self-control, politeness, moderation, humility, friendship, goodness, and kindness. Such an ethical framework shows that the rejection of oppressive behavior toward other human beings occupies a pivotal role in African understanding of what it means to be a human being (*Bumuntu*).

This openness to the other is part of the very nature of every human being as the "Fadenya-Badenya" paradigm teaches us. The African vision of personhood has a specific understanding of the individual and collective dimension of personhood which has an enlightening bearing on liberation theology. This vision of personhood was well captured in the Fadenya-Badenya paradigm to borrow the language of the Mande people. This anthropological paradigm points to a conception of the individual which is far from an "absolutized individualism," or a faceless token of the community. In the African worldview the *Muntu* is not a windowless monad. As the Mande well point out, each person is made up of two forces, Fadenya and

Badenya, which explain the constant tension between individuality and respect for the community (Bird and Kendall, 1987:14–16).

Fadenya or "Father-childness" is the centrifugal force of individualism which paves the way to individual greatness. It orients people toward heroic actions and a defense of personal dignity and honor that stimulates resistance and rebellion against oppressive traditions, debilitating conventions, and status quo. But since the search for personal fame can easily lead to self-aggrandizing passions, selfish pursuit of self-interests, and antisocial behavior, Fadenya is feared as a force of social disequilibrium, a force of envy, jealousy, abuse of power, competition, and self-promotion. The individual can find equilibrium only with the intervention of a counterpower, the centripetal force known as Badenya or "mother-childness." This force pulls the child back home, back to the mother's womb. It is a conservative force of submission to authority, stability, cooperation, and dependency on others. From Badenya arises social solidarity, benevolence, altruism, and hospitality. Fadenya corresponds to the Promethean impulse within the being: restless, heroic, rebellious and revolutionary, individualistic, and innovative, eternally seeking freedom, autonomy, change, and novelty. Badenya, on the other hand, represents the Saturnian impulse: conservative, stabilizing, controlling, that seeks to contain, sustain, order, and repress (Tarnas, 1991:492). Fadenya and Badenya stand as two sides of the *Bumuntu* within every *Muntu*.

The Fadenya-Badenya paradigm indicates that a healthy mode of being requires a harmonious balance between the individualistic and altruistic tendencies of each human being. Fadenya is a revolutionary power that stimulates rebellion against all forces of oppression. It is an indispensable engine of the struggle for liberation. On the other hand the Badenya dimension of humanity curbs human's libido dominandi, i.e., the drive to exploit others and be a "proud oppressor."

In conclusion, African traditional religions bring to liberation theology the notion that oppression occurs at the level of thought, speech, and deeds. This means that an African liberation theology intends to liberate people who are victims of evil thought (especially epistemic violence in the form of scientific, philosophical, and theological terrorism), evil speech (the badmouthing of Africans in literature, science, philosophy, and comparative religions), and evil deeds (including slave trade, colonialism, problematic trade policies, inhumane wages, and excessive taxes). Most importantly, according to this African mode of thinking, in the "master-slave" dialectic it is the oppressor who is inferior and not the oppressed. Through thought and deeds that destroy humanity in other humans, the oppressor destroys his own humanity and becomes a *Kintu*, a thing, a nonhuman. Liberation theology, in this context, is not merely about a compassionate liberation of others. One liberates oneself from oppressive instincts, from a self-inflicted inhumanity, and increases one's own humanity by rejecting an oppressive mode of being and by struggling for the liberation of others. Such are the principles that have guided traditional African liberation theology. We shall now examine how these principles played out historically and how they apply to local and global forces of oppression.

Liberation from Local and Global Forces of Oppression

Liberation from Local Forces of Oppression

What are the local forms of oppression and how did liberation theology address such a challenge? Oppression takes a myriad of forms; however, for the sake of clarity we have identified in the introduction "seven mortal sins." These seven types of oppressive behaviors fall into two major categories that constitute the major forces of oppression: religion and the state government. For the sake of brevity we shall focus here on the response of traditional liberation theology to sociopolitical forms of oppression.

The liberation struggle for decency and full humanity is as old as Africa itself. Indeed, well before the arrival of Christianity and Islam, Africans have challenged their own rulers, abusive priests, and abusive religious customs. Africa, like any other society in human history, has produced virtuous people and institutions, as well as corrupt and vicious individuals and oppressive institutions. Even ancestral traditions could turn oppressive in the hands of unscrupulous individuals or rulers. A deep-seated patriarchy shaped proverbs and the traditional wisdom itself. Both colonialism and slave trade would not have been successful without the "collaboration" of some Africans. Likewise neocolonialism is led among others by those *dictateurs aux dents longues* that continue to loot their own countries and transfer wealth to Swiss banks and elsewhere while their population starves. Indeed, Africa has known about the human condition and the paradoxes of human nature. It identified evil or harmful impulses in human heart, thought, speech, and actions, and referred to it with the concepts of *Mucima Mubi* or *mucima wa nshikanyi* (evil heart), and *butshi* (sorcery). Most people today regard African politicians as "witches" and the very word "politics" has become a synonym of harm, trickery, and lie. They look upon this "independence of dictators" as a betrayal of the ancestral tradition of sage kings. Given its use of religion and its direct impact on all aspects of social life, political tyranny plays a crucial role in the grand scheme of oppression.

That political power is dangerous in the hands of unscrupulous individuals is a point well known in Africa. If African historical memory celebrates some rulers as sage kings, many others are remembered as monsters that brought misfortune and bad luck to people. In Luba empire, Nkongolo Mwamba is remembered as a paradigmatic tyrant. Even Ngoie Nsanza, who is celebrated for his reign of justice, is remembered for establishing an oppressive penal code which inflicted terrible forms of punishment to criminals, including mutilation: the cutting off of a hand to a thief, the upper lip to a liar, an eye or the nose to one guilty of adultery, and an ear to one who does not listen and disobeys constantly.

The question before us is: how did people react in the face of oppressive behaviors or institutions? Did they passively submit to oppression by accepting that the perpetrators acted according the will of the ancestors? Here African liberation theology found its most explicit expression in the traditional doctrine of "sage king," in political institutions created to control the power of the king and make sure that the ancestral sage king principle was followed, and finally in the numerous resistance movements by which people strived to liberate themselves from the yoke of tyrants.

A careful examination of African history shows that most oppressive actions were met with a liberatory reaction. This reaction begins with the power of the word. At the core of African social life we find the institution of palaver, a legitimate discussion and debate which indicates that the will of the ancestor was not left to the canonical interpretation of kings, priests, or the privileged class of noble people. Indeed, Africans have agreed to disagree on the interpretation of the *Kishila-kya-bankambo* (the will of God and the will of the ancestors). The manipulation of religion and tradition by the powerful did not go unchallenged. Quite often it was rejected as a betrayal of the will of the ancestors. And indeed rebellion flourished whenever people had enough power to ascertain their resistance. A king was considered divine only insofar as his rule followed the will of God and the ancestors. Like in the Chinese doctrine of the Mandate of Heaven, once a king became oppressor to his people, he was ipso facto considered as a being abandoned by the ancestors and therefore a candidate to impeachment and even execution. Thus the Asante people destooled several of their kings. King Osei Kwame, for instance, was destooled in 1799 for absenting himself from the capital Kumasi and endangering the security of the nation in failing to perform his religious duties. Karikari was impeached in 1874 for extravagance, among other failings, and Mensa Bonsu for excessively taxing the Asante people. And the Asante were not an exception in that regard. Although the Zanj people of East Africa considered their ruler as a "supreme Lord" they never hesitated to depose and execute him in case he departed from the rule of equity (Davidson, 1994:36). In Africa as in other parts of the world, resistance against tyranny remains the first article of people's conception of political power. As the Luba proverb "Bulohwe I Bantu" put it, power is for the people and a ruler who tyrannizes the people ipso facto delegitimizes his authority and forfeits his right to rule. Throughout sub-Saharan Africa we find similar examples.

By glorifying for centuries sage kings at the expense of tyrants, African myths and popular traditions translate the peculiar aspiration of the African people to a good government and a radical rejection of despotism as immoral. Well before the United States declared independence from England, Africans overthrew many kings. Even Hegel who held African politics in extreme contempt declared that "when the Negroes are discontented with their king they express their dissatisfaction and warn him by sending parrots' eggs or a deputation, and finally when there is no change they depose and execute him" (Hegel, 1994:208).

What is most important is not merely rebellion against tyranny. African traditional religions produced a powerful antidote to tyranny, a political theology of good governance, enshrined in proverbs and investiture speeches. This doctrine begins with a distinction between a legitimate and an illegitimate ruler. The Baluba who make a distinction between Mulohwe (sage king) and Kilohwe (an inhuman tyrant) remind the ruler who has a penchant for tyrannical behavior that *bulohwe* is *Bantu* (power is the people). Likewise in South Africa where a clear distinction is made between the *Morena-Inkosi* (a king of the people) and the *Morena wa Mekopu* (the king of pumpkins), the tyrant is reminded that *Morena Ke Morena Ka Batho* (one is a king only when and as long as he is acknowledged by the people). It is significant to note that kings became kings during their investiture, often preceded by a divination which has to guarantee the legitimacy of the new ruler by confirming his acceptance by the ancestors.

Investiture happened after days of the rite of passage during which the future king had to symbolically die to his "ordinary nature" in order to be born as a new being capable of carrying the heavy duty of government with honesty, fairness, and passion for the common good. The criterion was that the will of the ancestors was to foster happiness and guarantee justice and the protection of the people. This vision is widespread in Africa as can be seen in the case of a Tswana Chief, who under pressure from his courtiers to act in an obviously prejudiced manner against another, retorted: "I cannot do that! How shall I face my fathers if I do so?" (Setiloane, 1993:148).

Finally and most importantly, African political theology of the sage king found its best articulation in investiture speeches. The investiture speech of the Ashanti, for example, stipulates that the king should not disclose the origin (ethnicity) of any person, should not curse people, should not be greedy or violent, should not call people "fools," and should never act without following the advice of his people (Ayittey, 1992:57). The investiture speech of the Asanti people of Bekwai warns the new king against the danger of drinking and other shameful behaviors and prohibits him from making civil wars and "gambling with the people." Everywhere rulers are told that they must listen to the advice and the wish of the people.

In conclusion, traditional religions generated a liberation theology based on five basic principles that constitute the traditional "pentagon of power."

1. African traditional religions built their political theology on the notion that life is the central gift from the ancestors and the creator. In virtue of its transcendent origin, life was regarded as sacred and the fundamental ethical criterion for distinguishing virtues from vices, good rulers from bad ones, liberation from oppression.

2. African traditional religions maintained that the *raison d'etre* of government is to ensure the welfare of all the people, by protecting life and being sure that people are not stripped of adequate means of existence.

3. African tradition acknowledges civil authority as vice regent of the Divinity on earth, however it does not view any individual civil authority as absolute.

4. A ruler is accepted as ruler only in so far as he conforms himself to the will of the ancestors and the creator, who established civil authority for the good ordering of society, and for the transmission of life and beneficence of the Divinity to the people.

5. When a civil authority ceases to be the transmitter of the graces and benefits of Divinity, i.e., to execute what has been entrusted to it, it forfeits its validity. At this level a "bellum justum" component emerges in traditional liberation theology. According to African traditional religion, such a forfeiture of validity by the king means an extrication of the people from his authority and rule. If the illegitimate

government refuses to resign, then it becomes the "abomination of desolation" standing in the ancestral shrine, a hindrance to people's access to the Divinity, hence the foundation of the legitimacy of uprising and resistance to the evil rule. It is then believed that it is against the will of the ancestors to fail to strike an evil regime, be it local or that of a foreign occupier. This is the foundation of Africa resistance to slave trade, colonialism, African dictators, and some ambiguous powers of globalization. This leads to the analysis of forces of foreign oppression.

Liberation from Outside Forces of Oppression

The fact that foreign forces, using a superior military might directly or indirectly seize control of African political and economic life implied not a greater prosperity for Africa but rather ipso facto African loss of freedom and various human rights. It implied slave labor, ridiculous salaries, heavy taxes, an unfair judicial system, appointment of token African rulers, transfer of wealth from Africa to Europe, and fake elections. Pseudodemocratic regimes ruled from Paris, Brussels, London, or Washington. African response came instantly by way of resistance movements. In 1891, when the British were trying to turn Ghana (then the Gold Coast) into their protectorate told the king Prempeh I of Asante that the Queen of England wanted to "protect" him and his kingdom, he replied: "The suggestion that Asante in its present state should come and enjoy the protection of Her Majesty the Queen and Empress of India I may say is a matter of very serious consideration, and which I am happy to say we have arrived at this conclusion, that my kingdom of Asante will never commit itself to any such policy. Asante must remain as of old at the same time to remain friendly with all white men" (Boahen, 1990:1). In 1895 Wobogo, the Moro Naba or King of Mosi (in modern Burkina Faso) told the French Captain Destenave: "I know the whites wish to kill me in order to take my country, and yet you claim that they will help me to organize my country. But I find my country good just as it is. I have no need of them. I know what is necessary for me and what I want: I have my own merchants; also consider yourself fortunate that I do not order your head to be cut off. Go away now, and above all, never come back" (Boahen, 1990:1).

Similar reaction is reported from Lat Dior, the Damel of Cayor (in modern Senegal) in 1883; from King Machemba of the Yao in modern Tanzania in 1890; from Hendrik Witbooi, a king in southwest Africa; and many other regions. In Central Africa, between 1885 and 1905, more than a dozen groups revolted in the Congo alone. Likewise a series of enlightened "sage kings" emerged in various parts of Africa challenging slave trade. In 1526, Affonso, King of Kongo, sent a letter of protest to the King of Portugal (Dom Joao). The letter first describes in detail the evils of the slave trade and then concludes with a decision to abolish it:

> To the most powerful and excellent prince Dom Joao, King our Brother
>
> Sir your Highness (of Portugal) should know how our Kingdom is being lost in so many ways . . . so great, Sir, is the corruption and licentiousness that our country is being completely depopulated, and Your Highness should not agree with this nor accept it as in your service. . . . That is why we beg of Your Highness to help and assist us in this matter, commanding your factors that they should not send here either merchants or wares, because it is our will that in these Kingdoms there should not be any trade of slaves nor outlet for them. (Davidson, 1991:223–24)

Affonso's analysis of the impact of slave trade on Kongo contradicts also the argument often used by some scholars who claim that the kingdoms of black Africa flourished because of the wealth gained by African kings through slave trade. But this phenomenon of enlightened kings is not unique to Central Africa. Another notorious case is reported in West Africa in the eighteenth century by the Swedish traveler Wadström. In a report to the British Privy Council Committee of 1789 on the political chaos caused by the slave trade in Africa, Wadström evokes the case of the enlightened king of Almammy who in 1787 enacted a law stating that no slave whatever should be marched throughout his territories. This same passion for moral correctness led the Asantehene of Ashanti (Ghana) to reject a European demand for enslaving people. In 1819 he replied to a European visitor that it was not his practice "to make war to catch slaves in the bush like a thief."

This resistance to the injustices of the global trade and global politics was deeply rooted in the traditional religious sense of dignity and justice. The few examples quoted above do not constitute a treatise of liberation theology. But they do wonderfully reflect the effects of a spirit of liberation theology at work, for those kings were influenced by a specific worldview steeped in ancestral spirituality. Indeed, traditional religions and their priests and diviners played a crucial role in formulating a liberation theology that provided moral legitimacy to resistance and even outright wars of liberation. The role of African traditional religions in liberation theology was twofold: First religion established the principle of just cause thus providing legitimacy and a powerful motivation for struggle against oppression. Secondly it established the principle of divine and ancestor assistance during wars of liberation. Such assistance was materialized in the "blessed water ritual" by which the ancestors bestowed strength, invulnerability, and even invisibility upon the warriors on the battlefield.

Thus, traditional religion, Africanized Christianity and Africanized Islam, spearheaded the "art of resistance" against slave trade and colonial oppression. Various "prophets" and "prophetesses" emerged on the political scene, preaching a kind of "social gospel," a "liberation theology." The Maji Maji uprising resorted to African traditional religion and the power of its "magic." In so doing it became the most serious challenge to colonial British rule in East Africa.

Germans too faced in their colony of Tanganyika the powerful prophet Kinjikitile Ngwale who resorted to traditional religious practices and worldview to preach that the war of liberation was ordained by God, and that the ancestors would return to life to assist the African people in this war. God and the ancestors, he added, want the unity and freedom of all the African people and want them to fight the German oppressors. The war raged for more than two years, from July 1905 to August 1907. Although Kinjikitile himself was captured early on and hanged by the Germans, his brother picked up his mantle, assumed the title of "Nyamguni," one of the three divinities in the region, and continued to administer the "Maji," a religiously blessed water aimed at rendering the warrior invulnerable (Mwanzi, 1990:80). This practice of blessed water is widespread in Africa. Among the Baluba it is referred to as "koya kizaba" (taking a bath in a magical water, blessed by the ancestors to gain extraordinary strength and invulnerability on the battlefield).

The traditional role played by women in African traditional religions brought them to the forefront in resistance movements. In the Zambezi valley, the Shona mediums instigated the famous rebellions of 1897, 1901, and 1904. In the Congo the notorious case remains that of the Christian independent church of Dona Beatrice: Kimpa Vita's struggle for freedom in the Kongo kingdom was so passionate that historians have called her "Jeanne d'Arc du Congo" in reference to the spirit of French Revolution. In Congo-Brazaville, the priestess Maria Nkoie instigated the Ikaya rebellion which lasted for five years, until 1921. And many other women have played a crucial role in the struggle for freedom. Almost all wars waged against Western conquest were backed by religious belief in justice and just cause. Enslaved Africans crossed the Atlantic carrying with them a liberation theology that was to have a global repercussion in the famous Haitian revolution and various slave rebellions in the United States and in Latin America.

The spirit of traditional religions impacted various charismatic figures converted to Christianity, such as Simon Kimbangu, and led them to challenge not only colonial governments but also the colonial Christianity that lent moral and spiritual legitimacy to foreign tyranny. Indeed, well before the rise of African theology and its process of Africanization of Christianity, and almost 250 years before the rise of the civil rights movement and the ensuing Afrocentric paradigm in the United States, Kimpa Vita, a young Congolese girl nicknamed "Jeanne d'Arc du Congo," after initiation in both traditional religions and Christianity, set up a radical movement to reform both religions. Preaching against some traditional customs, she also challenged the Portuguese slave traders and their understanding of Christianity and articulated her own version of Christian theology. Disgusted by racism within the sanctuary of Christianity, she taught her followers that Christ appeared to her as a black man in Sao Salvador and that all his apostles were black. She argued that Jesus identified himself with the oppressed black Africans and opposed the white exploiters and oppressors. She also created a Christian creed adapted to the African situation.

Persecuted by the Portuguese missionaries she was burned at the stake, but her liberation theology and her doctrine of the Africanization of Christianity was to continue in subsequent generations of new prophets. Beatrice Kimpa Vita did not only attack the structure of the global market of that time but also its religious foundation in a colonial version of Christianity. She was also capable of transcending the colonial mask to appreciate the values of Christianity, thus exhibiting that fundamental African spirit of religious tolerance and appreciation of the spiritual values and truth inherent in other religions. Her critical evaluation of African traditional religions and customs also exemplifies that traditional African power of self-criticism so relevant to issues of liberation theology.

This is the traditional spirit that had instigated the impeachment of many traditional kings and recently the democratic movements against African dictators. It is also to this traditional liberation theology that African Christian theologians have turned in their effort to Africanize Christianity and articulate a Christian theology that takes into account the well-being of the African people. The theme of the Africanization of Christianity is important for understanding the impact of traditional religious worldview on Christian liberation theology that is now dominant in Africa. It stems from the failure of Western Christianity to adequately address the needs of Africans. This brings us to one of the crucial issues of religious oppression.

Religious Oppression

It is widely acknowledged, by Christian and Muslim scholars alike, that in Africa the traditional religions, not Christianity or Islam, offer a great tradition of tolerance. According to the Catholic theologian Bénézet Bujo, religious wars were unknown in African traditional society (1992:55). Summarizing the Islamic view, Ali Mazrui, a Muslim scholar, is more explicit:

> Of the three principal religious legacies of Africa (indigenous, Islamic, and Christian), the most tolerant on record must be the indigenous tradition. One might even argue that Africa did not have religious wars before Christianity and Islam arrived, for indigenous religions were neither universalist (seeking to convert the whole of the human race) nor competitive (in bitter rivalry against other creeds). . . . Like Hinduism and modern Judaism—and unlike Christianity and Islam—indigenous African traditions have not sought to convert the whole of humanity. The Yoruba do not seek to convert the Ibo to the Yoruba religion—or vice versa—and neither the Yoruba nor the Ibo compete with each other for the souls of a third group, such as the Hausa. Because they are not proselytizing religions, indigenous African creeds have not fought with each other. Over the centuries, Africans have waged many kinds of wars with each other, but they were rarely religious ones before the universalist creeds arrived. (1999:77)

Writing from the perspective of the Yoruba religion of Nigeria, Abimbola observed that the Yoruba religion starts with myths of creation that maintain the idea of a universal common descent of all human beings from the same God creator, Obatala (Abimbola, 1990:138). Thus arises the African belief in the necessity of respect for all the religious traditions of humankind, as a condition for a peaceful coexistence among people and nations. Although in recent decades religious conflicts have erupted in Nigeria and the Soudan, religious crusades were alien to traditional religious spirit. This traditional spirit of religious tolerance epitomized by the extraordinary harmonious coexistence between Christians and Muslims in Senegal, and some other countries as well, constitutes in this era of rising fundamentalism one of the most important contributions of Africa to the liberation of the world from religious extremism and "sacred" violence.

Gender Oppression

African feminist philosophers and theologians such as Mercy Amba Oduyoye and many others have abundantly challenged the sexism inherent in African traditions and traditional religions. I also have elsewhere analyzed in detail the oppressive nature of African patriarchy (Nkulu-N'Sengha, 2001:69–108). In light of growing modern forms of sexism (including grotesque pornography, "leisure industry" or "sexual tourism," the global trade of women for prostitution, and the exclusion of women from priesthood) women are now turning toward ancestral notions of womanhood and dignity to combat the alienation generated by a modernity that purports to be essentially a force of liberation.

Conclusion: The Wisdom of the Poor

"Wisdom," says Ecclesiastes, "is better than strength; Nevertheless the poor man's wisdom is despised; and his words are not heard" (9:14-16). As a poor continent, Africa has been largely conceptualized as the unwise land of oppressive ancestral traditions awaiting for foreign liberators. Such a perception is in itself one of the major oppressive forces that not only Africa but the outside world needs to be liberated from. The wisdom of African liberation theology begins with faith in the self-liberation capacity of the African tradition. Such a tradition is grounded in ancestral spirituality. Africa has indeed a long tradition of ancestral wisdom which enabled life to thrive by constantly overcoming local and foreign structures of oppression. As Jacques Maquet (and Georges Balandier) pointed out in their classical *Dictionary of Black African Civilization*, "African wisdom is not merely a convenient expression; it is something that exists. It is a collection of unique precepts that enable the people of traditional Africa to settle as harmoniously as possible the disputes that mar human relationships" (Balandier and Maquet, 1974:336).

Overlooked and despised during the colonial era, this wisdom is being increasingly acknowledged as indispensable for solving many of the problems that Africa faces in modern times. This wisdom is well encapsulated in the key notion of Bumuntu that has shaped the African idea of genuine humanity and authentic mode of being, from the Nile to the Niger, from the Congo river to the Zambezi. For millennia, this Bumuntu wisdom of "the good life" has guided the African sense of good and evil, and the African understanding of oppression and liberation.

The effort to rediscover African traditional values is in itself a liberatory act. It takes the first step in the articulation of a genuine liberation theology. I have remarked that although 80 percent of Africans have converted to Christianity and Islam, traditional religions still remain the foundation of African identity and African spirituality and the soul and heart of African civilization, so much so that in Africa even Christianity and Islam are deeply shaped by a traditional worldview. This traditional spirit enables African Christians to challenge the oppressive nature of colonial and neocolonial Christianity. It is indeed the traditional spirit of Bumuntu wisdom that led the children of Soweto to face the machine guns of the apartheid regimes and elsewhere animated adult and school children to challenge the tyranny of Bokassa, Idi Amin, or Mobutu Sese Seko, and other ubuesque dictators. It is the same spirit of Bumuntu that produced Kimpa Vita and Wangari Mathai, Nelson Mandela and Desmond Tutu, Kwame Nkrumah and Patrice Lumumba. The same spirit led Sarawiwa to face the tyranny of oil companies such as Shell.

Although African ancestors did not produce a written treatise of a systematic liberation theology, such a theology existed in oral tradition and is well expressed in countless African resistance movements to local and foreign oppression. Nowadays such a theology exists in African independent movements as well as in writings by some Christian theologians who make extensive use of traditional religions and ancestral values in their articulation of the Africanization of Christianity which is perceived as a *sine qua non* condition for African spiritual liberation. It is a theology that repudiates religious patriotism, religious fanaticism, and religious imperialism. It is also a theology deeply grounded in the notion of human dignity we have referred to as Bumuntu. African liberation theology moves beyond the Cartesian "Cogito ergo sum" into an epistemology of solidarity and hospitality which maintains that "I am because we are; and since we are, therefore I am" as John Mbiti put it beautifully.

3 Studying Hinduism in Practice

Hillary Rodrigues

Introduction

This book is a collection of contributions written by specialists especially for readers relatively new to the academic study of the Hindu religious tradition. In accord with the intent of the *Studying Religions in Practice* series, to which this compilation belongs, the chapters are designed to serve two purposes. These are: 1) to highlight features of Hinduism as it is actually practiced, and 2) to illustrate some of the authentic experiences of researchers engaged in the study of those practices.

These contributions have other features that make this collection distinct. Although many of the authors may have strong affinities for the Hindu tradition, and some may even be deeply immersed in aspects of its practices, these are not chapters by Hindus telling the reader how they practice and experience their faith, and then explaining how or why these practices might make sense to non-Hindus. This book is grounded in the secular, scholarly study of Hinduism. It is also focused on the doings of Hindus, that is, their practices. This is because even well-written comprehensive introductory textbooks—and there are several in use in university undergraduate courses—cannot adequately convey the life of the Hindu religious tradition as it is experienced by Hindus. A textbook may talk about the Hindu caste system, and even describe how distinctions are made between the casteless Untouchables and high-caste Brahmins, but it rarely transports us into the midst of a scenario in which this distinction is played out. A textbook may tell us that the majority of Hindus live in small villages, that they enjoy varieties of folk entertainment with religious themes, and that modernization is bringing with it irreversible changes to rural life, but it does not carry us into the experiences of the people who are living those realities. And such books almost never reveal to the reader anything about the experiences of the researchers as they are making those discoveries. Effective textbooks are typically designed to convey information and serve as useful and comprehensive references on Hinduism.

This collection is intended to serve as a complement to a good textbook and a knowledgeable instructor. It makes no pretensions to providing a comprehensive coverage of the practices of Hinduism. Frankly, one should be highly suspicious of any book that makes such a claim. Hinduism is an inordinately complex and rich tradition, with an astounding array of practices. Its expressive forms vary considerably across regions of India, where it is widespread, in neighboring lands, such as Nepal, Sri Lanka, and Bali, where there are large Hindu populations, and across the globe, wherever Hindu communities of any reasonable size are found. Any attempt at an all-encompassing treatment of Hindu practices would require a small library of volumes. Nevertheless, this concise collection of chapters is felicitously broad in its temporal and topical coverage. When viewed as a whole, a knowledgeable reader will note that the chapters touch upon contemporary practices from half a century ago up to the present day, as they were actually observed. Within its corpus there are discussions of devotional worship, pilgrimage, folk dramas, music, dance, village life, temple traditions, exorcisms, possession, healings, the epics, rituals, oral traditions, women's practices, puranic myths, tantric, yogic, and other philosophies, as well as festival traditions. It illustrates the more marginalized realities of Hindu women, Dalits, the lowest members in the social hierarchy, and villagers, along with the views of the more dominant groups, such as urban, upper-caste Brahmin men. Its perspectives emanate from north and south India, as well as from the Hindu world beyond India.

Unlike other collections that concern practice, but which focus primarily on the translation of ancient texts that discuss religious practices, these chapters address current expressions of Hinduism. Thus the anthology is an excellent source for the study of contemporary Hinduism. Although some of the chapters address the changes that certain researchers have observed over decades of study, their contributions to this volume do not focus on how classical texts prescribe Hindu practice, but with how select groups of Hindus actually engage in their religion today. And, unlike the content of other collections that deal with the life of Hinduism, these chapters are not culled from larger works written by academics for the benefit of their scholarly peers. These are pieces written by highly trained, professional researchers and instructors specifically for readers with little or no background knowledge of the Hindu tradition. The contributors span a range from scholars at the early stages of their professional careers to those with emeritus professorial status or its equivalent. Many enjoy the reputation of eminence among their peers for their lifetime of contributions to the study of Hinduism. Some are scholars who do not or no longer work primarily within a university environment. Some tell stories about their journey through academia. All tell stories about their discoveries and processes of learning about Hinduism. Moreover, there is research material not published elsewhere, contained within some of these chapters. Apart from volumes in this series, there is currently no other published collection of contributions of this sort.

Another distinctive feature of this collection is the form in which the chapters are written. Authors were encouraged to comply with an innovative, experimental, prescribed structure, allowing moderate flexibility for the subject matter and the dispositions of the contributors. Having trained in both textual and anthropological methodologies, and being deeply committed to pedagogy, I was continually struck by how effective story telling can be in the process of teaching. Even a superficial probe into most religious traditions will reveal the enormously influential role that stories have in conveying religious teachings. Hinduism is especially instructive in that respect. In fact, I quickly recognized that when I taught my classes, my students most often remembered the myths that I recounted from epics, such as the *Rāmāyaṇa*, or from the Purāṇas, far better than the philosophical arguments and other material presented to them in a non-narrative manner. Moreover, when explaining where I took particular photographic slides (long before the advent of PowerPoint), I found that the stories I told about the circumstances surrounding those experiences, or the anecdotes that I used to illustrate particular points, such as interactions with religious specialists, my emotional responses to music or other performances, to sculpture or architecture, and so on, held my students' attention best. In evaluations at semester's end, there were frequent remarks on how much they enjoyed and learned from those aspects of the Hinduism course. Years, even decades later, former students I encountered would sometimes comment on how those stories inspired them to read or study further into Hinduism, long after they had graduated and gone on to other occupations. A few were even inspired to take up the academic study of religion. These observations and experiences are not unique, and are likely shared by most teachers. The narrative, particularly a personal one, is an undeniably compelling form of communication and can be a powerful teaching instrument. It is for this and numerous other reasons that the contributors begin their accounts with a self-implicated narrative, telling a story about their raw experiences while they were engaged in studying some feature of Hindu practice.

An early draft of my chapter included in this volume served as a guide to the authors. In it I begin with a description of some of my research experiences in Varanasi during two consecutive occurrences of the autumn navarātra, an annual goddess-centered celebration. The chapter provides a sense of the diversity of practices that take place in the city, both prior to and during the festival, as well as the challenges facing any researcher. It touches upon domestic and temple devotional rites (*pūjā*), urban pilgrimage, sacrifice, and various other aspects of the living practice of Hinduism. It then uses this descriptive narrative as a springboard for discussing the Hindu calendrical system, and introducing readers to some of the major festivals that are celebrated through the year.

Authors were instructed to tell their stories in a form that is not typical in scholarly papers, where narrative is often wholly absent. But even in such papers that include narratives, the story is kept brief, mostly stripped of its colorful descriptors and with little or nothing revealed of the researcher's personal response to the experience. Embedded within or immediately after the narrative, the scholar typically provides extensive interpretations and explanations often derived from their years of subsequent painstaking analytic work. There are obvious merits in that design, among which is its effectiveness in conveying information to one's academic peers. Among its demerits are the distance it constructs between the specialist and the novice, and the illusion it can perpetuate that the researcher possesses a mature understanding in the midst of raw experience. It is more akin to a polished performance. In contrast to that format, the intention in these chapters is pedagogic. Here the authors tell about their experiences in as honest a manner as they remember, including indications of their thoughts, and their sensory and emotional states. What were they seeing and hearing, what did the experience cause them to feel, and what did it make them wonder about? In so doing, and by minimizing specialized terminology, the aim is to first draw the reader into the experience alongside the researcher. The narrative is intended to be more of a description of raw experience than a well-processed explanation of the observed practices. This is because experience, whether it is that of the researcher or the observed practitioners, has a potency that derives from its immediacy. It is compelling because it carries qualities of sensory, emotional, and intellectual stimulation. Explanation, by contrast, is second-hand, a reflection upon experience.

By being drawn into companionship with the author through the narrative, the reader may be better able to share vicariously in the experience of observing and participating in the religious practices that are being described. They may find themselves having emotional responses, such as of excitement and awe, or even fear and revulsion, which resonate or contrast with those experienced by the researcher. They may find themselves asking questions about features of the experience described in the narrative that the researcher does not appear to ask. This is intended as a heuristic strategy. Moreover, the discussion that ensues in the chapter may not address any of the questions that may interest the reader. Authors were instructed to use the narrative as a launching point dicussing for any of a number of related topics. They might contextualize some features of the narrative with information. Alternately, they may go into a discussion about certain aspects of the experience, providing a much broader context and explanation about the phenomena described in the narrative. Some choose to touch on theoretical issues, while others offer advice to novice, would-be researchers.

In my own chapter, for instance, I do not provide theoretical explanations about *pūjā* or pilgrimage, or temple worship, or sacrifice, or renunciation and devotion. Nor do I go into extensive specific explanations about the nature of Durgā, her mythology, and the modes of her worship. Instead, I choose to inform about Hindu festivals and their place in the annual cycle. The readers are thus not provided with a neatly packaged story with its authoritative explanations and interpretations seemingly providing answers to all anticipated questions and an end to all further discussion. Instead, they are encouraged, if not induced, to turn to their instructors, read their textbooks more pointedly, and consult the suggested readings where many of their unanswered questions might be addressed in much greater detail. This process will have already transformed them into inquiring agents rather than passive recipients of knowledge. Readers may also find some answers to their inquiries, but certainly more questions, in other contributions in the anthology, because a discussion provided in one chapter may have instructional value and explanatory relevance for other narratives in the collection. Similarly, various narratives may touch upon overlapping subject matter, similar themes, and describe related forms of practice. Let me now turn to a brief account of the contents of the collection. My brevity is deliberate, because I do not wish to precede the authors' stories with lengthy summaries and analyses, which can diffuse their impact. Our intent is to let the phenomena of religious practices and their study take the lead, and to let reflections by the reader follow in their wake.

Brenda E. F. Beck's contribution centers on her early experiences in an Indian village in the 1960s. It tells how she, almost by happenstance, came upon aspects of Hinduism that served as the basis for some of her most significant scholarly contributions and current activities. In particular she discusses her discovery of the system of right and left castes, and the *Elder Brothers Legend*, a folk narrative, which she is now transforming into a series of animated films. She illustrates the value of fieldwork, and offers advice and guidance on how to benefit from it.

Jeffrey Brackett's chapter describes his visits to rural and urban temples to the monkey god Hanumān in the state of Maharashtra. These took place on different years on the occasion of the festival celebrating the deity's birth. His narrative illustrates the dazzling variety of temples dedicated to Hanumān, and leads to a discussion on why Hindu temples develop their distinctive popularity and eminence.

Paul B. Courtright tells about his investigation into the outlawed practice of *satī* (widow burning). These lead him to myths of the goddess Satī, which in turn are linked to places such as kankhal in north India. He demonstrates how such myths can be fertile sources for interpretation, yielding layers of meanings for whosoever contemplates them.

Patricia A. Dold describes her encounters at the renowned temple of kāmākhyā in Assam, with women who carry the tradition of singing devotional songs known as Nām to the goddess(es) abiding there. She tells of the ritual contexts in which these songs are performed, particularly the Debaddhanī festival, which entails phenomena such as supernormal empowerments, possession, and blood sacrifice. Her discussion focuses on the Mahāvidyās, the cluster of goddesses that figure most significantly as forms of kāmākhyā as she is actually worshipped today.

Jason D. Fuller recounts his first encounter with Hindu sacred space in an unexpected place, the temple complex at New Vrindaban in West Virginia. He also discovers experiential parallels during his visit to the Hare krishna temple in Mayapur, Bengal. This leads to a discussion of *Tīrthas*, Hindu conceptions of sacred crossing points that ford mundane and transcendental realms.

Anne-Marie Gaston gives an account of her absorption into Indian classical dance at a time when it was infrequently taken up by persons outside of the temple traditions within which it had formed, much less by foreigners. She tells of particularly memorable performances, choreography, and her progressive understanding of Hinduism through the medium of dance. This leads to a discussion of issues of purity and pollution, caste distinctions, as well as the aesthetic theories of Hinduism as they relate to dance.

Alf Hiltebeitel's piece deviates somewhat from the pervasive structure in the contributions because his topic does not submit particularly well to it. His concluding discussion is short because he embeds commentaries on context and theorizes within his lengthier narrative. He discusses his attempts to track a hypothesis within village enactments during a festival dedicated to Duryodhana, the villain of the *Mahābhārata* epic, who is worshipped as a god. His search for the widows of the kauravas, the family defeated by the heroic Pāṇḍavas, is based on various clues and hunches, most of which prove to be misguided. He thus offers valuable insights into the process of learning through fieldwork, while providing us with colorful descriptions of festival rituals.

Knut A. Jacobsen begins his chapter with a description of his observations at the kāpil Maṭh, perhaps the only monastery in India dedicated to the Sāṃkhya philosophical tradition. He witnesses the practices and participates in rituals that align with values promoted by Sāṃkhya, such as detachment, tranquility, and self-realization. We learn about the master-student relationship involved in the transmission of teachings, and he provides a more extensive discussion of Sāṃkhya teachings.

Jeffrey Lidke's story centers on his early experiences studying the *tablā* in Nepal, and performing as he gained greater proficiency. This forms the basis of a discussion on the intimate relationship between the performing arts and Hindu spirituality, which are particularly well articulated in aesthetic philosophies of Tantra.

William Sax's chapter recounts his experiences among the Harijans (Untouchables) of the Himalayas, where spirit possession and exorcism play significant roles in the diagnosis and treatment of maladies. He offers detailed descriptions of the ritual processes entailing music, chanting, and blood sacrifice, through which healing is enacted. His discussion probes the notion of possession in the social and religious lives of communities.

Bruce M. Sullivan describes his experiences studying the ancient dance dramatic form known as kūṭ iyāṭṭam, which originated within temples. This leads to a discussion of the classical Hindu theory of *rasa* (aesthetic enjoyment), which is the purpose of such dance dramas. He also tells of transformations that have been affecting the tradition as India modernizes.

Paul Younger tells of his experiences studying Indian religions in the early period after Indian independence, when hierarchical and colonial attitudes strongly prevailed, even among academics. He describes his progressive movement into the examination of Hindu temple traditions, particularly at Śrīraṅkam and Citamparam, and his study of festivals, including those not centered primarily on temples.

The contributors did not read each others' works and did not purposefully craft their contributions to resonate with them. And yet, as was suspected, thematic relationships and connections are everywhere evident. Lidke, for instance, makes passing reference to notions in Sāṃkhya and Yoga philosophy (which is discussed in greater detail by Jacobsen), to the *devadāsī* tradition (also discussed by Gaston), and to *rasa* theory (discussed by Gaston and Sullivan). The overall form of the anthology is intended to be synergistic in its effects. While the prescribed structure for each chapter was encouraged, the contributors followed it with varying degrees of rigor based on their capacities, professional habits, and the subject matter with which they were dealing.

These chapters may be used to get glimpses and insights into an assortment of Hindu practices. For instance, one might read Younger, Fuller, Brackett, Rodrigues, and Dold to get perspectives on pilgrimage, while aspects of temple traditions are found in Fuller, Brackett, Younger, Rodrigues, Dold, Courtright, and Jacobsen. Dimensions of Hindu philosophy are addressed in Jacobsen, Younger, Lidke, and Fuller. One can read about sacrifice, including blood sacrifice, in Rodrigues, Sax, Hiltebeitel, and Dold. Jacobsen and Dold offer translations and information on living, oral hymn and song traditions. Younger, Gaston, Sullivan, Beck and Hiltebeitel represent south Indian Hinduism in their pieces. Fuller and Lidke touch upon Hinduism outside of India. Women's religious practices are evidenced in Dold, Hiltebeitel, and Gaston, for instance, and the experiences of women scholars in Beck, Dold, and Gaston. Issues related to caste and untouchability are found in Beck, Sax, Gaston, Hiltebeitel, and Younger. Mythic tellings and enactments about gods and goddesses are touched upon in Beck, Hiltebeitel, Dold, Sullivan, Courtright, Rodrigues, and Younger. Possession and exorcism are treated in Hiltebeitel, Dold, and Sax. The crucially significant relationship between the teacher (*guru*) and the student is evident in Gaston, Lidke, and younger. Dold, too, reveals processes of transmission within women's oral traditions. The oft-ignored, but intimate relationship between the performance arts and the Hindu religion is explored in Gaston, Lidke, and Sullivan. Such Hindu aesthetic and philosophical notions as *rasa*, often rendered as taste, flavor, mood, emotional state or response, appear in the chapters by Lidke, Gaston, Sullivan, and Fuller. Priestly traditions and ritual performances are discussed in Sullivan, Rodrigues, Brackett, Hiltebeitel, and Younger. Aspects of village Hinduism are described in Beck, Hiltebeitel, Younger, and Sax. There are numerous other overlapping treatments of topics, which will be apparent even upon cursory reading. Since all the chapters deal with contemporary realities, they are a valuable resource for the study of modern Hinduism.

As the thematic overlaps mentioned above indicate, there were many options available in which to order the contents of this volume. However, no particular grouping seemed adequate. For instance, one could have placed Sullivan, Lidke, and Gaston's chapters under a category such as "Performance in the Hindu Tradition." But this would have excluded performative acts by mediums and healers in the chapters by Dold and Sax, for instance. And, by labeling those chapters as dealing with performance, it might have done disservice to the discussions of philosophy, social structure, and other such themes embedded in them. In other words, any viable grouping seemed to diminish the richness of the constituent chapters, undercutting potential benefits derived from such categorizations. My decision, therefore, has been arbitrarily to simply place the chapters in alphabetic order following the author's surnames.

On Transliteration and Pronunciation

Transliteration is the method in which words that are typically written in foreign scripts are depicted in the English or Latin-based alphabet. Since the languages of India, such as Sanskrit, Tamil, and Hindi, have their own alphabets that do not always correspond with the english alphabet, the scholarly convention is to use diacritic marks. Diacritics are dots and dashes that are placed above or below certain letters in an alphabet giving it a sound variant. For instance, the Sanskrit alphabet has three sibilant letters, or "s" sounds. one sibilant sounds like the common "s" in "sassy," but there are two others, which sound more like the "s" in "sugar," or "Sean." These are rendered "ś" (as for the god, Śiva), and "ṣ" (as for the god Kṛṣṇa). You will sometimes see these gods' names written as Shiva or krishna, to clarify the pronunciation without using diacritics.

We have decided to use diacritics, both because they are widely used by most scholars, and because they actually give you a much better indication of how to pronounce a word. When you see a diacritic dot under a letter, place your tongue near the roof of your mouth, and then say it as you would in English. If you see a dash over a vowel, as in the word Hanumān, for instance, just extend the sound of that vowel, so it sounds like "Hanumaan." And the letter "c" in Sanskrit is always pronounced like the "ch" in "chair," and not with the "k" sound as in "cat." So "Cōla dynasty" is pronounced like "Chōla dynasty," and not "Kōla dynasty." There is much more that one can say about proper pronunciation, but this should suffice to enable you to read the essays in this volume effectively. You should consult a good textbook on Hinduism if you are interested in learning more about Sanskrit transliteration and pronunciation.

In this book, we opted to use diacritic marks for most terms, but not for place names, or names and terms that are normally rendered without diacritics even in India. So you might see "Varanasi" instead of "Vārāṇasī" and "Ramakrishna" instead of "Rāmakṛṣṇa." Since India has changed the names of many cities in the last few decades, you might often see references to cities by their older and more commonly used names. Sometimes the alternate name is placed in parenthesis beside the first occurrence. So you might see Bombay (Mumbai) or Kolkata (Calcutta) or Varanasi (Banāras). On occasion, you might also encounter "Gaṅgā" instead of "the Ganges," because it struck the author as more appropriate to call the river by the name of the living goddess that it is believed to be by Hindus, rather than by the mundane english equivalent.

In some cases, authors chose to transliterate terms according to regional conventions. So, although the terms will be spelled consistently in a particular chapter, you might find variations in the spellings of the same word in different chapters throughout this volume. For instance, you will see the name of the great south Indian temple to Śiva rendered as "Citamparam," a spelling derived from the Tamil script, while the derivation from Sanskrit would be "Cidambaram." Since it is a place name, it might also be written "Chidambaram." We have included a list of such spelling variants here.

List of Common Variant Spellings

Brahmin	Brāhmaṇa	
Brahminic	Brahmanic	
Cidambaram	Chidambaram	Citamparam
Gaṇeśa	Ganesha	Ganesh
Gaṅgā	Ganges	
Kṛṣṇa	Krishna	
Kolkata	Calcutta	
Madras	Chennai	
Mumbai	Bombay	
Nataraja	Naṭarāja	
Sāṃkhya	Sāṅkhya	
Śiva	Shiva	
Tamil Nadu	Tamilnadu	Tamilnātu
Varanasi	Banāras	
Vrindaban	Brindavan	

4

Buddhism And Jainism

Eugene F. Gorski

Hinduism Challenged

In India in the late fifth century BCE, a spiritual vacuum arouse out of a complex matrix of factors that challenged Hinduism and give rise to Buddhism and Jainism. The first factor was that of a spiritual malaise. By this time, the doctrines of *karma* and *samsara*, which had been controversial at the time of Yajnavalkya, were universally accepted by the people.[1] "Bad" karma meant that individuals would be reborn as slaves, animals, or plants. "Good" karma would ensure their rebirth as kings or gods. But this was not a fortunate occurrence: even gods would exhaust this beneficent karma, die, and be reborn in a less exalted state on Earth. As this teaching took hold, the mood of India changed, and many people became depressed with the fear of being doomed to one transient life after another. Not even good karma could save them. As they reflected on their community, they could see only pain and suffering. Wealth and material pleasure were darkened with the grim reality of old age and mortality. As this gloom became more and more intense people sought to find a way out.

People became increasingly unsatisfied with the old Vedic rituals that could not provide a solution to this problem. The very best these rituals could do was provide a rebirth in the domain of the gods, but this could be only a temporary release from the relentless

54

and suffering-producing cycle of samsara. Some even rejected the spirituality of the *Upanishads*, which was not for everyone. It was a full-time task, demanding hours of effort each day, and it was incompatible with the duties of a householder. And at this time the revolution that produced bhakti devotion as the universally accessible means to salvation had not yet taken place. So, because of the prevailing malaise of doom and despair, many people in India were looking for a spiritual solution and longing for a *jina*, a spiritual conqueror or a Buddha, an enlightened one who had woken up to a different dimension of existence.

Social, Political, and Economic Change

In addition to the spiritual malaise of this time, there was a social crisis. The people of northern India were undergoing major political and economic changes. The Vedic system had been the spirituality that supported a highly mobile society, constantly engaged in migration. But the peoples of sixth and fifth centuries were settling down in increasingly larger communities that were focused on agricultural production. There was also political development. The small chiefdoms had been absorbed into the larger units of kingdoms. As a result, the *Kshatriya* kingly warrior class had become more prominent. The new kingdoms stimulated trade in the Ganges basin. This generated more wealth, which the kings could spend on luxury goods, on their armies, and on the new cities that were becoming centers of trade and industry.

This new urbanization was another blow for Vedic spirituality, which was not well suited to urban culture and civilization. The kings began to shrug off control of the priests, and the urban republics tended to ignore the Brahmin class altogether and put a limit on the traditional sacrifices. The lavish sacrifices had been designed to impress the gods and enhance the prestige of the patrons. By the fifth century, the eastern peoples realized that their trade and culture brought much more wealth and status than the Vedic sacrifice rites. Instead of conforming to the old traditional ways, the new cities encouraged personal initiative and innovation; individualism was replacing tribal, communal identity; the lower classes of the Vedic system were acquiring wealth and status that once would have been inconceivable.

These massive social changes brought about by urbanization were unsettling and left many people feeling disoriented and lost. The tensions were especially acute in the East, where urbanization was more advanced and where the next phase of the Indian Axial Age began. Here, life probably was experienced as particularly ephemeral, transient, plagued by disease and anomie, confirming the now well-established belief that life was *dukka*, suffering. The urban class was ambitious and powerful, but the gambling, theater, prostitution, and spirited tavern life of the towns seemed disarming to the people who still trusted in the older values.

Radical Dissent

Life was becoming more and more aggressive than before, in strong contrast to the older ideal of *ahimsa* that had become so crucial in north India. In the kingdoms there was infighting and civil strife. The economy was moved by greed and rugged competition. Life was experienced as even more violent and terrifying than when cattle rustling had been the backbone of the economy. The Vedic religion impressed people as increasingly out of touch with the violence of contemporary public life. People needed a different religious situation.

These ideas of radical dissent, along with the spiritual malaise and social, economic, and political crisis of the time, formed the complex matrix from which Buddhism and Jainism emerged during the Axial Age to vex the course of Hinduism. The founders of these religions, Siddhattha Gotama and Mahavira, provided alternative solutions to what had become the central problem of Indian life: how to find self-transcendence and salvation from the continual cycle of rebirths in the frightening and suffering-producing world. The Buddhists and Jains, of the warrior tribes and the *Kshatriya* caste, were more than ready to contest the Brahmins' claim to cultural control. They did not appreciate either the social or the religious implications of the Brahmins' teaching. Among the ranks of the Buddhists and Jains there were persons of brilliant mind for whom the costly sacrifices prescribed by the priests were not satisfactory. They and others like them had no interest in priestly sacrifices that did not immediately give them solace or fulfill their spiritual needs; they sought near-at-hand practical modes of release from their growing sense of the essential misery of existence. Like the authors of the *Upanishads,* they considered the world flawed and a cause of suffering. So they rejected the religion controlled by the Brahmins as being ineffectual for souls inwardly pained. Their radicalism was in their rejection of the sacrificial system of the *Bramanas* as well as their refusal to give the Brahmins first place of prescriptive rights in their urgent search for ways to liberation from the plight of suffering and the cycle of rebirths.

Buddhism

Buddhism emerged from the complex matrix of radical dissent, spiritual malaise, and the social, economic, and political crisis of the Indian Axial Age. About its founder, the Buddha, historians are confident of a few key facts. He was born into the family of King Shuddhodana and Queen Maya about the year 566 BCE in a region of the Indian subcontinent that now lies in southern Nepal. This date has been questioned recently by a group of historians who place his birth in the fifth century BCE. Most scholars now think that the Buddha in fact lived around 490 to 410. He was a member of the Shakya tribe, his clan name being Gotama, his given name Siddhattha. It is common to refer to him as *Siddhattha Gotama* or, more commonly as *Shakyamuni,* "The Sage of the Shakya Tribe." He was one among the thousands of brave individuals who searched in the northeastern forests of India to end samsara, the transmigration of life, during the Axial Age. Like many others, Gotama had become convinced that conquering the suffering of samsaric existence was the highest aspiration of life. Nothing else was of equal importance. And like others, he willingly gave up everything to attain that goal.

He departed from his princely existence and began his search for salvation as a wandering mendicant. For six years following his departure from palace life, he made serious efforts to attain his spiritual goal. As he engaged in this quest, he came to the conclusion that the philosophy of the Brahmins was unacceptable and their claims unsubstantiated. He also denied the saving efficacy of the *Vedas* and the ritual observances based on them. But he did take up the options available to him for practicing the ascetic and contemplative disciplines. Quickly he mastered the extreme ascetic method for reaching union with Brahman but found it did not bring him what he was looking for. After many years of frustrating searching, he decided to abandon the well-trodden spiritual paths passed on to him by his teachers and to devise his own path. Within a short time after this decision, he went to a nearby river, cleansed himself of the dust that had accumulated on his body for many months, and then ate a bowl of milk rice. According to his new, self-taught approach to the spiritual journey, he would have to care for his body because physical well-being was necessary to pursue liberation from samsara. The traditional harsh forms of self-mortification he had followed previously had to be abandoned. Shortly later, on the evening of the full moon in the month of Vesakha (which is between April and May) he sat beneath the *bodhi* tree near the village of Bodhgaya in the present Indian state of Bihar. Resting in the shade of that tree released an old memory of sitting under a rose-apple tree as a child during a clan agricultural festival. Gotama recalled that as his father was engaged in a ceremonial plowing action, he became restless and bored. And with nothing else to do, he began to pay close attention to his breath. In those moments, he experienced a heightened sense of awareneness and a pervasive serenity that diminished his boredom and restlessness. Remembering that time of his childhood, Siddhattha thought that this gentle practice of awareness meditation might be useful for the spiritual practices he wanted to devise for himself.

This form of meditation was different from the practices of his teachers in that it emphasized the quality of *mindfulness*. While the goal of other meditations was to become absorbed in exceptional states of mind, *his* mindfulness meditation aimed at attaining a heightened awareness of the immediate present moment, so that one became attentive to what was occurring in the mind, the body, and the external environment and observing these processes without judgment. By putting aside goals and releasing preconceptions and judgments, the Buddha believed the mind would become more open to insight into the nature of the world and self. Gotama sat beneath the huge tree, practicing his meditation, and vowed not to leave the spot until he realized the liberating knowledge he had sought for so many years.

In his mindfulness he scrutinized his behavior, carefully noting the ebb and flow of his feelings and sensations as well as the fluctuations of his consciousness. He made himself aware of the constant stream of desires, irritations, and ideas that coursed thorough his mind in the space of a single hour. By this introspection, he was becoming acquainted with the working of his mind and body in order to exploit their capacities and use them to best advantage. Finally, at dawn, he was convinced that he had attained the knowledge that liberates and conquers samsara. At this moment Gotama earned the title, the *Buddha*, which means the "awakened one."

For forty-nine days, the Buddha enjoyed his liberation. He then decided to teach others the knowledge with which he had been enlightened. He found five former disciples and delivered to them a discourse that is sometimes called the "Buddha's First Discourse and Turning the Wheel of Dhamma." This formal talk consisted of a concise formulation of the insights that he had received under the bodhi tree. It contained what the Buddhist tradition calls the "Four Noble Truths," considered by many to be the essence of Buddhism. Most of the Buddha's subsequent teachings might be considered explanations or amplifications of these basic points. As the four truths are discussed here, other teachings in the Pali scriptures will be used to clarify them.

The First Noble Truth: Suffering

The first noble truth is that life is *dukka*—suffering—and that craving for things of the world is responsible for suffering. It was not only the traumas of old age, sickness, and death that made life so unsatisfactory. "Human existence was filled with countless frustrations, disappointments, and its nature was impermanent. Pain, grief and despair are *dukka*," he explained. "Being forced into proximity with what we hate is suffering; being separated from what we love is suffering; not getting what we want is suffering."[2] Suffering includes a whole range of human experiences from the usual events of getting sick, growing old and dying, to not getting what we want and getting what we do not want. Suffering is the fundamental quality of the whole of existence. The very makeup of human existence is entangled in suffering. The whole of human life—not only certain occasions—is suffering. In his mindfulness he also observed how one craving after another took hold of him, how he was ceaselessly yearning to become something else, go somewhere else, and get something he did not have.

We might ask, Why did the Buddha teach that suffering is comprehensive and constant and not simply episodic in human life? Mark W. Muesse suggests the reason the Buddha taught this "is because we do no fully appreciate the extent to which we suffer or feel the unsatisfactoriness of existence."[3] The First Noble Truth is not a statement of a self-evident fact of life; rather, for individuals it is a challenge to discover for themselves the depth and breadth of *dukka* by the means of introspection and observation. The Buddha himself hinted at much when he said, "'This Dhamma that I have attained is profound, hard to see and hard to understand, peaceful and sublime, unattainable by mere reasoning, subtle, to be experienced by the wise.'"[4] Muesse adds, "I would even go so far as to say that one cannot realize the nature and extent of *dukka* until the moment of complete awakening, as the Buddha himself did on the full moon of Vesakha. The true depth of suffering can only be seen from the perspective of the enlightened mind."[5] Recognizing that suffering is manifested not only in particular experiences, but in the whole of existence requires persistent and attentive awareness.

The Second Noble Truth: The Cause of Suffering

In the Second Noble Truth, the Buddha states that the root of suffering is desire, or craving. This aspect of the Buddha's teaching distinguishes it the most from other religious perspectives.

The cause of suffering is *tanha*, desire. Desires are problematic when they are self-centered and become intense craving: that is, when an object of desiring becomes a matter of necessity, as if our lives depended on it. Or when we already possess what we desire and believe that losing it would be devastating to our existence. And such craving can lead to the point where relationships to objects, people, values, beliefs, ideas, power, status, experience, and sensation have the nature of attachments or clinging. The problem is not with the objects of attachment themselves, but with the nature of a person's relationships to them, which can become addictions. Since everything in the world is of constant change, nothing can support a person's attachments; all things to which we become attached are subject to change, and this causes suffering. To allay this suffering we seek something else to cling to, but the more we try to secure happiness through acquisition the more we suffer. Attachment can also include an aversion to an object or situation, causing a negative relationship that is just as difficult to relinquish as an attachment. Both Hinduism and Buddhism recognize attachments as mechanisms that lead to samsara and suffering. The Buddha's answer to the dual dangers of attachments and aversion is equanimity, the Middle Way between the two extremes.

Now that the effects of *tanha* and attachments have been discussed, we ask in turn about their antecedent causes. What makes us have desires that become attachments? The cause is ignorance: ignorance of the true nature of ourselves and the world. We develop strong desires and attachments when we are ignorant of the fact that the world and self are really impermanent; they are not things, they are only processes. In the mind of the Buddha, change and impermanence are constant, persistent. Even solid objects are in constant flux. The Buddha viewed the cosmos as a complex arrangement of processes rather than a set of things. It is not only that things change, but that change is the only thing there is. Unlike the Vedanta tradition of Hinduism, the Buddha held that the soul or true self of the human person is impermanent.

No-Self Anatta

On his spiritual journey, the Buddha eventually became convinced that the ultimate cause of his suffering and unfulfilled longing was delusion about himself. He failed to see that he was selfless. The human person as "me" or "I" forms a distorting lens through which the world takes on a false character. In that lens the universe is misinterpreted as structured around "me," and the world process is accordingly experienced as a stream of objects of my desires and aversions, hopes, and fears that give rise to grasping. This covetous-ness expresses itself in egotism, injustice, and cruelty, in a pervasive self-regarding anxiety in face of life's uncertainties, in the inevitability of final decay and death—all of which comprehensively constitute the "suffering of human existence," *dukka*. The salvation Siddhattha searched for was liberation from the suf-fering caused by the powerful illusion of "me" or "self." It involved the recognition of his having *no* self: his selflessness. Being liberated from the illusory and falsely evaluating "me" was for him to exchange the realm of ego-infected consciousness for the sublime freedom of *nirvana*.

What the Buddha came to perceive and teach his followers about selflessness is called *anatta* in Pali. However, the Sanskrit term, *anatman* ("no-self") makes it evident that the Buddha denies the reality of the *atman,* the Hindu concept of the permanent, immortal, substantial soul or true self. Most interpreters of Buddhism hold that *anatta* was meant to be a doctrine or concept or an ontological statement-theory about the nonexistence of the conscious subject. But it is perhaps more appropriate to hold that it was intended to refer to an *anti-concept* as well as an *axiological or value-oriented, realistic prescription for a certain kind of moral practice.* It is more a denial of what humans ordinarily believe themselves to be. Let us develop this position, first focusing on *anatta* as an anti-concept.

Anatta as Anti-Concept and Axiological Prescription

The Buddha held that the concept of the self can promote fruitless speculation and contribute to human-kind's suffering. Instead of putting forth another view of self, the Buddha simply indicates that the concept of the self is an inept way of thinking about human beings. While it is permitted to refer to the self reflexively, as in talking about ourselves, the Buddha insisted that we should never consider that it refers to anything substantial or permanent. However, one should not think that the Buddha denies human existence or suggests that human life is unreal or an illusion. *Anatta* means essentially that human beings do not exist in the way they think they do, that is, as separate, substantial selves. To hold this is to hold to an illusion, an unsubstantiated belief in the same way a rainbow is an optical illusion, created by the convergence of various conditions.[6] To the Buddha, atman is an illusion supported by changing conditions. That is why no one is able to identify or pinpoint the soul or essential self. The Buddha taught that the problems of human beings arise when they ascribe reality to this illusion. Belief in a permanent, substantial self is the origin of suffering; it sets into motion a series of thoughts, words, and actions that bring on anguish and disappointment. The so-called self is not a thing; it is no-thing, nothing; it is insubstantial; it lacks permanence and immortality. The Buddha's denial of self states that no concept is able to express the reality of who we are. His intention is merely to attempt to disrupt human beings' old habits about who they are.

Instead of viewing individuals as immortal souls in perishable bodies, the Buddha saw the human person as a complex of interconnected and ever-in-flux energies or forces that he called the "Five Aggregates of

Being." These are (1) matter, one's physical makeup; (2) sensation or feeling, the way one judges experiences as pleasant, unpleasant, or neutral (such judgments condition one's tendencies of attachment and aversion); (3) perception and apperception; (4) mental formations, the sources of desire, craving, and intention; mental formations are, in the Buddha's thinking, the sources of karma; therefore as long as there is craving, there will be rebirth; (5) consciousness, the process of awareness. There is nothing about these components that endures. All of them are in flux. Neither is there a permanent agent of subject that underlies these processes.

The Buddha's teaching, then, about *anatta* is an anti-concept. Furthermore, it is appropriate to understand it also as an axiological or value-oriented and practical ethical prescription about how one should direct his or her life in order to attain salvation. A person should live in a way that is selfless, that is, without being attached to the notion of "my self"—and this is truly a way of being that is "authentically myself." It is the distinctive and famous path to axial self-transcendence that Gotama personally chose to follow. It led to the overturning of the delusion of self and discovering nirvana, the Place of Peace, of inner freedom and the extinction of suffering.

The Third Noble Truth: The Cessation of Suffering

The Buddha's good news for humanity can be found in the Third and Fourth Noble Truths. The Third Noble Truth is direct and clear: "Now this, bhikkus, is the noble truth of the cessation of suffering: it is the remainderless fading away and cessation of the same craving, the giving up and relinquishing of it, freedom from it, non-reliance on it."[7] One does not have to suffer. If *tanha*, thirst or craving, is the cause of suffering, then clearly the solution is to cease from craving, and when persons end craving, attachments dissolve, and they are liberated from the cycle of suffering and rebirth. The reason to end craving is *nibbana*, in Pali, or *nirvana* in Sanskrit. *Nirvana* means the eradication of desire, the cessation of thirst, and the destruction of the illusion that one is a separate, substantial self. It is the end of suffering, the point where a person ceases craving for reality to be other than that what it is, radically accepting the way the world and the self truly are. The *method* for quenching thirst is set forth in the Fourth Noble Truth. But before we focus about the way to the goal, let us discuss the goal itself.

Nirvana is experienced at death, but a form of it can be realized in one's historical lifetime. One who achieves this is called an *arahant:* he or she has fully realized the truth of the Buddha's vision and is free from craving, aversion, and ignorance. *Arahants* continue to experience physical pain and other forms of old karma. However, even with physical pain, one does not suffer. Suffering is distinguished from pain; pain is a bodily sensation, while suffering pertains to the mental anguish that comes from resisting pain or merely resisting the way things are. The *arahant* does not generate new karmas but still must experience effects of the old ones. When at death nirvana is experienced, all karmic forces that sustain existence are dissipated, and the *arahant* is released from rebirth. The image that is frequently associated with final nirvana is a candle, the flame of which has gone out because the fuel and the oxygen have been exhausted. In a parallel fashion, without karma to perpetuate rebirth, the flame of the candle belonging to the *arahant* "goes out."

The Buddha's disciples, of course, were strongly interested in what occurs at final nirvana. One of the central issues of the Axial Age, as we have seen, was the matter of an individual's destiny after death. So the disciples were curious: whether an *arahant* exists after death or does not exist after death; or both exists and does not exist after death; or neither exists nor does not exist after death. But the Buddha refused to respond because knowing the answer was not essential to seeing nirvana, and dwelling on such questions was an obstacle to the goal. The Buddha was generally reticent about issues that were not essential to the termination of suffering.

It should be noted that, for the Buddha, freedom from suffering was not received as a grace or gift from God. Like the path of knowledge in Hinduism, the Buddha's Middle Way required great effort and discipline because human beings are the cause of their own suffering and only they themselves can find freedom from it. The Buddha only shows the way to that freedom.

The Fourth Noble Truth: The Eightfold Path to Enlightenment

In this final truth, the Buddha shows the way to enlightenment with an outline of what the discipline involves. "Now this, bhikkus, is the noble truth of the way leading to the cessation of suffering: It is this Noble Eightfold Path that is right understanding, right intention, right speech, right action, right livelihood, right mindfulness and right concentration."[8] The Noble Eightfold Path the Buddha followed and taught was in the middle between simply giving in to the sensual, vulgar desires of an ordinary foolish person and depriving oneself of even the very necessities of existence. Traditionally, the eight components of the plan of action have been divined into three sections: *conduct*, or developing ethical behavior; *concentration*, or developing the mind by meditation; and *study*, or cultivating the wisdom that enabled persons to see themselves and all things as they truly are. For this reason the Noble Path is sometimes called the "Triple Practice." By following his middle path and thus avoiding the two extremes, Gotama achieved, at Bodhgaya in Bihar, the enlightenment for which he passionately searched.

Right Understanding

The Buddha recognized that to begin engaging in the Eightfold Path requires some initial understanding of his teaching about the Middle Way and the Four Noble Truths, and that this understanding is achieved by study, discussion, and reflection. The result of such study and reflection is, however, only a glimmer of the truth that the practitioner sees that prompts him or her to take the path at the outset.

Right Intention

The interior motive bridges right understanding and the next division of the triple practice, developing moral conduct. Right intention involves the determination to practice specific virtues that neutralize the conditioned tendencies of individuals toward greed, hatred, and harming. The virtues that exert the counter-acting effect are nonattachment, goodwill, and harmlessness.

Right Speech–Action–Livelihood

Developing moral conduct, the second part of the triple practice, is the chief part of the Buddha's path. This moral behavior is not commanded either by a god or by the Buddha. It is rooted, the Buddha believed, in the very nature of human beings. He also held that karma is generated only by intentional acts; the source of karma is the aggregate of mental formations, the idea of desire and intention. An appropriate way to discuss the moral dimension of the Buddha's teaching is to start with what he called the "Five Precepts":

1. "I will refrain from harming sentient beings."
2. "I will refrain from taking what is not offered"; that is, one promises not to steal or to covet.
3. "I will refrain from sexual misconduct."
4. "I will refrain from false speech"; not only lying and slandering, but also gossiping, cursing, loud talk, idle chatter.
5. "I will refrain from stupefying drink"; intoxicants.[9]

Right Mindfulness–Concentration

Virtuous moral behavior is central to the holy life, but the Buddha considered it equally important to discipline the mind. As self-absorbed habits hinder the basic compassion of the human heart, so misled habits of the thinking mind obstruct the ability to understand the world and the self as they truly are. For the Buddha, the mind meant the complex of thoughts, sensations, feeling, and consciousness that in each moment arise and fall away. The mind has great power and potential; however, in its unenlightened condition it is out of control, unruly and undisciplined. And to bring it under control requires skill, persistent training, and patience.

Right concentration involves the practice of meditation to strengthen the virtues of attentiveness and nonattachment. The Buddha intended the practice of meditation to heighten consciousness of the world and self by being attentive to the events of ordinary life in the present moment. The fundamental meditative practice, based on the Buddha's own experiences, involved attending to the breath and observing without judgment the coming and going of thoughts, sensations, feeling, and perceptions. As these phenomena come to awareness, the subject notes them and allows them to fall away without dwelling on them. Simply by being observant of the mind, the body, and the surrounding world, the Buddha held it was possible to gain an insight into the true essence of the world and the self, and on the basis of such insight to act and think accordingly. He believed this meditative practice would disclose the illusionary nature of self and the origin of suffering in the mind's tendency to thirst for new pleasures and to avoid unpleasant experiences. He also held that meditation could hold back the mind's inclination to make spontaneous judgments and to become absorbed in thoughts about the future and the past, all of which were considered to be unwholesome habits.

In the development of mindfulness and the practice of contemplation, the Buddha also fostered the skillful states of a lucid, conscious mind, completely alert, filled with compassion and loving welfare for all beings.[10] By performing these mental exercises at sufficient depth, they could, he was convinced, transform the restless and destructive tendencies of his conscious and unconscious mind. At each stage of his journey into the depths of his mind, he intentionally evoked the emotion of love and directed it to the four corners of the Earth without omitting a single plant, animal, friend, or foe from its embrace. This outpouring of loving kindness was a fourfold program. First, he developed an attitude of friendship for everything and for everybody. Next, he cultivated an empathy with their pain and suffering. In the third stage of his mindfulness, he evoked a "sympathetic joy" that rejoiced in the happiness of others, without envy or a sense of personal diminishment. Finally, he aspired to an attitude of complete equanimity toward others, feeling neither attraction nor antipathy.

This expression of universal love was a difficult challenge because it involved Gotama's turning away completely from the egotism that always is concerned with how other people and things might benefit or detract from the self. He was learning to surrender his entire being to others, and thus to transcend the ego in compassion and loving kindness for all creatures.[11]

Enlightenment

In the Buddhist tradition there are two levels of understanding. The first is attained by mere reasoning. The second form is the understanding that occurs in enlightenment; it is the content of enlightened experience. Gotama's great experience of enlightenment was the first most significant event in the history of Buddhism. His followers who follow his Eightfold Path aspire to achieve that same enlightened experience. When they arrive at this goal, then in light of the eternal reality of being itself—the transcendent stream of Universal Being—they see themselves and the world around them, as he himself saw, as passing, unsubstantial expressions of the Absolute. This is seeing reality as it is, unfettered by expectation, belief, or defilement of any kind. In this form of comprehension, one knows for certain the authenticity of the Four Noble Truths without reliance on authorities other than one's own experience. To comprehend the Buddha's teaching at this level means to live one's life in accord with the truth. One no longer seeks for or aspires to nirvana. Nirvana has been seen.

In written accounts of the Buddha's enlightenment, he is described as rapt in ecstatic joy, imbued with a compassionate love of all sentient beings, "as a mother toward the only child," and endowed with the equanimity of a perfectly liberated person. In monastic commentaries, this state of even-mindedness is described as the opposite of three kinds of experience: the pleasure that comes with attachment, the displeasure due to aversion, and an ignorant kind of indifference. What the Buddha experienced was nirvana: It transformed his life.

Nirvana

What was nirvana? It was the extinguishing of the fires of greed, hatred, and delusion, the elimination of the craving, hatred, and ignorance that subjugate humanity. And even though the Buddha was still subject to physical ailments and other vicissitudes, nothing could cause him serious mental pain or diminish his inner peace of complete selflessness. The Buddha would continue to suffer; he would grow old and sick like everybody else; but by following his Noble Eightfold Path, he had found the inner haven that enables a person to live with suffering, take possession of it, affirm it, and experience in its midst a profound serenity.

The Buddha was convinced that nirvana was a transcendent state because it lay beyond the capacities of those who had not achieved the inner awakening of enlightenment. And while no words could adequately describe it, in mundane terms it could be called "Nothing" since it corresponded to no recognizable reality. But those who had been able to find this sacred peace realized that they lived a limitlessly richer life.[12] Later monotheists would speak about God in similar terms, claiming that God was "nothing" because "he" was not another being; and that it was more precise to state that he did not exist because human notions of existence were too limited to apply to the divine reality.[13] They would also state that a selfless, compassionate life would bring people into God's presence.

But, like other Indian sages and mystics, the Buddha found the idea of a personalized deity too limiting. He always denied the existence of a supreme being because such a deity would become another block to enlightenment. The Buddhist Pali texts never mention Brahman. Gotama's rejection of God was a calm and measured posture. He simply put the notion serenely out of his mind.

When Gotama made an effort to give his disciples a hint of what nirvana was like, he used both negative and positive terms. Nirvana was the "extinction of greed, hatred and delusion"; it was "taintless," "unweakening," "undisintegrating," "inviolable," "non-distress," "unhostility," and "deathless." Nirvana was "the Truth," "the Subtle," "the Other Shore," "Peace," "the Everlasting," "the Supreme Goal," "Purity, Freedom, Independence, the Island, the Shelter, the Harbor, the Refuge, the Beyond."[14] It was the supreme goal of humans and gods, an incomprehensible serenity, an utterly safe refuge. Many of these images are suggestive of words later used by monotheists to describe their experiences of the ineffable God.

The Buddha as Teacher

After the important event of his enlightenment, for nearly a half-century the Buddha traveled the Gangetic basin teaching his doctrine and building a community of followers. After his initial enlightenment at Bodhgaya, the second most significant occurrence in the history of Buddhism is Gotama's first sermon, which was given at Sarnath. In this presentation to his first five followers, he began to expound the Middle Path and the Four Noble Truths as the kernel of his awakening experience. The principle conception of his teaching was the doctrine of *anatta*, "No Self," and the invitation to his listeners to a way of life that leads to the Axial ideals of self-transcendence and salvation from the suffering and dissatisfaction that is part and parcel of human existence.

At the age of eighty, the Buddha peacefully died and passed into final nirvana. After his death, the Sangha or Buddhist community continued his teaching, and with grand success. They gathered together to consider how to preserve the Buddha's teaching. Early Buddhist councils led to the creation of authoritative texts and to the discussion of important doctrinal issues. This ultimately divided the community into several sects. Of the eighteen different varieties of Buddhist schools, only the Theravada school remains, making it the oldest extant Buddhist tradition. It probably represents the form closest to the way Buddhism was practiced around the time of the Buddha.

Around the first century CE the Mahayana form of Buddhism began to take shape in northwestern India; it added a substantially different dimension and new views about the Buddha and his role in making salvation accessible to humanity. New narratives were created that ascribed to the Buddha divine, godlike status. Mahayana developed the idea of the *bodhisattva*, an enlightened being who remained in the samsaric circle or in the heavenly domain in order to help others attain enlightenment and salvation. Mahayana was carried to China, Korea, and Japan. It eventually became the most popular form of Buddhism but has also fragmented over time into new schools. Out of the Mahayana emerged the third major form of Buddhism, the Vajrayana, practiced for centuries in Tibet and Mongolia.

Gotama's doctrine of "No Self" is at the heart of both the Theravada and the Mahayana schools of Buddhism. In Theravada there is a psychological realization of *anatta* which is the loss of "conceit of I am." This constitutes the attainment of the state of enlightenment, the state of be an *arahant*. In Mahayana the same concept of liberation from self applies, but here the aim is not to become an *arahant* but a *bodhisattva*, an enlightened person whose openness to the Transcendent is expressed in unlimited compassion for all sentient beings. For to live as a "self" is to seek happiness for oneself. But transcending the ego, becoming a manifestation of the universal Buddha nature, is to seek the happiness of all.

Today there are a total of approximately 329 million Buddhists in many areas of the world, including Sri Lanka, Burma, Thailand, Cambodia, Laos, China, Korea, Japan, Tibet, Mongolia, Europe, and the United States. One hundred twenty-four million Buddhists are of the Theravada branch; 20 million are of the Vajrayana; 185 million are of the Mahayana.[15] In chapter 7 we explore the Mahayana tradition in tandem with Shinto as these religions developed and are practiced in Japan.

Jainism

Almost all estimates indicate that there are 350 million Buddhists in the world today and fewer than 5 million Jains, almost all of them in India, mostly in Mumbai and other large urban centers.[16] While they account for less than 5 percent of the Indian population, their influence on the religious, social, political, and economic life of India has been, and is, quite out of proportion to their numbers. In Europe, largely in the United Kingdom, there are presently estimated to be 25,000 Jains. Some estimates suggest a similar number may be found in North America. There is a vast disparity in the number of Buddhists and Jains, but the two traditions share similar histories, beliefs, and practices. Both reject the authority of the *Vedas*, and both accept rebirth and karma and aspire to release from samsara.

Modern history specifies the origins of Jainism in the same cultural environment that gave rise to Hinduism and Buddhism. Jainism grew from the struggle for enlightenment of its main figure, Vardhamana Jnatrputra (c. 497–425 BCE), called the *Jina* ("Conqueror") or *Mahavira* ("Great Hero"). Sometimes he is referred to by outsiders as the founder of Jainism, but Jains themselves see their religion as a tradition going back dozens of generations before Mahavira. Devout adherents of Jainism insist that their religious tradition is eternal, based on truths that have no beginning in time. At certain moments in the universal life cycle, these truths have been forgotten and lost, but then rediscovered and reintroduced to humanity. When an Axial Age sage named Vardhamana Mahavira began to teach the doctrines of Jainism, he was only communicating a religion that had been taught many times before by others. Each of these former teachers was a *Tirkanthara*, a word that means "bridge builder" ("those who find a ford over the river of suffering"). The *Tirthankaras* were exceptional individuals who showed the way to salvation by their words and example. In the last turn of the universal cycle, there have been twenty-four *Tirthankaras*. The most recent was Vardhamana, portrayed mythically as being of supernatural birth and the twenty-third and last in a long line of *Tirthankaras*. He is not considered to be the founder of Jainism, only its reformer and reviver. It should be noted that there is no historical evidence to support the existence of the first twenty-two *Tirthankaras*.

Modern scholarship locates the origins of Jainism in the person of Vardhamana Mahavira of the Axial Age, who according to tradition was born into the *Kshatriya* in 599 BCE. Both Buddhist and Jain texts indicate that the Buddha and Mahavira were contemporaries living in the same region of northeastern India, in Bihar state. The texts indicate that they knew of each other but never actually met. However, if the

Buddha in fact lived around 490 to 410, as most scholars now think, then the traditional dates of Mahavira would be inaccurate.

After the death of his parents, at the age of thirty Mahavira gave up his princely life and became a wondering monk in search of liberation from death and rebirth, following a harsh lifestyle as a *samana,* a renouncer of wealth and life in society. For the next twelve years, he practiced intense asceticism, including fasting for long periods of time, mortification of the flesh, meditation, and the practice of silence. He scrupulously avoided harming other living beings, including animals and plants. By dedication to these austere practices he merited a title given to him by his admirers, the *Mahavira,* meaning the "Great Hero." At the age of forty-two, after twelve years of uncompromising dedication to self-discipline, he believed he was simply the latest in a long line of *jinas* who achieved complete victory over his body and the desires that bound him to the world of matter and sin; he had crossed the river of *dukka* (suffering) to find access to liberation and enlightenment. In his enlightened state he attained a transcendent knowledge that gave him a unique perspective of the world. He was able to perceive all levels of reality simultaneously, in every dimension of time and space, as though he were a god. In fact, for Mahavira, God was simply a creature who had accomplished supreme knowledge by perceiving and respecting the single divine transcendent soul that existed in every single creature. This state of mind could not be described, because it entirely transcended ordinary consciousness. It was a state of absolute friendliness with all creatures, however lowly. He had crossed the river of *dukka* to find access to liberation and enlightenment.

For the next thirty years he roamed around the Ganges region teaching others his principles and practices for achieving liberation from samsara, for which he used both the terms *moksha* and *nirvana.* Like the Buddha, he drew men and women and children from all social strata. His followers were called "Jainas," or now, according to a more modern pronunciation, "Jains," because they were disciples of the *jina.* Some legends indicate that at one point Mahavira had gathered more than 400,000 disciples. He organized his followers into an order of monks, nuns, and laypersons. To attain liberation, one had to become a monk because of the austere discipline required to achieve it. Laypersons expected to strive for *moksha* in a future lifetime when circumstances were more favorable for such a pursuit. His teaching became the basis of the *Agam Sutras,* one of the most important scriptures in Jainism. According to tradition, Mahavira died and attained final nirvana at the age of seventy-two, after thirty years of successful teaching and organizing. He is now, according to all Jain sects, at the top of the universe, where all perfect ones go, enjoying complete self-transcendent bliss in a state no longer subject to rebirth. After his death, the Jains would develop an elaborate prehistory, claiming that in previous eras there had been twenty-four of these ford makers who had discovered the bridge to salvation.

Mahavira taught his followers in conformity with this vision. Like Buddhists and Hindus, he appropriated many of the basic assumptions and beliefs circulating in the Ganges basin in the early Indian Axial Age, but he reinterpreted them to fit his particular enlightened view of the world. We now explore how

Mahavira understood these concepts, including his idea of time, the structure of the world, the nature of the soul, karma, and the path to salvation.

Time

Mahavira was of the belief that the world was never created and will never be destroyed. Cosmic time, therefore, is infinite, but it does conform to a cyclical pattern. Each cycle has two half-segments, a period of decline and a period of ascendancy. Each segment is further divided into six unequal parts. The half-cycles are incalculably long. One half-cycle is a time of decline. During the first part of this period, people are very tall and live lives that are very long. They are exceedingly happy, wise, and virtuous, with no need of religion or ethics. All of their needs are provided by wish-granting trees. As the cycle proceeds, conditions become progressively worse. The world and life are gradually tainted with corruption and deterioration; ethics and religion are then introduced; writing is invented, since peoples' memories begin to fail. During these times the *Tirthankaras* appear. When the lowest point of the cycle of decline is reached, people will be only about three feet tall and live twenty years. Like animals, they will live in caves and pursue all sorts of immoral activity.

But as time reaches its lowest point, it begins to ascend, and the world becomes increasingly better. People then start to live longer, healthier lives, to conduct themselves in more compassionate ways, and to experience greater happiness. When this cycle reaches its apex, time begins again its downward motion. The pattern is repeated over and over again, forever. According to Jain belief, we are presently in the fifth stage of the cycle of descent, a period when things are bad and will become even worse. The current era began a little over 2,500 years ago and will continue for a total of 21,000 years. When this period ends, Jainism will be lost and will be reintroduced by the next *Tirthankaras* after the half-cycle of ascent commences again.

Structure of the World

According to the teaching of Mahavira, the physical world is made up of three levels: the underworld; the surface of the world, or the middle realm; and the heavens. In the underworld are a series of seven or eight hell realms, and each of these is colder than the next. The hell realms are for the punishment of the wicked as a means of purifying negative karma. The Jain hells are more like a purgatory than a location of ultimate condemnation. When souls have suffered sufficiently for their sins, they may be reborn in another realm. The middle level is the place of life; it is known by the name of *Jambudvipa,* or the island of the rose-apple tree. It is a name used also by Buddhists and Hindus. The upper level of the world is the realm of the gods. It has sixteen heavens and fourteen celestial abodes. And then, above the ceiling of the universe is a crescent-shaped structure where the *Tirthankaras* and the completely liberated souls dwell. This is the ultimate goal and destination of those who attain *moksha*.

Nature of the Soul

Mahavira, like the sages who wrote the *Upanishads,* believed that the soul was real, not illusionary as the Buddha thought. Mahavira considered the soul to be a living, luminous, and intelligent entity within the material body; it was unchanging in essence, but its characteristics were subject to change. It was also his conviction that there were an infinite number of souls, each an actual, separate individual. Therefore, Mahavira would not have accepted the Vedantic idea that soul and ultimate reality are consubstantial, since that view denies individuality. Furthermore, all souls are of equal value; one is no better than another. Souls may be embodied in gods and in humans, as well as in animals and plants, and even, according to some, stones, minerals, bodies of water, fire, and the winds. By the karmas of former lives they had been brought to their present existence. Therefore, all beings share the same nature and must be treated with equal respect and care that persons would want to receive themselves.[17]

Karma

In its pure state, the soul enjoys perception, knowledge, happiness, power, all of which are perfect. However, at the present time, all souls, with the exception of the completely liberated ones, are defiled because they are embodied and tainted with karma. The Jain understanding of karma is of a fine, material substance that clings to and stains the soul. Karmas are invisible particles, floating throughout the world. When a soul commits a karmic act, it attracts these fine articles, which adhere to the soul and weigh it down. These karmas accumulate and, in due course, color the soul. We cannot see a soul because of our defiled state; but if we could, we could with ease detect a soul's moral and spiritual quality. The souls that are worse are stained black, and the purest are white. And in between, from bad to good, the soul may be blue, gray, red, lotus-pink, or yellow. Like in Buddhism and Hinduism, karma determines persons' future births and keeps them bound to the material, samsaric world.

Since they are imprisoned in matter, souls do not enjoy omniscience as they do in their pure state. Karmic stains cause our perceptions to be distorted and our knowledge of the world limited. These distortions urge the soul to seek pleasure in material possessions and fleeting enjoyments, which further lead to self-absorbed thoughts and anger, hatred, greed, and other states of the mind. These, in turn, bring about the further accumulation of karma. Consequently, the cycle is a vicious one.

The limitations that result from karmic defilement also mean that we are unable to understand the great richness and complexity of reality. The Jains propose that reality is many sided; this means that the world is made up of an infinite number of material and spiritual substances, each with an infinite number of qualities and manifestations. Since the universe is complex and our knowledge is limited, all claims of truth must be tentative. The Jains refer to the principle as "non-absolutism," which means making no categorical or unconditional statements.

Path to Liberation

In Mahavira's teaching, liberation meant the release of one's true self from the constraints of body and thus the achievement of salvation, inner control, and transcendent peace of mind, enlightenment, all being the great values of the Axial Age. The path to liberation is simple. At first, preventing the flow of new karma and then, second, eliminating the old karmas that have already accumulated and weigh the soul down.

To attain the first goal, Mahavira urged his followers to fulfill five Great Vows. The first and foremost of these vows is *ahimsa,* to avoid harming any living beings. The Jains take this rule further than the Buddhists, who drew the line at sentient life, not at life itself. The Jains are convinced that even unintentionally injuring another creature causes negative karma. In line with these beliefs, Jains are vegetarians and refuse to use leather or other animal products. Most avoid agriculture, because the plow might inadvertently damage a worm, and other kinds of occupations that might cause harm to other forms of life. Some, especially the monks, use a cloth to cover a glass when they drink so as to strain out insects that may have fallen into the liquid; and they sweep the pathways before them to avoid stepping on bugs. *Ahimsa,* however, means more than avoiding physical injury to life. It also involves what the Jains call *ahimsa* of the mind and *ahimsa* of speech. The former is the practice of right thought. Evil thoughts are held to generate negative karma. The latter is speaking in a nonhurtful way, using kind, compassionate language.

Achieving salvation is centered on not harming one's fellow creatures. Until persons had acquired this empathetic view of the world, they could not attain salvation. Consequently, nonviolence was a strict religious duty. All other ethical and religious practices were useless without *ahimsa,* and this could not be achieved until the Jain had acquired a state of empathy, an attitude of positive benevolence, with every single creature. All living creatures should be of support and assistance to one another. They should relate to every single human being, animal, plant, insect, or pebble with friendship, goodwill, patience, and gentleness.

The other four vows are connected to *ahimsa* and the cessation of karmic accumulation. They are always to speak the truth; not to steal or take what is not given; chastity, which is understood as celibacy for the monks, and faithfulness in marriage for the laypeople; and last, nonattachment to people and material things.

Preventing new karmas from staining the soul is the first step to liberation; purification of the stains of old karmas is the next. Good deeds and asceticism are the principle means of eliminating the accumulation of karmas. Those who desired to attain perfect enlightenment must, like Mahavira, practice fasting, engage in certain types of meditation, penance, yoga, study, and recitation of the scriptures. These acts purge the soul of its karmic deposit. They lead to transcendence over one's own physical state and to a trance state marked by complete disassociation from the outer world. This trance state is believed to be like the one Mahavira entered into in the thirteenth year of his seeking and assured him of his final liberation.

The ultimate ascetic observance, assumed by many throughout history, is fasting to death. The fast is the symbol and producer of absolute renunciation. Before this point, the ascetic has abstained from all but food and water. And then in a profound meditative state, food and water are given up, ending for good all attachments to samsara. This fast is not considered an act of violence, but a gesture of compassion, because there is no anger or pain associated with it.

The purging of all karmas restores the soul to its pure, undefiled state. It then has perfect knowledge, perfect perception and power. It is no longer weighed down by the burden of its karma, so it ascends to the very ceiling of the universe, where it enjoys the bliss of nirvana in the company of other liberated beings.

Similar to the Buddha and the Upanishadic sages, Mahavira taught a path of self-salvation. Since each individual soul is responsible for its own karmas, only the individual person is able to reverse the karmic accumulations. The purpose of the monastic community was to provide a supportive context for the pursuit of nirvana. Because the Jain search for nirvana required a more austere asceticism than the Buddha's Middle Way, taking on the life of a monk or nun was more vital to the realization of nirvana in Jainism than in Buddhism. The monks were also responsible for safeguarding the Mahavira's teaching, first in oral tradition and then in writing.

Although there are in Jainism differences of doctrine and practice, they should not be overemphasized. According to the contemporary Jains scholar, Nathmal Tatia, all Jains agree on the central message of Jainism, which is nonviolence, non-absolutism, and nonattachment.[18] These basic observances are the elements in the Jain quest for personal liberation from samsara and the communitarian goal of peace throughout the world.

Conclusion

With this we conclude our study of Jainism and the Indian Axial Age. We next turn our attention to East Asia and ancient China.

Notes

1. Thomas J. Hopkins, *The Hindu Religious Tradition* (Encino, CA, and Belmont, CA: Dickenson, 1971), 50–51.

2. *Vinaya: Mahavagga* 16. This text is part of the *Vinaya Pitaka*, the *Book of Monastic Discipline*, which codifies the rule of the Buddhist order. Cited in Karen Armstrong, *The Great Transformation: The Beginning of Our Religious Traditions* (New York/Toronto: Knopf, 2006), 278.

3. 3. Mark W. Muesse, *Religions of the Axial Age: An Approach to the World's Religions* (Chantilly, VA: Teaching Company, 2007), part 1, 175.

4. 4. Ibid.

5. 5. Ibid.

6. 6. Ibid., part 2, 16.

7. 7. Cited in Ibid., part 2, 23.

8. 8. Ibid., 26.

9. 9. Ibid., 28–29.

10. *Majjhima Nikaya* (MN) 38. Cited in Armstrong, *The Great Transformation*, 278. The Pali scriptures include four collections of the Buddha's sermons (*Majjhima Nikaya, Digha Nikaya, Anguttara Nikaya,* and *Samyutta Nikaya*) and an anthology of minor works, which include *Udana,* a collection of the Buddha's maxims, and the *Jataka,* stories about the past lives of the Buddha and his companions.

11. Hermann Oldenberg, *Buddha: His Life, His Doctrine, His Order* (London and Edinburgh: Williams & Norgate, 1882), 299–302.

12. Muesse, *Religions of the Axial Age,* part I, 97–98.

13. Karen Armstrong, *A History of God: The 4000-Year Quest of Judaism, Christianity and Islam* (New York: Knopf, 1993).

14. *Sutta-Nipata* 43:1–43; cited in Armstrong, *Great Transformation*, 282. The *Sutta-Nipata* is an anthology of early Buddhist poetry.

15. Major Religions of the World Ranked by Number of Adherents. Available at: http://www.adherents.com/adh_branches.html.

16. Ibid.

17. Muesse, *Religions of the Axial Age,* part 2, 59–62.

18. *That Which Is: Tattvartha Sutra,* trans. Nathmal Tatia (San Francisco: HarperCollins, 1994).

5

Sikh Dharam

Pashaura Singh

The Tradition Defined

Sikh religion originated in the Punjab ('five rivers') region of northwest India five centuries ago. It is a monotheistic faith that stresses the ideal of achieving spiritual liberation within a person's lifetime through meditation on the divine Name. It is also oriented toward action, encouraging the dignity of regular labor as part of spiritual discipline. Family life and social responsibility are important aspects of Sikh teachings. Notably, the Sikh tradition is the youngest of the indigenous religions of India where the Sikhs constitute about 2 percent of India's 1 billion people. What makes Sikhs significant in India is not their numbers but their contribution in the political and economic spheres. The global Sikh population is approximately 23 million; that is more than the worldwide total of Jewish people. About 18 million Sikhs live in the state of Punjab, while the rest have settled in other parts of India and elsewhere, including substantial communities established through successive waves of emigration in Southeast Asia, East Africa, the United Kingdom, and North America. In the last century, about a quarter of a million Sikhs immigrated to the United States of America.

Origins of the Tradition

The Sikh tradition is rooted in a particular religious experience, piety, and culture and is informed by a unique inner revelation of its founder, Guru Nānak (1469–1539), who declared his independence from the other thought forms of his day. He tried to kindle the fire of autonomy and courage in those who claimed to be his disciples (*sikh*, 'learner'). Notwithstanding the influences he absorbed from his contemporary religious environment, that is, the devotional tradition of the medieval *sant*s (poet-saints) of North India with whom he shared certain similarities and differences, Guru Nānak laid down the foundation of 'true teaching, practice, and community' from the standpoint of his own religious ideals. Among the religious figures of North India, he had a strong sense of mission that compelled him to proclaim his message for the ultimate benefit of his audience and to promote socially responsible living.

Nānak was born to an upper-caste professional Hindu family in the village of Talwaṇḍī, present-day Nankana Sāhib in Pakistan. Much of the material concerning his life comes from hagiographical *janam-sākhī*s (birth narratives). His life may be divided into three distinct phases: his early contemplative years, the enlightenment experience accompanied by extensive travels, and a foundational climax that resulted in the establishment of the first Sikh community in western Punjab. In one of his own hymns he proclaimed, 'I was a minstrel out of work, the Lord assigned me the task of singing the divine Word. He summoned me to his court and bestowed on me the robe of honoring him and singing his praise. On me he bestowed the divine nectar (*amrit*) in a cup, the nectar of his true and holy Name' (*Ādi Granth* p.150). This hymn is intensely autobiographical, explicitly pointing out Guru Nānak's own understanding of his divine mission, and it marked the beginning of his ministry. He was then thirty years of age, had been married to Sulkhanī for more than a decade, and was the father of two young sons, Sri Chand and Lakhmi Dās. He set out on a series of journeys to both Hindu and Muslim places of pilgrimage in India and elsewhere. During his travels he came into contact with the leaders of different religious persuasions and tested the veracity of his own ideas in religious dialogues.

At the end of his travels, in the 1520s, Guru Nānak purchased a piece of land on the right bank of the Rāvī River in West Punjab and founded the village of Kartarpur ('Creator's Abode'; today in Pakistan).

There he lived for the rest of his life as the 'Spiritual Guide' of a newly emerging religious community. His attractive personality and teaching won him many disciples who received the message of liberation through religious hymns of unique genius and notable beauty. They began to use these hymns in devotional singing (*kīrtan*) as a part of congregational worship. Indeed, the first Sikh families who gathered around Guru Nānak in the early decades of the sixteenth century at Kartarpur formed the nucleus of a rudimentary organization of the Nānak-Panth, the 'path of Nānak,' the community constituted by the Sikhs who followed Guru Nānak's path of liberation. In his role as what the sociologist Max Weber dubbed an 'ethical prophet,' Guru Nānak called for a decisive break with existing formulations and laid the foundation of a new, rational model of normative behavior based on divine authority. Throughout his writings he conceived of his work as divinely commissioned, and he demanded the obedience of his audience as an ethical duty.

Guru Nānak prescribed the daily routine, along with agricultural activity for sustenance, for the Kartarpur community. He defined the ideal person as a Gurmukh ('one oriented toward the Guru'), who practiced the threefold discipline of 'the divine Name, charity, and purity' (*nām-dān-iśnān*). Indeed, these three features, *nām* (relation with the Divine), *dān* (relation with the society), and *iśnān* (relation with the self) provided a balanced approach for the development of the individual and the society. They corresponded to the cognitive, the communal, and the personal aspects of the evolving Sikh identity. For Guru Nānak the true spiritual life required that 'one should live on what one has earned through hard work and that one should share with others the fruit of one's exertion' (*Ādi Granth* p.1,245). In addition, service (*sevā*), self-respect (*pati*), truthful living (*sach achār*), humility, sweetness of the tongue, and taking only one's rightful share (*haq halāl*) were regarded as highly prized ethical virtues in pursuit of liberation. At Kartarpur, Guru Nānak gave practical expression to the ideals that had matured during the period of his travels, and he combined a life of disciplined devotion with worldly activities set in the context of normal family life. As part of Sikh liturgy, Guru Nānak's *Japjī* (Meditation) was recited in the early hours of the morning and *So Dar* (That Door) and *Ārti* (Adoration) were sung in the evening.

Guru Nānak's spiritual message found expression at Kartarpur through key institutions: the *sangat* ('holy fellowship') where all felt that they belonged to one large spiritual fraternity; the *dharamsala*, the original form of the Sikh place of worship that developed later into the *gurdwārā*; and the establishment of the *langar*, the interdining convention which required people of all castes to sit in status-free lines (*pangat*) to share a common meal. The institution of *langar* promoted the spirit of unity and mutual belonging and struck at a major aspect of caste, thereby advancing the process of defining a distinctive Sikh identity. Finally, Guru Nānak created the institution of the Guru ('Preceptor'), who became the central authority in community life. Before he passed away in 1539, he designated one of his disciples, Lehnā, as his successor by renaming him Angad, meaning 'my own limb.' Thus, a lineage was established, and a legitimate succession was maintained intact from the appointment of Guru Angad (1504–52) to the death of Guru Gobind Siṅgh (1666–1708), the tenth and the last human Guru of the Sikhs.

Successors of Guru Nānak

The early Sikh Gurus followed a policy of both innovation and preservation. The second Guru, Angad, consolidated the nascent Sikh Panth in the face of the challenge offered by Guru Nānak's eldest son, Sri Chand, the founder of the ascetic Udāsī sect. Guru Angad further refined the Gurmukhi script for recording the compilation of the Guru's hymns (*bāṇī*). The original Gurmukhi script was a systematization of the business shorthands (*laṇḍelmahājanī*) of the type Guru Nānak doubtless used professionally as a young man. This was an emphatic rejection of the superiority of the Devanagri and Arabic scripts (along with Sanskrit and the Arabic and Persian languages) and of the hegemonic authority they represented in the scholarly and religious circles of the time. The use of the Gurmukhi script added an element of demarcation and self-identity to the Sikh tradition. In fact, language became the single most important factor in the preservation of Sikh culture and identity and the cornerstone of the religious distinctiveness that is part and parcel of the Sikh cultural heritage.

A major institutional development took place during the time of the third Guru, Amar Dās (1479–1574), who introduced a variety of innovations to provide greater cohesion and unity to the ever-growing Sikh Panth. These included the establishment of the city of Goindval, the biannual festivals of Dīvālī and Baisākhī that provided an opportunity for the growing community to get together and meet the Guru, a missionary system (*mañjīs*) for attracting new converts, and the preparation of the Goindval *pothī*s, collections of the compositions of the Gurus and some of the medieval poet-saints.

The fourth Guru, Rām Dās (1534–81), founded the city of Rāmdāspur, where he constructed a large pool for the purpose of bathing. The city was named Amritsar, meaning 'the nectar of immortality.' To build an independent economic base, the Guru appointed deputies (*masand*) to collect tithes and other contributions from loyal Sikhs. In addition to a large body of sacred verse, he composed the wedding hymn (*lāvān*) for the solemnization of a Sikh marriage. Indeed, it was Guru Rām Dās who for the first time explicitly responded to the question 'Who is a Sikh?' with the following definition: 'He who calls himself Sikh, a follower of the true Guru, should meditate on the divine Name after rising and bathing and recite *Japjī* from memory, thus driving away all evil deeds and vices. As day unfolds he sings *gurbāṇī* (utterances of the Gurus); sitting or rising he meditates on the divine Name. He who repeats the divine Name with every breath and bite is indeed a true Sikh (*gursikh*) who gives pleasure to the Guru' (*Ādi Granth* pp. 305–306). Thus, the liturgical requirements of the reciting and singing of the sacred word became part of the very definition of being a Sikh. The most significant development was related to the self-image of Sikhs, who perceived themselves as unique and distinct from the other religious communities of North India.

The period of the fifth Guru, Arjan (1563–1606), was marked by a number of far-reaching institutional developments. First, at Amritsar he built the Harimandir, later known as the Golden Temple, which acquired prominence as the central place of Sikh worship. Second, he compiled the first canonical scripture, the *Ādi Granth* (Original Book), in 1604. Third, Guru Arjan established the rule of justice and humility (*halemi rāj*) in the town of Rāmdāspur, where everyone lived in comfort (*Ādi Granth* p. 74). He proclaimed, 'The divine rule prevails in Rāmdāspur due to the grace of the Guru. No tax (*jizyah*) is levied, nor any fine; there is no collector of taxes' (*Ādi Granth* pp. 430, 817). The administration of the town was evidently in the hands of Guru Arjan, although in a certain sense Rāmdāspur was an autonomous town within the context and the framework of the Mughal rule of Emperor Akbar. Fourth, by the end of the sixteenth century the Sikh Panth had developed a strong sense of independent identity, which is evident from Guru Arjan's assertion 'We are neither Hindu nor Musalmān' (*Ādi Granth* p.1,136).

Fifth, dissentions within the ranks of the Sikh Panth became the source of serious conflict. A great number of the Guru's compositions focus on the issue of dealing with the problems created by 'slanderers' (*nindak*), who were rival claimants to the office of the Guruship. The Udāsīs and Bhallās (Guru Amar Dās' eldest son, Bābā Mohan, and his followers) had already established parallel seats of authority and had paved the way for competing views of Sikh identity. The rivalry of these dissenters was heightened when Guru Arjan was designated for the throne of Guru Nānak in preference to the former's eldest brother, Prithī Chand, who even approached the local Mughal administrators to claim the position of his father. At some point Prithī Chand and his followers were branded *miṇā*s ('dissembling rogues').

Finally, the author of *Dabistān-i-Mazāhib* (The School of Religions), a mid-seventeenth-century work in Persian, testifies that the number of Sikhs had rapidly increased during Guru Arjan's period and that 'there were not many cities in the inhabited countries where some Sikhs were not to be found.' In fact, the growing strength of the Sikh movement attracted the unfavorable attention of the ruling authorities because of the reaction of Muslim revivalists of the Naqshbandiyyah Order in Mughal India. There is clear evidence in the compositions of Guru Arjan that a series of complaints were made against him to the functionaries of the Mughal state, giving them an excuse to watch the activities of the Sikhs. The liberal policy of Akbar may have sheltered the Guru and his followers for a time, but in May 1606, within eight months of Akbar's death, Guru Arjan, under torture by the orders of the new emperor, Jahangīr, was executed. The Sikh community perceived his death as the first martyrdom, which became a turning point in the history of the Sikh tradition.

Indeed, a radical reshaping of the Sikh Panth took place after Guru Arjan's martyrdom. The sixth Guru, Hargobind (1595–1644), signaled the formal process when he traditionally donned two swords symbolizing the spiritual (*pīrī*) as well as the temporal (*mīrī*) investiture. He also built the Akāl Takhat (Throne of the Timeless One) facing the Harimandir, which represented the newly assumed role of temporal authority. Under his direct leadership the Sikh Panth took up arms in order to protect itself from Mughal hostility. From the Sikh perspective this new development was not taken at the cost of abandoning the original spiritual base. Rather, it was meant to achieve a balance between temporal and spiritual concerns. A Sikh theologian of the period, Bhāī Gurdās, defended this martial response as 'hedging the orchard of the Sikh faith with the hardy and thorny *kikar* tree.' After four skirmishes with Mughal troops, Guru Hargobind withdrew to theSivalik Hills, and Kiratpur became the new center of the mainline Sikh tradition. Amritsar fell into the hands of the *miṇā*s, who established a parallel line of Guruship with the support of the Mughal authorities.

During the time of the seventh and eighth Gurus, Har Rai (1630–61) and Har Krishan (1656–64), the emphasis on armed conflict with the Mughal authorities receded, but the Gurus held court and kept a regular force of Sikh horsemen. During the period of the ninth Guru, Tegh Bahadur (1621–75), however, the increasing strength of the Sikh movement in rural areas again attracted Mughal attention. Guru Tegh Bahadur's ideas of a just society inspired a spirit of fearlessness among his followers: 'He who holds none in fear, nor is afraid of anyone, Nānak, acknowledge him alone as a man of true wisdom' (*Ādi Granth* p. 1,427). Such ideas posed a direct challenge to the increasingly restrictive policies of the Mughal emperor, Aurangzīb (r. 1658–1707), who had imposed Islamic laws and taxes and ordered the replacement of Hindu temples by mosques. Not surprisingly, Guru Tegh Bahadur was summoned to Delhi by the orders of the emperor, and on his refusal to embrace Islam he was publicly executed in Chāndnī Chowk on November 11, 1675. The Sikhs perceived his death as the second martyrdom, which involved larger issues of human rights and freedom of conscience.

Tradition holds that the Sikhs who were present at the scene of Guru Tegh Bahadur's execution shrank from recognition, concealing their identity for fear they might suffer a similar fate. In order to respond to this new situation, the tenth Guru, Gobind Siṅgh, resolved to impose on his followers an outward form that would make them instantly recognizable. He restructured the Sikh Panth and instituted the Khālsā ('pure'), an order of loyal Sikhs bound by a common identity and discipline. On Baisākhī Day 1699 at Anandpur, Guru Gobind Siṅgh initiated the first 'Cherished Five' (*pañj piare*), who formed the nucleus of the new order of the Khālsā. The five volunteers who responded to the Guru's call for loyalty, and who came from different castes and regions of India, received the initiation through a ceremony that involved sweetened water (*amrit*) stirred with a two-edged sword and sanctified by the recitation of five liturgical prayers.

The inauguration of the Khālsā was the culmination of the canonical period in the development of Sikhism. The most visible symbols of Sikhism known as the five Ks—namely, uncut hair (*kes*), a comb for topknot (*kaṅghā*), a short sword (*kirpan*), a wrist ring (*karā*), and breeches (*kachh*)—are mandatory to the Khālsā. Guru Gobind Siṅgh also closed the Sikh canon by adding a collection of the works of his father, Guru Tegh Bahadur, to the original compilation of the *Ādi Granth*. Before he passed away in 1708, he terminated the line of personal Gurus and installed the *Ādi Granth* as the eternal Guru for Sikhs. Thereafter, the authority of the Guru was invested together in the scripture (*Guru Granth*) and in the corporate community (Guru Panth).

Evolution of the Panth

The historical development of the Sikh Panth took place in response to four main elements. The first of these was the ideology based on religious and cultural innovations of Guru Nānak and his nine successors. This was the principal motivating factor in the evolution of the Sikh Panth.

The second was the rural base of the Punjabi society. Guru Nānak founded the village of Kartarpur to sustain an agricultural-based community. Its location on the bank of the river Rāvī, provides extremely fertile soil for agriculture. Guru Nānak's father, Kālū Bedī, and his father-in-law, Mūlā Chonā, were village revenue officials (*patvārī*) who must have been instrumental in acquiring a parcel of land at Kartarpur. Since the Mughal law recognized Guru Nānak's sons as the rightful owners of their father's properties, Guru Angad had to establish a new Sikh center at Khadur. It confirmed an organizational principle that the communal establishment at Kartarpur could not be considered a unique institution but rather a model that could be cloned and imitated elsewhere. Similarly, Guru Amar Dās founded the city of Goindval. Interestingly, the location of Goindval on the right bank of the Beās River was close to the point where the Mājhā, Mālvā, and Doāba areas converge. This may help account for the spread of the Panth's influence in all three regions of the Punjab. Guru Rām Dās founded the city of Rāmdāspur (Amritsar). During the period of Guru Arjan the founding of the villages of Taran Taran, Sri Hargobindpur, and Kartarpur (Punjab) in the rural areas saw a large number of converts from local Jāṭ peasantry. Further, Guru Tegh Bahadur's influence in the rural areas attracted more Jāṭs from the Mālvā region, and most of them became Khālsā during Guru Gobind Singh's period. It may have been the militant traditions of the Jāṭs that brought the Sikh Panth into increasing conflict with the Mughals, a conflict that shaped the future direction of the Sikh movement.

The third factor was the conflict created within the Sikh community by dissidents, which originally worked to counter and then, paradoxically, to enhance the process of the crystallization of the Sikh tradition. Guru Nānak's son, Sri Chand, was the first dissident who lived a life of celibacy. Although he failed to attract much support from early Sikhs, he created his own sect of Udāsīs (renunciants). This group was closer to the Nātha Yogīs in its beliefs and practices. Similarly, the followers of Mohan (Guru Amar Dās' elder son), Prithī Chand (*miṇā*), Dhir Mal (Guru Har Rai's elder brother, who established his seat at Kartarpur, Jalandhar), and Rām Rai (Guru Har Krishan's elder brother, who established his seat at Dehrā Dūn) posed a challenge to the mainline Sikh tradition. All these dissidents enjoyed Mughal patronage in the form of revenue-free grants (*madad-i-māsh*). Their proestablishment stance triggered the mainline tradition to strengthen its own resources.

Finally, the fourth element was the period of Punjab history from the seventeenth to the eighteenth centuries in which the Sikh Panth evolved in tension with Mughals and Afghans. All four elements combined to produce the mutual interaction between ideology and environment that came to characterize the historical development of Sikhism.

Worldview

The nature of the Ultimate Reality in Sikh doctrine is succinctly expressed in the Mūl Mantar ('seed formula'), the preamble to the Sikh scripture. The basic theological statement reads as follows: 'There is one

Supreme Being ('1' *Oankar*), the Eternal Reality, the Creator, without fear and devoid of enmity, immortal, never incarnated, self-existent, known by grace through the Guru. The Eternal One, from the beginning, through all time, present now, the Everlasting Reality' (*Ādi Granth* p. 1). The numeral '1' at the beginning of the original Punjabi text represents the unity of Akāl Purakh (the 'Timeless One,' God), a concept that Guru Nānak interpreted in monotheistic terms. It affirms that Akāl Purakh is one without a second, the source as well as the goal of all that exists. He has 'no relatives, no mother, no father, no wife, no son, no rival who may become a potential contender' (*Ādi Granth* p. 597). The Sikh Gurus were fiercely opposed to any anthropomorphic conceptions of the divine. As the creator and sustainer of the universe, Akāl Purakh lovingly watches over it. As a father figure, he runs the world with justice and destroys evil and supports good (*Ādi Granth* p. 1,028). As a mother figure, the Supreme Being is the source of love and grace and responds to the devotion of her humblest followers. By addressing the One as 'Father, Mother, Friend, and Brother' simultaneously, Guru Arjan stressed that Akāl Purakh is without gender (*Ādi Granth* p. 103). Paradoxically, Akāl Purakh is both transcendent (*nirguṇa*, 'without attributes') and immanent (*saguṇa*, 'with attributes'). Only in personal experience can he be truly known. Despite the stress laid on *nirguṇa* discourse within the Sikh tradition, which directs the devotee to worship a nonincarnate, universal God, in Sikh doctrine God is partially embodied in the divine Name (*nām*) and in the collective Words (*bāṇī*) and the person of the Guru and the saints.

Guru Nānak's cosmology hymn in *Mārū Rāg* addresses the basic questions about the genesis of the universe: 'For endless eons, there was only darkness. Nothing except the divine Order (*hukam*) existed. No day or night, no moon or sun. The Creator alone was absorbed in a primal state of contemplation. . . . When the Creator so willed, creation came into being. . . . The Un-manifested One revealed itself in the creation' (*Ādi Granth* pp. 1,035–36). Guru Nānak maintained that the universe 'comes into being by the divine Order' (*Ādi Granth* p. 1). He further says: 'From the True One came air and from air came water; from water he created the three worlds and infused in every heart his own light' (*Ādi Granth* p. 19). Guru Nānak employed the well-known Indic ideas of creation through five basic elements of air, water, ether, fire, and earth. As the creation of Akāl Purakh, the physical universe is real but subject to constant change. It is a lush green garden (*jagg vaṛi*), where human beings participate in its colorful beauty and fragrance (*Ādi Granth* p. 118). For Guru Nānak the world was divinely inspired. It is a place that provides human beings with an opportunity to perform their duty and achieve union with Akāl Purakh. Thus, actions performed in earthly existence are important because 'all of us carry the fruits of our deeds' (*Ādi Granth* p. 4).

For the Gurus, human life is the most delightful experience that one can have with the gift of a beautiful body (*Ādi Granth* p. 966). It is a 'precious jewel' (*Ādi Granth* p. 156). Indeed, the human being has been called the epitome of creation: 'All other creation is subject to you, [O Man/Woman!], you reign supreme on this earth' (*Ādi Granth* p. 374). Guru Arjan further proclaimed that human life provides an individual with the opportunity to remember the divine Name and ultimately to join with Akāl Purakh (*Ādi Granth* p.15). But rare are the ones who seek the divine Beloved while participating in worldly actions and delights.

The notions of *karma* (actions) and *saṃsāra* (rebirth or transmigration) are central to all religious traditions originating in India. *Karma* is popularly understood in Indian thought as the principle of cause and effect. This principle of *karma* is logical and inexorable, but *karma* is also understood as a predisposition that safeguards the notion of free choice. In Sikh doctrine, however, the notion of *karma* undergoes a radical change. For the Sikh Gurus, the law of *karma* is not inexorable. In the context of the Guru Nānak's theology, *karma* is subject to the higher principle of the 'divine order' (*hukam*), an 'all-embracing principle' which is the sum total of all divinely instituted laws in the cosmos. The law of *karma* is replaced by Akāl Purakh's *hukam*, which is no longer an impersonal causal phenomenon but falls within the sphere of Akāl Purakh's omnipotence and justice. In fact, the primacy of divine grace over the law of *karma* is always maintained in the Sikh teachings, and divine grace even breaks the chain of adverse *karma*.

Sacred Life and Literature

Sacred life

The Sikh view of sacred life is intimately linked with the understanding of the nature of *gurmat* ('Guru's view or doctrine') whereby one follows the teachings of the Gurus. Guru Nānak employed the following key terms to describe the nature of divine revelation in its totality: *nām* (divine Name), *śabad* (divine Word), and *guru* (divine Preceptor). The *nām* reflects the manifestation of divine presence everywhere around us and within us, yet the people fail to perceive it due to their *haumai* or self-centeredness. The Punjabi term '*haumai*' ('I, I') signifies the powerful impulse to succumb to personal gratification so that a person is separated from Akāl Purakh and thus continues to suffer within the cycle of rebirth (*saṃsāra*). Akāl Purakh, however, looks graciously upon the suffering of people. He reveals himself through the Guru by uttering the *śabad* (divine Word) that communicates a sufficient understanding of the *nām* (divine Name) to those who are able to 'hear' it. The *śabad* is the actual 'utterance,' and in 'hearing' it a person awakens to the reality of the divine Name, immanent in all that lies around and within.

The institution of the Guru carries spiritual authority in the Sikh tradition. In most of the Indian religious traditions the term 'Guru' stands for a human teacher who communicates divine knowledge and provides his disciples with a cognitive map for liberation. In Sikhism, however, its meaning has evolved in a cluster of doctrines over a period of time. There are four focal points of spiritual authority, each acknowledged within the Sikh tradition as Guru: doctrine of eternal Guru; doctrine of personal Guru; doctrine of Guru Granth; and doctrine of Guru Panth. First, Guru Nānak uses the term 'Guru' in three basic senses: the Guru is Akāl Purakh; the Guru is the voice of Akāl Purakh; and the Guru is the Word, the Truth of Akāl Purakh. To experience the eternal Guru is to experience divine guidance. In Sikh usage, therefore, the Guru is the voice of Akāl Purakh, mystically uttered within human heart, mind, and soul (*man*).

Second, the personal Guru functions as the channel through whom the voice of Akāl Purakh becomes audible. Nānak became the embodiment of the eternal Guru only when he received the divine Word and conveyed it to his disciples. The same spirit manifested itself successively in his successors. In Sikh doctrine, a theory of spiritual succession was advanced in the form of 'the unity of Guruship' in which there was no difference between the founder and the successors. Thus they all represented one and the same light (*jot*) as a single flame ignites a series of torches.

Third, in Sikh usage, the *Ādi Granth* is normally referred to as the *Guru Granth Sāhib*, which implies a confession of faith in the scripture as Guru. As such, the *Guru Granth Sāhib* carries the same status and authority as did the ten personal Gurus from Guru Nānak through Guru Gobind Siṅgh, and therefore, it must be viewed as the source of ultimate authority within the Sikh Panth. In actual practice, it performs the role of Guru in the personal piety and corporate identity of the Sikh community. It has provided a framework for the shaping of the Sikh Panth and has been a decisive factor in shaping a distinctive Sikh identity. The *Ādi Granth* occupies a central position in all Sikh ceremonies, and its oral/aural experience has provided the Sikh tradition with a living presence of the divine Guru. Indeed, the *Guru Granth Sāhib* has given Sikhs a sacred focus for reflection and for discovering the meaning of life. It has functioned as a supratextual source of authority within the Sikh tradition. In a certain sense Sikhs have taken their conception of sacred scripture farther than other people of the Book such as Jews and Muslims.

Finally, the key term Guru Panth is normally employed in two senses: first, the Panth of the Guru, referring to the Sikh community; and second, the Panth as the Guru, referring to the doctrine of Guru Panth. This doctrine fully developed from the earlier idea that 'the Guru is mystically present in the congregation.' At the inauguration of the Khālsā in 1699 Guru Gobind Siṅgh symbolically transferred his authority to the Cherished Five when he received initiation from their hands. Thus the elite corps of the Khālsā has always claimed to speak authoritatively on behalf of the whole Sikh Panth, although at times non-Khālsā Sikhs interpret the doctrine of Guru Panth as conferring authority on a community more broadly defined. As a practical matter, consensus within the Sikh community is achieved by following democratic traditions.

In order to achieve a state of spiritual liberation within one's lifetime one must transcend the unregenerate condition created by the influence of *haumai*. In fact, *haumai* is the source of five evil impulses traditionally known as lust (*kām*), anger (*krodh*), covetousness (*lobh*), attachment to worldly things (*moh*), and pride (*hankār*). Under the influence of *haumai* a person becomes 'self-willed' (*manmukh*), one who is so attached to his passions for worldly pleasures that he forgets the divine Name and wastes his entire life in evil and suffering. This unregenerate condition can be transcended by means of the strictly interior discipline of *nām simaran* or 'remembering the divine Name.' This threefold process ranges from the repetition of a sacred word, usually Vahigurū (Praise to the Eternal Guru), through the devotional singing of hymns with the congregation to sophisticated meditation on the nature of Akāl Purakh. The first and the third levels of this practice relate to private devotions, while the second refers to corporate sense. On the whole the discipline of *nām simaran* is designed to bring a person into harmony with the divine order (*hukam*).

The person thus gains the experience of ever-growing wonder (*vismād*) in spiritual life and achieves the ultimate condition of blissful 'equanimity' (*sahaj*) when the spirit ascends to the 'realm of Truth' (*sach khaṇḍ*), the fifth and the last of the spiritual stages, in which the soul finds mystical union with Akāl Purakh.

The primacy of divine grace over personal effort is fundamental to Guru Nānak's theology. There is, however, neither fatalism nor any kind of passive acceptance of a predestined future in his view of life. He proclaimed, 'With your own hands carve out your own destiny' (*Ādi Granth* p.474). Indeed, personal effort in the form of good actions has a place in Guru Nānak's view of life. His idea of 'divine free choice,' on the one hand, and his emphasis on the 'life of activism' based on human freedom, on the other, reflect his ability to hold in tension seemingly opposed elements. Guru Nānak explicitly saw this balancing of opposed tendencies, which avoids rigid predestination theories and yet enables people to see their own 'free' will as a part of Akāl Purakh's will, as allowing Sikhs the opportunity to create their own destinies, a feature stereotypically associated with Sikh enterprise throughout the world. Sikhism thus stresses the dignity of regular labor as an integral part of spiritual discipline. This is summed up in the following triple commandment: engage in honest labor (*kirat karanī*) for a living, adore the divine Name (*nām japan*), and share the fruit of labor with others (*vaṇḍ chhakaṇā*). The formula stresses both the centrality of meditative worship and the necessity of righteous living in the world.

Scriptures and Other Literature

The *Ādi Granth* is the primary scripture of the Sikhs. It contains the works of the first five and the ninth Sikh Gurus, four bards (Sattā, Balvaṇḍ, Sundar, and Mardānā), eleven Bhaṭṭs (eulogists associated with the Sikh court), and fifteen Bhagats ('devotees' such as Kabīr, Nāmdev, Ravidās, Shaikh Farid, and other medieval poets of *sant, ṣūfī*, and *bhakti* origin). Its standard version contains a total of 1,430 pages, and each copy corresponds exactly in terms of the material printed on individual pages. The text of the *Ādi Granth* is divided into three major sections. The introductory section includes three liturgical prayers. The middle section, which contains the bulk of the material, is divided into thirty-one major *rāg*s or musical patterns. The final section includes an epilogue consisting of miscellaneous works that could not be accommodated in the middle section.

The second sacred collection, the *Dasam Granth* is attributed to the tenth Guru, Gobind Siṅgh, but it must have extended beyond his time to include the writings of others as well. Mani Siṅgh, who died in 1734, compiled the collection early in the eighteenth century. Its modern standard version of 1,428 pages consists of four major types of compositions: devotional texts, autobiographical works, miscellaneous writings, and a collection of mythical narratives and popular anecdotes.

The works of two early Sikhs, Bhāī Gurdās (1551–1637) and Bhāī Nand Lāl Goyā (1633–1715), make up the third category of sacred literature. Along with the sacred compositions of the Gurus, their works are approved in the official manual of the *Sikh Rahit Maryādā* (Sikh Code of Conduct) for singing in the *gurdwārā*s.

The last category of Sikh literature includes three distinct genres: the *janam-sākhī*s (birth narratives), the *rahit-nāmā*s (manuals of code of conduct), and the *gur-bilās* (splendor of the Guru) literature. The *janam-sākhī*s are hagiographical accounts of Guru Nānak's life, produced by the Sikh community in the seventeenth century. The *rahit-nāmā*s provide rare insight into the evolving nature of the Khālsā code in the eighteenth and nineteenth centuries. The *gur-bilās* mainly focus on the mighty deeds of two warrior Gurus, Hargobind and particularly Gobind Siṅgh.

Institutions and Practices

The Khālsā and the Rahit

From the perspective of ritual studies, three significant issues were linked with the first *amrit* ceremony. First, all who chose to join the order of the Khālsā through the ceremony were understood to have been 'reborn' in the house of the Guru and thus to have assumed a new identity. The male members were given the surname Siṅgh ('lion'), and female members were given the surname Kaur ('princess'), with the intention of creating a parallel system of aristocratic titles in relation to the Rājput hill chiefs of the surrounding areas of Anandpur. Second, the Guru symbolically transferred his spiritual authority to the Cherished Five when he himself received the nectar of the double-edged sword from their hands and thus became a part of the Khālsā Panth and subject to its collective will. In this way he not only paved the way for the termination of a personal Guruship but also abolished the institution of the *masand*s, which was becoming increasingly disruptive. Several of the *masand*s had refused to forward collections to the Guru, creating factionalism in the Sikh Panth. In addition, Guru Gobind Siṅgh removed the threat posed by the competing seats of authority when he declared that the Khālsā should have no dealings with the followers of Prithī Chand (*miṇā*), Dhir Mal, and Rām Rai. Finally, Guru Gobind Siṅgh delivered the nucleus of the Sikh Rahit (Code of Conduct) at the inauguration of the Khālsā. By sanctifying the hair with *amrit*, he made it 'the official seal of the Guru,' and the cutting of bodily hair was thus strictly prohibited. The Guru further imposed a rigorous ban on smoking.

All Sikhs initiated into the order of the Khālsā must observe the Rahit as enunciated by Guru Gobind Siṅgh and subsequently elaborated. The most significant part of the code is the enjoinder to wear five visible symbols of identity, known from their Punjabi names as the five Ks (*pañj kakke*). These are unshorn hair (*keś*), symbolizing spirituality and saintliness; a wooden comb (*kaṅghā*), signifying order and discipline in life; a miniature sword (*kirpan*), symbolizing divine grace, dignity, and courage; a steel 'wrist ring' (*karā*), signifying responsibility and allegiance to the Guru; and a pair of short breeches (*kachh*), symbolizing moral restraint. Among Sikhs the five Ks are outer symbols of the divine Word, implying a direct correlation between *bāṇī* ('divine utterance') and *bāṇā* ('Khālsā dress'). The five Ks, along with a turban for male Sikhs, symbolize that the Khālsā Sikhs, while reciting prayers, are dressed in the word of God. Their minds are thus purified and inspired, and their bodies are girded to do battle with the day's temptations. In addition, Khālsā Sikhs are prohibited from the four cardinal sins (*chār kurahit*): 'cutting the hair, using tobacco, committing adultery, and eating meat that has not come from an animal killed with a single blow.'

Worship, Practices, and Lifecycle Rituals

The daily routine of a devout Sikh begins with the practice of meditation upon the divine Name. This occurs during the *amritvelā*, the 'ambrosial hours' (that is, the last watch of the night, between 3 and 6 a.m.), immediately after rising and bathing. Meditation is followed by the recitation of five liturgical prayers, which include the *Japjī* of Guru Nānak. In most cases the early morning devotion concludes in the presence of the *Guru Granth Sāhib*, in which the whole family gathers to receive the divine command (*vāk lainā* or 'taking God's Word') by reading a passage selected at random. Similarly, a collection of hymns, *Sodar Rahiras* (Supplication at That Door), is prescribed for the evening prayers, and the *Kīrtan Sohila* (Song of Praise) is recited before retiring for the night.

Congregational worship takes place in the *gurdwārā*, where the main focus is upon the *Guru Granth Sāhib*, installed ceremoniously every morning. Worship consists mainly of the singing of scriptural passages set to music, with the accompaniment of instruments. The singing of hymns (*kīrtan*) in a congregational setting is the heart of the Sikh devotional experience. Through such *kīrtan* the devotees attune themselves to vibrate in harmony with the divine Word, which has the power to transform and unify their consciousness. The exposition of the scriptures, known as *kathā* ('homily'), may be delivered at an appropriate time during the service by the *granthī* ('reader') of the *gurdwārā* or by the traditional Sikh scholar (*gyani*). At the conclusion of the service all who are present join in reciting the *Ardās* ('Petition,' or Sikh Prayer), which invokes divine grace and recalls the rich common heritage of the community. Then follows the reading of the *vāk* (divine command) and the distribution of *karāh prasād* (sanctified food).

The central feature of the key lifecycle rituals is always the *Guru Granth Sāhib*. When a child is to be named, the family takes the baby to the *gurdwārā* and offers *karāh prasād*. After offering thanks and prayers through *Ardās*, the *Guru Granth Sāhib* is opened at random and a name is chosen beginning with the same letter as the first composition on the left-hand page. Thus, the process of *vāk lainā* (divine command) functions to provide the first letter of the chosen name. The underlying principle is that the child derives his or her identity from the Guru's word and begins life as a Sikh. To a boy's name the common surname Singh is added, and to a girl's name Kaur is added at the end of the chosen name. In some cases, however, particularly in North America, people employ caste names (for example, Ahluwalia, Dhaliwal, Grewal, Kalsi, Sawhney, or Sethi) as the last elements of their names, and for them Singh and Kaur become middle names. In addition, the infant is administered sweetened water that is stirred with a sword, and the first five stanzas of Guru Nānak's *Japjī* are recited.

A Sikh wedding, according to the *Ānand* (Bliss) ceremony, also takes place in the presence of the *Guru Granth Sāhib*, and the performance of the actual marriage requires the couple to circumambulate the sacred scripture four times to take four vows. Before the bridegroom and the bride make each round, they listen to a verse of the *Lāvān*, or 'wedding hymn' (*Ādi Granth* pp. 773–74), by the fourth Guru, Rām Dās, as given by a scriptural reader. They bow before the *Guru Granth Sāhib* and then stand up to make their round while professional musicians sing the same verse with the congregation. During the process of their clockwise movements around the scripture, they take the following four vows: to lead an action-oriented life based upon righteousness and never to shun the obligations of family and society; to maintain a bond of reverence and dignity between them; to keep enthusiasm for life alive in the face of adverse circumstances and to remain removed from worldly attachments; and to cultivate a 'balanced approach' (*sahaj*) in life, avoiding all extremes. The pattern of circum-ambulation in the *Ānand* marriage ceremony is the enactment of the primordial movement of life, in which there is no beginning and no end. Remembering the four marital vows is designed to make the life of the couple blissful.

The key initiation ceremony (*amrit sanskār*) for a Sikh must take place in the presence of the *Guru Granth Sāhib*. There is no fixed age for initiation, which may be done at any time the person is willing to accept the Khālsā discipline. Five Khālsā Sikhs, representing the collectivity of the original Cherished Five, conduct the ceremony. Each recites from memory one of the five liturgical prayers while stirring the sweetened water (*amrit*) with a double-edged sword. The novice then drinks the *amrit* five times so that his body is purified from the influence of five vices; and five times the *amrit* is sprinkled on his eyes to transform his outlook toward life. Finally, the *amrit* is poured on his head five times to sanctify his hair so that he will preserve his natural form and listen to the voice of conscience. Throughout the procedure the Sikh being initiated formally takes the oath each time by repeating the following declaration: '*Vahigurū jī kā khālsā! Vahigurū jī kī fateh!*' (Khālsā belongs to the Wonderful Lord! Victory belongs to the Wonderful Lord!) Thus, a person becomes a Khālsā Sikh through the transforming power of the sacred word. At the conclusion of the ceremony a *vāk* is given and *karāh prasād* is distributed.

Finally, at the time of death, both in the period preceding cremation and in the postcremation rites, hymns from the *Guru Granth Sāhib* are sung. In addition, a reading of the entire scripture takes place at home or in a *gurdwārā*. Within ten days of the conclusion of the reading, a *bhog* ('completion') ceremony is held, at which final prayers are offered in memory of the deceased.

Ethics and Human Relations

The *Ādi Granth* opens with Guru Nānak's *Japjī* where the fundamental question of seeking the divine Truth is raised as follows: 'How is Truth to be attained, how the veil of falsehood torn aside?' Guru Nānak then responds: 'Nānak, thus it is written: submit to the divine order (*hukam*), walk in its ways' (*Ādi Granth* p.1). Truth obviously is not obtained by intellectual effort or cunning but only by personal commitment. To know truth one must live in it. The seeker of the divine Truth, therefore, must live an ethical life. An immoral person is neither worthy of being called a true seeker nor capable of attaining the spiritual goal of life. Any dichotomy between spiritual development and moral conduct is not approved in Sikh ethics. In this context Guru Nānak explicitly says: 'Truth is the highest virtue, but higher still is truthful living' (*Ādi Granth* p. 62). Indeed, truthful conduct (*sach achār*) is at the heart of Sikh ethics.

The central focus in the Sikh moral scheme is the cultivation of virtues such as wisdom, contentment, justice, humility, truthfulness, temperance, love, forgiveness, charity, purity, and fear of Akāl Purakh. Guru Nānak remarked, 'Sweetness and humility are the essence of all virtues' (*Ādi Granth* p. 470). These virtues not only enrich the personal lives of individuals but also promote socially responsible living. The Gurus laid great stress on the need to earn one's living through honest means. In particular, living by alms or begging is strongly rejected. Through hard work and sharing, Sikh ethics forbid withdrawal from social participation. The Sikh Gurus offered their own vision of the cultivation of egalitarian ideals in social relations. Such ideals are based on the principle of social equality, gender equality, and human brotherhood/ sisterhood. Thus, it is not surprising that any kind of discrimination based on caste or gender is expressly rejected in Sikh ethics.

The key element of religious living is to render service (*sevā*) to others in the form of mutual help and voluntary work. The real importance of *sevā* lies in sharing one's resources of 'body, mind, and wealth' (*tan-man-dhan*) with others. This is an expression toward fellow beings of what one feels toward Akāl Purakh. The service must be rendered without the desire for self-glorification, and in addition, self-giving service must be done without setting oneself up as a judge of other people. The Sikh Prayer (*Ardās*) holds in high esteem the quality of 'seeing but not judging' (*anadith karanā*). Social bonds are often damaged beyond redemption when people, irrespective of their own limitations, unconscionably judge others. The Sikh Gurus emphasized the need to destroy this root of social strife and enmity through self-giving service.

Finally, Sikhism is dedicated to human rights and resistance against injustice. It strives to eliminate poverty and to offer voluntary help to the less privileged. Its commitment is to the ideal of universal brotherhood, with an altruistic concern for humanity as a whole (*sarbat da bhala*). In a celebrated passage from the *Akāl Ustat* (Praise of Immortal One), Guru Gobind Siṅgh declared that 'humankind is one and that all people belong to a single humanity' (verse 85). Here it is important to underline the Guru's role as a conciliator who tried to persuade the Mughal emperor Bahādur Shāh to walk the ways of peace. Even though Guru Gobind Siṅgh had to spend the major part of his life fighting battles that were forced upon him by Hindu hill *rājā*s and Mughal authorities, a longing for peace and fellowship with both Hindus and Muslims may be seen in the following passage from the *Akāl Ustat*: 'The temple and the mosque are the same, so are the Hindu worship [*pū jā*] and Muslim prayer [*namāz*]. All people are one, it is through error that they appear different.... Allāh and Abhekh are the same, the Purāṇ a and the Qur ān are the same. They are all alike, all the creation of the One' (verse 86). The above verses emphatically stress the irenic belief that the differences dividing people are in reality meaningless. In fact, all people are fundamentally the same because they all are the creations of the same Supreme Being. To pursue this ideal, Sikhs conclude their morning and evening prayers with the words 'Says Nānak: may thy Name and glory be ever triumphant, and in thy will, O Lord, may peace and prosperity come to one and all.'

Society: Caste and Gender Issues

Guru Nānak and the succeeding Gurus emphatically proclaimed that the divine Name was the only sure means of liberation for all four castes: the Khatrī, originally the Kṣatriya (warrior), the Brāhman. (priest), theŚūdra (servant/agriculturalist), and the Vaiśya (tradesman). In the works of the Gurus, the Khatrīs were always placed above the Brāhman s in the caste hierarchy while theŚudras were raised above the Vaiśyas. This was an interesting way of breaking the rigidity of the centuries-old caste system. All the Gurus were Khatrīs, which made them a top-ranking mercantile caste in Punjab's urban hierarchy, followed by Arorās (merchants) and Ahlūwālīās (brewers). In the rural caste hierarchy an absolute majority (almost two-thirds) of Sikhs are Jāṭs (peasants), followed by Rāmgar.hīās (artisans), Rāmdāsīās (cobblers), and Mazhabīs (sweepers). Although Brāhman s are at the apex of the Hindu caste hierarchy, Sikhs place Brāhman s distinctly lower on the caste scale. This is partly because of the strictures the Sikh Gurus laid upon Brāhman pride and partly because the reorganization of Punjabi rural society conferred dominance on the Jāṭ caste.

Doctrinally, caste has never been one of the defining criteria of Sikh identity. In the Sikh congregation there is no place for any kind of injustice or hurtful discrimination based upon caste identity. In the *gurdwārā* Sikhs eat together in the community kitchen, share the same sanctified food, and worship together. The *Sikh Rahit Maryādā* explicitly states, 'No account should be taken of caste; a Sikh woman should be married only to a Sikh man; and Sikhs should not be married as children.' This is the ideal, however, and in practice most Sikh marriages are arranged between members of the same endogamous caste group. Caste, therefore, still prevails within the Sikh community as a marriage convention. Nevertheless, intercaste marriages take place frequently among urban professionals in India and elsewhere.

The Sikh Gurus addressed the issues of gender within the parameters established by traditional patri-archal structures. In their view an ideal woman plays the role of a good daughter or sister and a good wife and mother within the context of family life. They condemned both women and men alike who did not observe the cultural norms of modesty and honor in their lives. It is in this context that images of the immoral woman and the unregenerate man are frequently encountered in the scriptural texts. There is no tolerance for any kind of premarital or extramarital sexual relationships, and rape in particular is regarded as a violation of women's honor in Punjabi culture. Rape amounts to the loss of family honor, which in turn becomes the loss of one's social standing in the community. The notion of family honor is thus intimately linked to the status of women.

The issue of gender has received a great deal of attention within the Sikh Panth. It is notable that the Sikh Gurus offered a vision of gender equality within the Sikh community and took practical steps to foster respect for womanhood. They were ahead of their times when they championed the cause of equal access for women in spiritual and temporal matters. Guru Nānak raised a strong voice against the position of inferiority assigned to women in society at the time: 'From women born, shaped in the womb, to woman betrothed and wed; we are bound to women by ties of affection, on women man's future depends. If one woman dies he seeks another; with a woman he orders his life. Why then should one speak evil of women, they who give birth to kings?' (*Ādi Granth* p. 473). He sought to bring home the realization that the survival of the human race depended upon women, who were unjustifiably ostracized within society. Guru Amar Dās abolished the customs among women of the veil and of *satī* (self-immolation) and permitted the remarriage of widows. He further appointed women as Sikh missionaries. Indeed, Sikh women were given equal rights with men to conduct prayers and other ceremonies in *gurdwārā*s. In actual practice, however, males dominate most Sikh institutions, and Sikh women continue to live in a patriarchal society based on Punjabi cultural assumptions. In this respect they differ little from their counterparts in other religious communities in India. Although there is a large gap between the ideal and reality, there is clear doctrinal support for the equality of rights for men and women within the Sikh Panth.

Modern Expressions

The modern religious and cultural transformation within the Sikh tradition took place during the colonial period on the initiatives of the Singh Sabhā (Society of the Singhs). This reform movement began in 1873 at Amritsar. The principal objective of the Singh Sabhā reformers was to reaffirm the distinctiveness of Sikh identity in the face of the twin threats posed by the casual reversion to Hindu practices during Sikh rule and the explicit challenges from actively proselytizing religious movements such as Christian missionaries and the Ārya Samāj. The Tat Khālsā (Pure Khālsā), the dominant wing of the Singh Sabhā movement, succeeded in eradicating all forms of religious diversity by the end of the nineteenth century and established norms of religious orthodoxy and orthopraxy. The reformers were largely successful in making the Khālsā ideal the orthodox form of Sikhism, and they systematized and clarified the Khālsā tradition to make Sikhism consistent and effective for propagation.

Indeed, the Tat Khālsā ideal of Sikh identity, which was forged in the colonial crucible, was both old and new. In addition to the economic and military policy of the British, there were other elements that meshed together to produce a great impact on the emerging Sikh identity. These additional elements in the larger colonial context were new patterns of administration, a new technology, a fresh approach to education, the entry of Christian missionaries, and the modernist perspective based on the scientific paradigm of the Enlightenment. All these factors produced a kind of Neo-Sikhism, characterized by a largely successful set of redefinitions in the context of the notions of modernity and religious identity imposed by the dominant ideology of the colonial power closely associated with Victorian Christianity. As such, modern Sikhism became a well-defined 'system' based on a unified tradition, and the Tat Khālsā understanding of Sikh identity became the norm of orthodoxy.

Among the 23 million Sikhs in the postmodern world, however, only approximately 15 to 20 percent are *amrit-dhārī*s (initiated), those who represent the orthodox form of the Khālsā. A large majority of Sikhs, however, about 70 percent, are *kes-dhārī*s, that is, those who 'retain their hair' and thus maintain a visible identity. These Sikhs follow most of the Khālsā Rahit without having gone through the initiation ceremony. The number of Sikhs who have shorn their hair, and are thus less conspicuous, is quite large in the West in general, and in particular in North America and the United Kingdom. Popularly known as *monā* (clean-shaven) Sikhs, they retain their Khālsā affiliation by using the surnames Singh and Kaur. These Sikhs are also called *ichhā-dhārī*s because they 'desire' to keep their hair but cut it under some compulsion. They are frequently confused with *sahaj-dhārī* (gradualist) Sikhs, those who have never accepted the Khālsā discipline. Although *sahaj-dhārī* Sikhs practice *nām simaran* and follow the teachings of the *Ādi Granth*, they do not observe the Khālsā Rahit and in general do cut their hair. The number of *sahaj-dhārī*s declined during the last few decades of the twentieth century, although they have not disappeared completely from the Sikh Panth. Finally, there are those who violate the Khālsā Rahit and cut their hair after initiation. These lapsed *amrit-dhārī*s, who are known as *patit* or *bikh-dhārī* (apostate) Sikhs, are found largely in the diaspora. There is thus no single way of being a Sikh, and the five categories of Sikhs are not fixed permanently. Punjabi Sikhs frequently move between them according to their situation in life.

Transmission of the Tradition Outside of India

There are now more than 1 million Sikhs who have settled in foreign lands as a result of successive waves of emigration over the past 100 years. It is not surprising to find the establishment of more than 400 *gurdwārā*s in North America and the United Kingdom alone. The recent years have witnessed among the Sikhs of North America a revived interest in their inherited tradition and identity. This awakened consciousness has produced a flurry of activities in children's education. Sikh parents realize that worship in *gurdwārā*s is conducted in Punjabi, which scarcely responds to the needs of children born in North America. At schools these children are being trained to be critical and rational, and they are therefore questioning the meaning of traditional rituals and practices. Traditionally trained *granthī*s and *gyanī*s are unable to answer their queries.

Moreover, without adequate knowledge of Punjabi, the language of the *Ādi Granth*, the new generation of Sikhs is in danger of being theologically illiterate.

Moreover, a steady process of assimilation is in progress among second- and third-generation Sikhs. Western culture has added new challenges and obstructions to the Sikh tradition. This situation has created new responses from the Sikh community. Many Sikh parents have started home-based worship in both Punjabi and English in order to meet new challenges from the diaspora situation. They have introduced another innovative feature in the form of Sikh Youth Camps to pass on the Sikh traditions to the children. These camps last one or two weeks. Through them a spiritual environment is created which provides the children with continuous exposure to Sikh values and traditions.

Finally, in the 1970s a group of Caucasian Americans and Canadians converted to the Sikh faith at the inspiration of their Yoga teacher, Harbhajan Singh Khalsa (Yogi Bhajan), who founded the Sikh Dharma movement. These so-called white, or *gorā*, Sikhs, male and female alike, wear white turbans, tunics, and tight trousers. They live and raise families in communal houses, spending long hours in meditation and chanting while performing various postures of Tantric *yoga*. They have thus introduced the Sikh tradition into a new cultural environment. Most Punjabi Sikhs have shown an ambivalent attitude toward these converts. On the one hand, they praise the strict Khālsā-style discipline of the white Sikhs; and on the other hand, they express doubts about the mixing of the Sikh tradition with the ideals of Tantric *yoga*.

Relations With Other Religions

The ability to accept religious pluralism is a necessary condition of religious tolerance. Religious pluralism requires that people of different faiths be able to live together harmoniously, which provides an opportunity for spiritual self-judgement and growth. It is in this context that Sikhism expresses the ideals of coexistence and mutual understanding. Sikhism emphasizes the principles of tolerance and the acceptance of the diversity of faith and practice. It is thus able to enter freely into fruitful interreligious dialogue with an open attitude. Such an attitude signifies a willingness to learn from other traditions and yet to retain the integrity of one's own tradition. It also involves the preservation of differences with dignity and mutual respect.

The Sikh Gurus were strongly opposed to the claim of any particular tradition to possess the sole religious truth. Indeed, a spirit of accommodation has always been an integral part of the Sikh attitude toward other traditions. The inclusion of the works of the fifteen medieval non-Sikh saints (*bhagat bāṇī*, 'utterances of the Bhagats'), along with the compositions of the Gurus, in the foundational text of the Sikhs provides an example of the kind of catholicity that promotes mutual respect and tolerance. For instance, the Muslim voice of the devotee Shaikh Farid is allowed to express itself on matters of doctrine and practice. This is the ideal that Sikhs frequently stress in interfaith dialogues.

The presence of the *bhagat bāṇī* in the Sikh scripture offers a four-point theory of religious pluralism. First, one must acknowledge at the outset that all religious traditions have gone through a process of self-definition in response to changing historical contexts. Thus, in any dialogue the dignity of the religious identities of the individual participants must be maintained. One must be able to honor a commitment as absolute for oneself while respecting different absolute commitments for others. For this reason the quest for a universal religion and the attempt to place one religious tradition above others must be abandoned. Second, the doctrinal standpoints of different religious traditions must be maintained with mutual respect and dignity. Third, all participants must enter into a dialogue with an open attitude, one that allows not only true understanding of other traditions but also disagreements on crucial doctrinal points. Finally, the 'other' must somehow become one's 'self' in a dialogue, so that the person's life is enriched by the spiritual experience.

The Tradition in the Study of Religions

The first North American conference on Sikh Studies was held in 1976 at the University of California, Berkeley. At that conference it was generally felt that the Sikh tradition was indeed 'the forgotten tradition' in scholarly circles in North America. In particular, Mark Juergensmeyer argued that in the textbooks in world religions the study of Sikhism was either completely ignored or misrepresented. He examined the various reasons for this treatment. He suggested that there are two prejudices in Indian Studies that function against the study of the Sikh tradition. The first prejudice is that against the modern age. Many scholars, following the Orientalist perspective, have been more interested in the classical texts on Indian philosophy rather than a medieval devotional tradition. Since Sikh tradition is relatively modern, it has been completely ignored in Indian Studies. The other prejudice that faces Sikh Studies in Indian literature is the prejudice against regionalism. Sikhism is not only relatively modern but also almost exclusively Punjabi. In his arguments, Juergensmeyer made the case for the utility of Sikhism for the studies of religion.

In the last two decades the study of Sikh tradition has received a great deal of scholarly attention, and there are now five programs of Sikh and Punjab Studies established in North America with the active financial support of the Sikh community. In the West, Sikh Studies is a new field that is slowly gaining the academic respectability that it richly deserves. It provides interesting data to scholars of Religious Studies to address the fundamental question of how Sikhism has become meaningful to 23 million followers around the world. Its doctrines, myths, rituals, practices, and symbols are the channels of the expression of a faith in which one may grow and fulfill one's life. Throughout Sikh history the faith of its adherents has kept them steadfast in the face of adverse circumstances.

Suggested Further Readings

Cole (1982, 1984); Grewal (1991, 1998); McLeod (1989, 1997, 1999, 2003); Oberoi (1994); H. Singh (1983, 1992–98); N.-G. Singh (1993); N. Singh (1990); P. Singh (2000, 2003); Thursby (1992, 1993).

6

Background to Daoism

Livia Kohn

In This Chapter

Daoism forms an integral part of Chinese culture and has not only contributed considerably to its shaping and development, but is also deeply embedded in it. In the time before even the first traces of Daoism appear on the historical horizon—usually associated with the philosopher Laozi, dated to around 500 B.C.E.—various cultural perceptions and religious practices were established that have had a lasting effect on Daoist philosophy, cosmology, ritual, and religious cultivation ever since. The four most notable ones form the contents of this chapter.

Main Topics Covered

- Shang ancestors and divination
- The *Yijing*
- Philosophical Schools
- Confucianism

Shang Ancestors and Divination

The Shang dynasty (*c.* 1600–1028 B.C.E.) is the earliest Chinese state documented in writing as well as archaeological finds—its predecessor, the Xia dynasty (*c.* 2100–1600 B.C.E.), and its contemporary, the western culture in Sichuan, are only known from excavated tombs and artifacts. Ruling the central area of China with a capital in what is today Henan, the Shang state worked through an extensive administrative bureaucracy, constituted by the king as central ruler, his relatives, local aristocrats, and educated upper-class officials.

Shang Ancestors

The dominant belief of the dynasty was that the otherworld was similarly organized as the Shang bureaucracy. Populated by nature deities such as sun, moon, rain, and thunder as well as a plethora of ancestors—most importantly those of the ruling house and its original founder, known as Shangdi or Highest Ruler—the realm beyond had a major impact on all events and occurrences on earth. Ancestors not only served as intermediaries to the great nature deities but also influenced events on earth by bestowing either blessings or curses on human actions.

As a result, all actions involving the ruler, from the most mundane to the most decisive, had to be submitted to the ancestors' inspection and were either supported or rejected. All events likely to occur were posted to the ancestors for their prediction and guidance. Different ancestors, moreover, were responsible for different areas of life. They received regular offerings based on a complex ritual schedule that followed a calendar consisting of a ten-day week and twelve-year cycle. Both are still in use in China today, notably for fortune-telling purposes.[1]

Ancestor Worship and Divination

The key religious activity of the Shang dynasty involved ancestral sacrifices and divination. Ancestral sacrifices consisted of regular offerings of food and drink in special ritual vessels, usually cast from bronze. They came in all shapes and sizes and were richly ornamented with supernatural figures and intricate patterns. These vessels are the famous Shang bronzes, exhibited in numerous museums around the world, and the object of more or less skilled forgeries since the Song dynasty.

Divination, unlike fortune-telling from palms, playing cards, or dreams, is the reading of divine guidance through secondary signs. A well-known Western example is the auguries of ancient Rome, where the flight pattern of birds was interpreted to foretell the success or failure of an upcoming battle. Shang rulers employed the so-called oracle bones. Discovered by accident by local farmers in Henan in the 1920s, the bones were first taken to be dragon bones and ground up as potent aphrodisiacs. Once identified by archaeologists, they were brought to museums and gradually their writing, the earliest form of Chinese characters, was deciphered and has since been called the oracle-bone script.

Oracle Bones

Oracle bones were originally carapaces of turtles, seen as symbols of the cosmos with their square base (earth) and round top (heaven). Later, when China ran out of turtles and even could not import more from Vietnam, shoulder blades of cattle were used. Trained technicians drilled holes into them at specific spots, then heated them over a fire. As a result, in the drilled area the bone would crack. The cracks were interpreted by professional diviners to mean either yes or no. Even today the character for divination is the image of a crack: 卜 . Both question and answer were recorded by scribes, leaving a good record of the concerns and tendencies of the ancient Chinese. Questions could be both simple and more complicated, including the outcome of warfare, the birth of son or daughter, the relief for the king's toothache. Over the years, the bones were reused, so that many have inscriptions on both sides.

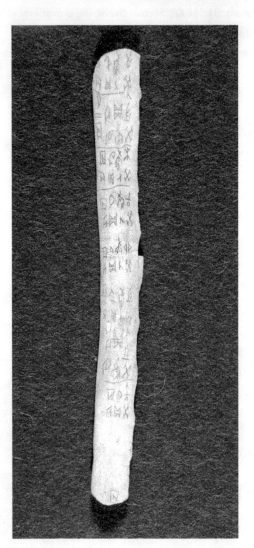

While it is clear that oracle-bone divination was a very involved ritual that required various specialists, scholars are divided with regard to its exact nature. Was the divination in essence a bureaucratic and rather rational method of learning the ancestors' intention (e.g. David Keightley)? Or was it a more ecstatic and shamanic rite that involved direct contact with the otherworld and was undertaken to the accompaniment of music and dance, and possibly with the help of alcoholic drinks and psychedelic drugs (e.g. Chang Kwangchih)? Similarly it is not clear whether the bronze vessels, undoubtedly used to present offerings to the ancestors, were mere vessels for food and drink or, through their animal designs and intricate patterns, represented the divine conveyance of shamanic priests in their excursion to the heavens. Both methods, the rational divination according to signs and the ecstatic/ shamanic way of connecting to the gods have continued actively in Chinese culture, so history does not provide an answer.

Figure 6.1 An oracle bone of the Shang dynasty (British Museum, London, UK/The Bridgeman Art Library.)

Impact on Daoism

Daoists incorporated a heavy dose of Shang religion into their beliefs and practices. The Daoist otherworld is hierarchically organized and populated by nature deities and ancestors, joined in due course by pure divine emanations of the Dao and lofty spirit immortals; regular rituals to these various deities are essential to maintain harmony in the cosmos. The gods have to be appeased to prevent disasters but they can also be enticed to give guidance to human beings; communication with them is a bureaucratic act that involves the written language, no longer in the form of oracle-bone inscriptions but through petitions, contracts, mandates, and other formal documents. Daoist priests are intermediaries of the divine realm and occupy official positions in the otherworld; equipped with special passports and sacred passwords, they can—like shamans—travel into the spheres beyond.

The *Yijing*

Another early feature of Chinese culture that exerted a strong impact on Daoism is the *Yijing* or *Book of Changes*. Historically it supplanted Shang oracle-bone divination when the dynasty changed to the Zhou (1028–221 B.C.E.).

Belief in Heaven

Without giving up on nature gods and ancestors, the Zhou put their dominant faith in Heaven (*tian*). Unlike the Highest Ruler of the Shang, this was not a former human being and thus not guided by personal whims and moods. Rather, Heaven was a process, an abstract representation of the cycles and patterns of nature, a nonhuman force that interacted closely with the human world in a nonpersonal way.

For example, if people behaved in a morally upright way and the ruler did well, Heaven responded by creating harmony through appropriate weather patterns, fertility, and general wellness. It thereby showed its approval and granted the dynasty the right to rule, known as the "Mandate of Heaven." On the other hand, if people behaved badly and the government mismanaged the realm, Heaven showed its displeasure by sending along floods, droughts, earthquakes, locust plagues, epidemics, and the like. These were signs that the ruling dynasty had forfeited its Mandate and that it was time for a change. In Zhou thinking, Heaven thus represented the sum-total of human and natural activities, matching their impulses with appropriate responses.

The notion that humanity and nature/Heaven existed in a close, if not immediate, relationship has remained central to Chinese thinking, and even in 1976 it was very clear to all Chinese that the massive earthquake in August was a harbinger of the death of Chairman Mao in September—both equally signifying upheaval and major change. Daoists adopted this thinking, and the entire complex of Daoist ethics revolves around it (see Chapter 6).

Textual History

The *Yijing*, then, is a divination manual that—rather than providing yes/no answers as the oracle bones did—helps people determine the inherent tendencies in the course of Heaven and aids them in making good decisions through formal judgments and advice. Compiled into a coherent book by Confucius around 500 B.C.E., its system claims to go back to prehistory when a mythical ruler named Fu Xi discerned its original symbols from constellations in the stars. King Wen, the mastermind behind the Zhou conquest, supposedly first standardized its basic judgments.

Named one of the Six Classics by Confucius, the *Yijing* became part of literati training and was adopted by the Chinese upper classes. Many used it to gain personal readings on official careers and family concerns; some studied it in more detail and wrote commentaries and interpretations. In recent years, the text has also made inroads in the West, where translations have multiplied—some highly specialized such as, for example, a women's version called *The Kuan-yin Book of Changes*. Numerous people all over the world still explore the ancient classic for spiritual advice, use it for divination, and trust in its workings.

The Eight Trigrams

The system of the *Yijing* is based on the two cosmic forces yin and yang, which are symbolized by written lines: an unbroken line indicates yang, while a broken line shows yin. The two lines, like the binary pattern at the base of computing, are combined two by two into four symbols: double yang, yang over yin, double yin, and yin over yang. Next the lines are combined into eight symbols of three lines each, known as trigrams and linked symbolically with cosmic phenomena. The eight trigrams (*bagua*) are as follows:

heaven (*qian*, creative)	☰	earth (*kun*, receptive)	☷
fire (*li*, clinging)	☲	water (*kan*, abysmal)	☵
wind (*sun*, gentle)	☴	lake (*dui*, joyous)	☱
thunder (*zhen*, arousing)	☳	mountain (*gen*, still)	☶

These trigrams are still in wide use today. For example, they signify the Eight Corners of the house or room in fengshui and are commonly found on mirrors and other protective devices. In Daoist cosmology,

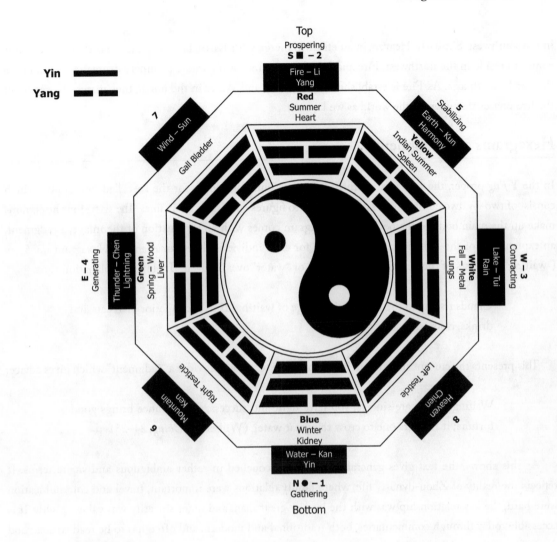

Figure 6.2 The eight trigrams

they have played an important role in signifying different cosmic directions and dimensions. For example, they were arranged in two different patterns, laid out on a geographical grid, that represented the state before creation or "Former Heaven" (*xiantian*) and the forces of the universe after creation or "Later Heaven" (*houtian*), states that also apply to the human body as pre- and postnatal.

Thus, before creation or birth in this body, Heaven (*qian*) is due south, while Earth (*kun*) is due north, Fire (*li*) and Water (*kan*) are to the east and west. In the course of creation, described as the union of Heaven and Earth, *kun* desires to join with *qian* and moves south. After connecting with *qian*, it establishes itself in the southwest. Similarly, Heaven, in an effort to merge with Earth, begins to move north and eventually comes to reside in the northwest. Fire and Water in the meantime rotate by ninety degrees and end up on the north–south axis. As Fire is established in the south and Water in the north, they match the set-up of the five phases that governs the world as we know it.

Hexagrams and Judgments

In the *Yijing* proper, the trigrams are further used as building blocks for the so-called hexagrams, which consist of two-by-two combinations of trigrams into figures consisting of six lines. The sixty-four hexagrams make up the main body of the book. Each hexagram comes with an explanation of the image, a judgment, an explanation of the judgment, and a fortune for each individual line. For example, Hexagram no. 5, *xu* ("waiting") consists of the trigrams *kan* and *qian* or "water" over "heaven." Its image explanation runs:

> Clouds rise up to the heaven, the image of waiting. Thus the superior man eats and
> drinks, is joyous and of good cheer.

This presents the current situation in its essence. The text then provides a "judgment" which gives advice:

> Waiting. If you are sincere, you have light and success. Perseverance brings good
> fortune; it furthers one to cross the great water. (Wilhelm, *I Ching*, 24–25)

As this shows, the text gives general advice, often couched in rather ambiguous and vague terms. It reflects the reality of Zhou-dynasty life, where family relations were important, travel and communication were hard, the key relationship was with the lord or great man, and inner sincerity was valued highly. It is accessible today through commentaries, both traditional and modern, and often has to be read with a good dose of intuition and personal feeling.

Divination Methods

There are two methods of obtaining a hexagram-fortune from the *Yijing*, both leading to an answer for a specific question one has in mind. The first, more traditional method is complicated. It involves the use of fifty milfoil stalks (long stems of a plant). First, one stalk is put aside, then the remaining forty-nine are divided into two piles. Four stalks are then counted off between each finger until there remain either one, two, three, or none. These remaining numbers are interpreted according to yin and yang—1 = strong yang, 2 = strong yin; 3 = weak yang, 0 = weak yin—and the resulting line is written down, adding a little cross on the side if the line is strong. This is repeated five more times to obtain six lines total. The lines are written down from the bottom to the top. The resulting hexagram can then be looked up in the book. Every line that has a cross next to it, moreover, can be changed into its opposite, again beginning from the bottom and working upward. In this way further hexagrams are obtained to indicate later developments.

The second method to obtain a hexagram is a great deal easier and more popular today. It involves three identical coins, in which head is designated yang and tail means yin. Yang, moreover, counts 3, while yin counts 2. Throwing the three coins at any one time will result a total count of 6, 7, 8, or 9. These translate into lines: 9 = strong yang, 6 = strong yin, 7 = weak yang, and 8 = weak yin. Again, the line is written down, the throwing of coins repeated, and the hexagram obtained.

Role in Daoism

Daoists as much as other Chinese literati have used the *Yijing* for millennia to give guidance and to support them in their decision making. In alchemy, moreover, Daoists have used the hexagrams to symbolize the waxing and waning of yin and yang through the seasons, placing them in a series of twelve hexagrams that each show either an increase or decrease in yang lines:

This sequence shows the increase of yang between the winter and summer solstices—the latter located in the center of the line and symbolized by the six-yang hexagram "heaven"—followed by the increase of yin as the year once again moves toward winter. The system allows a subtle patterning of seasonal change which in turn creates the optimal conditions for the concoction of an elixir or the growth of the immortal embryo. Besides applying the *Yijing* in its originally intended mode as a divination manual, Daoists also employ its symbols to express subtle cosmological and internal transformations. In cosmological and alchemical treatises, the trigrams show the directions and dimensions of the universe while the hexagrams signify subtle stages and times of cultivation.

Philosophical Schools

The Zhou dynasty ruled China for almost a millennium, from 1028 to 221 B.C.E. However, it did not maintain power steadily or without challenge for this entire period, but underwent various changes and transformations. One change occurred in 771 B.C.E., when the dynasty was attacked by Central Asian tribes and had to move its capital east to what is today Luoyang. Another major change occurred in the fifth century (479 B.C.E.), when it lost all but the most elementary ritual powers and a number of independent states or dukedoms emerged that in fact shaped the politics of the country. Historians have called this latter phase of Zhou rule the Warring States period, since the various states were not satisfied with the land and populace they controlled, but strove to enlarge their sphere of influence and made war with increasing frequency.

The Iron Age

One reason why war was more of an option than before is that around 500 B.C.E., China was undergoing tremendous economic and political changes. The arrival of iron-age technology created better ploughshares, wagon axles, and weapons. It not only caused an increase in food production which resulted in massive population growth but also led to greater mobility and wealth among the people, inspiring them to strive for more power, land, and goods. Rather than fighting for this by engaging in combat among select troops and feudal leaders, local lords began to set large infantry armies against each other, disrupting agricultural cycles and causing devastation in vast sections of the country. The overall result was a time of great unrest and transition which left many people yearning for the peace and stability of old.

Philosophical Tendencies

It was also a time of great learning and increased literacy as the cumbersome writing of the oracle-bone script had given way to more manageable characters, known as the greater and lesser seal scripts, which are still used in chops today. Literacy and learning, moreover led to the arising of several philosophical schools. They all had in common that they bemoaned the current state of affairs, looked backward to the good times of antiquity, and proposed various social and individual measures that would lead not only to overall harmony but also to greater success in rulership, conquest, and population retention. Besides the theoretical and cosmological speculation typical of Western philosophy, Chinese philosophers thus also engaged in political doctrines and proposed practical methods for the recovery of long-lost harmony.

Six Schools

The earliest document of Daoism, Laozi's *Daode jing*, dates from this time and has to be read in this context. Daoism forms one of six philosophical schools of ancient China, two of which have left no serious imprint on the Chinese religious scene. They are the Mohists (named after Master Mo, *c.* 479–438) who preached universal love and equal goodness towards all; and the Logicians who insisted that all ills could be cured if one only rectified language to be perfectly logical: "A white horse is not a horse" is one of their standard sayings, insisting that everyone use the correct term and thus, by rectifying his or her mind, contribute to the harmony of the world.

The remaining three schools have remained present in Chinese thinking; they have variously impacted Daoism in the course of its history. They are Confucianism, Legalism, and Yin-Yang cosmology. Especially the latter has become the foundation of much of Daoist thought and cosmic patterning (see Chapter 4).

Legalism

Legalism was first formulated by the philosopher Xunzi (c. 300–230) in the third century B.C.E. Reflecting Warring States reality, he assumed that people's nature is originally evil and that everyone is set only on personal profit, no matter what the cost to others. Life accordingly is a battle for limited resources and the bottom line is "every man for himself." To make social harmony possible, there have to be strict rules and enforceable laws joined by punishments that will make everyone sit up and listen.

The Legalists served as advisers to the First Emperor (Shihuang) of China, whose dynastic name Qin gave us the name "China." The unifier of the warring states in 221 B.C.E., he is best known for building sumptuous palaces, the Great Wall, and the Terracotta Army. Standardizing measures, wheel sizes, coins, and the Chinese script, he created a new political entity on Chinese soil, advancing the kingdom of the Zhou to the status of empire. He also ruled with strict laws and executed ruthless punishments to the point where soon after his death in 210 B.C.E. the populace rose in rebellion and brought about a new dynasty, the Han.

Beyond aiding greatly in the unification of China, the Legalists are responsible for codifying Chinese law. They created a long-lasting system of mutual responsibility, dividing all neighborhoods and villages into groups of five families who would be punished or rewarded summarily for the deeds of any one of them. They made widespread use of the death penalty, also for entire clans and household groups; of physical punishments, from flogging through locking into the cangue—a square board locked around the person's neck—to dismemberment; and of forced labor and exile, usually in the far reaches of the Chinese empire where the climate was harsh, the food was rough, and no one knew the finer sides of culture. Prisons were run by Confucian trained magistrates but were only used to keep criminals out of circulation while they awaited trial. After trial and sentencing, also run by the magistrate, the culprit would be executed, sent away, or flogged. The system was harsh and relentless, with minimal chances of escape.

Daoists have always been radically opposed to the Legalist position and relegated their drastic punishments to the hells and underworld prisons. Still, Daoist organizations and monasteries had to work in an environment that was dominated by Chinese law, and time and again they adopted strict rules and measures even within their groups.

Confucianism

Confucianism has provided the social conscience not only of China but also of Daoism. Its five virtues (benevolence, righteousness, wisdom, propriety, and honesty) are the leading light of all Chinese ethics and form an important goal of Daoist cultivation. Its emphasis on family values and loyalty to the ruler, its political vision of harmony and Great Peace have continued to inspire Daoists—who were not, as commonly thought, apolitical and detached, but who developed a complex political philosophy and took an active interest in running the government at various times in history. Vice versa, Daoist mystical thought and cultivation practices have exerted a strong influence on Confucianism, especially in the Song and late imperial periods.

Basic Tenets

At the root of the teaching is Confucius (552–479 B.C.E.) with his sayings as documented in the *Lunyu* (Analects). Following him, and matching the dominant trend of Warring States philosophy, Confucians look back to the Golden Age of the past. Unlike Legalists who see people as inherently evil and establish harsh laws, and unlike Daoists who find people naturally good and suggest perfect alignment with natural spontaneity, Confucians understand that people can be either good or evil and should be taught to do the right thing. The right thing, then, is the correct understanding of social hierarchies and the practice of morality and social awareness.

Without denying the value of all-encompassing nature, of cosmological alignment with Heaven, of laws, and of ancestral advice, Confucianism focuses on ritual formality (*li*) as its

Figure 6.3 Confucius (Bibliothèque Nationale, Paris, France/The Bridgeman Art Library.)

key method of bringing the world back to the Golden Age. Representing the image of a ritual vessel, the word *li* means "to arrange in order" and designates ways of how people in society should best interact in a well-ordered fashion. In practice it means three things: interpersonal politeness, governmental organization, and religious devotion.

Etiquette and Politeness

First, among personal relationships *li* means etiquette, politeness, and good social behavior. It manifests in respecting the social boundaries, notably the five relationships (ruler-minister, father-son, husband-wife, older-younger brother, friend-friend), honoring one's elders and caring for one's juniors. The key virtues here are benevolence (*ren*), a general sense of consideration and kindness, and filial piety (*xiao*), the devotion of the younger toward their seniors.

Reciprocity is essential. A senior person has to be generous, giving, and gentle toward the younger generation, while a junior person needs to behave with respect, circumspection, and obedience. If both sides fulfill their roles, society and by extension the world will function with utmost harmony; if one side fails, the other is released from its obligation and revolution can occur. Flexibility is equally important. Everyone living in a Confucian society (nowadays especially Singapore, Taiwan, Korea, and Japan) has to know how to work in all different roles and positions, since no one can always be senior or junior at all times. Comparable to Immanuel Kant's concept of "the unenforceable"—a level of social control between legal sanctions and personal restraint—the system works by evoking shame and embarrassment, social ostracism and loss of face. There are no formal punishments for failure to work within the rules, yet the moral structure is pervasive and has worked effectively for millennia.

> The Master said: Guide them by edicts, keep them in line with punishments, and the common people will stay out of trouble but will have no sense of shame. Guide them by virtue, keep them in line with *li*, and they will, besides having a sense of shame, reform themselves. (*Lunyu* 2.3)

Institutional Correctness

On a second level, *li* is applied to public organizations and government institutions. Each agency has to know exactly what to do and when to do it and has to be able to sit back and do nothing at certain times as much as it needs to be forceful and vigorous on occasion. Timing—the realm of the cosmologists—is very important. In ancient China, where politics were intricately linked with the will of Heaven and the ancestors, numerous government offices dealt with divination, astronomy, calendar science, and the like. Officials in these agencies had to have a clear definition of their role and had to be able to advance and retire in the right measure and at the right moment.

Their key virtues are righteousness or social responsibility (*yi*) and loyalty to the ruler (*zhong*). Government is centralized and hierarchical, but its open flow of administration—matching the naturalistic vision of Dao—depends on the proper functioning of individual officials. Guidelines and rules abound, formulated early in the *Liji* (Book of Rites), but again there are no serious laws involved, the most dire punishment being release from office.

Ritual Propriety

Third and last, *li* also means religious ritual, the practices used to communicate with the ancestors, the various gods of earth and nature, and with Heaven. In the ideal Confucian system, every Chinese family takes care of their ancestors, every household worships a stove god, every village a village god, and every town a city god—all to maintain the proper order within the larger cosmic realm seen as the direct continuation of life on earth. In addition, the ruler and his officials present regular seasonal sacrifices to Heaven and Earth, reporting activities and ensuring the proper blessings in the form of right weather and good fortune. The ritual aspect of Confucianism is not as well known but it has pervaded traditional Chinese society and is still present in popular stove and village gods as well as the great Altar to Heaven, one of the main Beijing tourist attractions in the south of the city.

Learning

To become adapt in the complexity of society and religious worship, people should study, especially history and literature as contained in the Six Classics (the *Books of Changes, Rites, Songs, Music,* and *History*, as well as the *Spring and Autumn Annals*). They should also practice the six arts of the gentleman: poetry, calligraphy, numbers, music (lute), archery, and charioteering. Some are inherently more apt to learn and become ideal Confucian gentlemen (*junzi*) than others, but there is hope for everyone. Learning, moreover, is not a burden but a pleasure, an exciting adventure of becoming increasingly aware of oneself and the social intricacies in one's surroundings, an ongoing effort at creating the ideal human being in the ideal human society.

Connection to Daoism

Daoists do not quite share this enthusiasm for learning—they tend to be more in favor of unlearning and forgetting with the goal of reaching a more natural state of mind—but they appreciate the social awareness and cosmic harmony proposed by Confucians. Plus, not only did the *Daode jing* arise in a dialogue with

Confucian thought, but throughout history Daoists have lived and breathed Confucian society all around them. The need for proper social graces, the unfolding of essential virtues, and the vision of a well-integrated and harmonious society have pervaded Daoism from the very beginning, making Confucianism another important factor in the background of the tradition.

Key Points You Need to Know

- Daoism is deeply embedded in Chinese culture and has incorporated several important elements that are present in Chinese history even before the beginnings of Daoism.
- From Chinese religion as known already from Shang dynasty documents and artifacts, Daoism has inherited its belief in a bureaucratically organized otherworld, its veneration of ancestors, its emphasis on the written language in ritual, and possibly its shamanic/ecstatic tendencies.
- The *Yijing* or *Book of Changes* is important as a divination manual but also plays a key role in Daoist cosmological speculation and alchemy.
- Daoists do not share the urge to punish with Legalists but have had to live in a society dominated by Legalist-inspired laws and have created similar rules and organizations within their tradition.
- Confucianism focuses on ritual formality (*li*) as its key method, sees society as hierarchically structured, emphasizes life-long learning, and proposes a set of virtues that have played an important role in Daoist communities and practice.

Discussion Questions

1. What is divination and what are some of its main methods in China and the West?
2. How does the *Yijing* work?
3. What are some key points of difference between Legalists and Confucians?

Note

1. The twelve-year cycle, based on the time it takes for the planet Jupiter to circle the sun, is familiar in the West through zodiac charts.

Further Reading

Allan, Sarah. 1991. *The Shape of the Turtle: Myth, Art, and Cosmos in Early China.*

Albany, NY: State University of New York Press.

Chang, Kwang-chih. 1980. *Shang Civilization.* New Haven, CT: Yale University Press.

Eno, Robert. 1990. *The Confucian Creation of Heaven: Philosophy and the Defense of Ritual Mastery.* Albany, NY: State University of New York Press.

Graham, A. C. 1989. *Disputers of the Tao: Philosophical Argument in Ancient China.* La Salle, IL: Open Court Publishing Company.

Keightley, David N. 1978. *Sources of Shang History: The Oracle Bone Inscriptions of Bronze Age China.* Berkeley and Los Angeles, CA: University of California Press.

Wilhelm, Richard. 1950. *The I Ching or Book of Changes*, Bollingen Series XIX. Princeton, NJ: Princeton University Press.

Figure Credits

7 Chinese Philosophy III: Confucianism

Ray Billington

A s we saw earlier, in philosophical and religious terms there have been three major influences in China. One is Taoism, in both its *tao-chia* and *tao-chiao* expressions; the second is Buddhism, which, while not native to China, was to establish so firm a hold there in its Mahayana mode that the Chinese could be forgiven for looking on it as native to themselves; the third, and the most typically Chinese of all, is Confucianism. This philosophy—and we shall see that, of all the schools discussed in this book, it has least claim to be termed a religion—has made such an indelible mark on Chinese personal and socio-political life that Confucianism and China are almost as ineradicably linked as Hinduism and India.

The great name in this school is of course Confucius himself, but there have been a host of Confucian scholars and philosophers over the centuries. We shall look at two of these who, by the pure originality of their thinking, have made distinctive contributions relevant to the theme of this book: Mencius, living two centuries later than Confucius, and his direct ideological descendant (he could be described as the Huxley to Confucius's Darwin); and, in the twelfth century CE, Chu Hsi, the outstanding mentor of Neo-Confucianism, which was effectively a synthesis of Taoism, Buddhism and Confucianism. Other teachers will be mentioned in passing, in relation to particular debates in which the major protagonists were engaged.

Confucius

This name, with which even children in the West are familiar, is the Latinised form of **K'ung Tzu** (sometimes transcribed as K'ung Fu-tzu), or Master K'ung. He lived from 551 to 479 BCE, during the so-called Spring and Autumn Period (722–481) of the Chou Dynasty (1111–249). Tradition had it that during its founding era this dynasty had been ruled by men who were highly principled, in particular the kings Wen and Wu. By K'ung's time, however, Chou had fallen prey to internal conflicts and attacks from beyond, and his own state of Lu (now Shantung) was in fact ruled by usurpers. This may help to explain why it was that he experienced frustration in his chosen calling as a civil servant, and why at the age of fifty he resigned to become a peripatetic teacher, a role that many other learned Chinese, including Mencius, also assumed. He gathered a large number of students around him, amounting eventually to some three thousand.

According to tradition, Master K'ung spent his final years writing a number of books, including the *Shi Ching* (Book of Songs), the *Shu Ching* (Book of Writings), and the *Ch'un Ch'iu* (Spring and Autumn Annals). All we can say for sure is that these books are among the Confucian classics and reflect K'ung's teaching. His philosophy is expressed most directly, however, in the work that, along with the *Tao Te Ching*, is at the peak of Chinese philosophical writing, the ***Analects***. It is generally held that K'ung did not write this work, but that it was compiled by his disciples after his death. Here is the essence of Confucianism, and it is significant that Chan Wing-Tsit, in his comprehensive compilation *A Source Book in Chinese Philosophy*, uses only this work to illustrate K'ung's teaching. It was, along with Mencius and two other Confucian classics, the *Ta Hsueh* and the *Chung Yung*, one of the so-called 'Four Books' (*ssu-chu*), which were used as the basis of Chinese civil service examinations from 1313 CE until as recently as 1905.

Almost any extract from the *Analects* will illustrate why it is that the name of Confucius has become synonymous with sound common sense (reflected in the phrase, 'Confucius, he say . . .'). In Book II,15–17, we read:

> The Master said, He who learns but does not think is lost. He who thinks but does not learn is in great danger . . . Shall I teach you what knowledge is? When you know a thing, to recognise that you know it; and when you do not know a thing, to recognise that you do not know it. That is knowledge.

(Perhaps even more basic is his laconic statement in IX,17 that he had 'never seen anyone whose desire to build up his moral power was as strong as sexual desire'.)

Master K'ung's prime consideration, and the central theme of the Analects, was how people might live harmoniously together. He was therefore concerned with ethics rather than metaphysics, although Mencius and other successors were to develop this strand in their teaching. From K'ung's point of view, it was a difficult enough task to cope with other people here and now without introducing speculation (for he viewed it as no more than that) about a future life, or a divine being who might influence events in this world from some invisible world beyond. He frequently referred to 'the Way of Heaven' (*t'ien*) and even referred to the emperor as 'Son of Heaven' (*t'ien-tzu*), but the word is normally used with an ethical connotation, signifying the highest pinnacle of human behaviour. Any ruler, as we shall see, was held by K'ung to be uniquely placed both to practise the virtues himself and to set an example for others. K'ung was questioned about *t'ien* apropos of 'God in heaven' but was at best agnostic and generally sceptical on the matter. It seemed to him absurd to believe that the 'will of heaven' could be modified as a direct consequence of prayers sent 'up' by people on Earth: so the sensible procedure was to forget about praying and tackle the problems of living as they stared one in the face. In this, to be sure, all people have the examples of their ancestors to inspire them; but K'ung refused to speculate about any influence that the spirits of the dead might have on the human situation. *Analects* XI,11 states:

> Tzu-lu asked how one should serve ghosts and spirits.
> The Master said, How can there be any proper service of spirits until living men
> have been properly served?
> Tzu-lu then ventured upon a question about the dead (whether they are conscious).
> The Master said, Until a man knows about the living, how can he know about the
> dead?

This perspective is reminiscent of the New Testament words: 'He who does not love his brother whom he has seen, cannot love God whom he has not seen' (I John 4:21); but K'ung's philosophy is totally humanistic in its suggestion that relationships with others should be based on secular, rather than spiritual, considerations. To make the love of God one's ultimate aim in human encounters, rather than to have regard for others for their own sakes, would have seemed to him an unrealistic diversion from the clearly defined, self-disciplined way that he was offering to his followers.

The way of Confucius is based on two definable and unambiguous human qualities, which have given Confucianism its distinctive stamp. They may be described as the *yin* and the *yang* of relationships, in the sense that each, while apparently poles apart (like justice and mercy), needs to be tempered by the other. They are *jen*, or loving kindness, and *li*, or propriety.

The Chinese pictogram for *jen* gives a clear indication of its meaning. It shows the sign for a human being, together with the sign for 'two'. Thus *jen* embraces all the qualities that enable one human being to express ideal behaviour towards another. It is the equivalent of the Greek word *agape*, for which, as for *jen*, the word 'love' is too general and too vague a translation. It is based on sympathy for others, an empathy with them, and a desire for them to achieve their best good. It is mirrored in Kant's description of goodwill, which to him was the ideal basis of all human intercourse. It meant that no other person was to be treated as a means to an end (that is, one's own selfish end) but rather should be treated as at all times an end in him or herself. 'Respect for persons' would be a not inapposite translation of this quality, fostered by a sense of mutuality (*shu*) and loyalty (*chung*) in any relationship. Master K'ung himself, when asked if there was a single saying that one could act on all day and every day, gave the simple and straightforward guideline already quoted on page 5: 'Never do to others what you would not like them to do to you' (XV,23). This expression of the Golden Rule in negative form is probably easier to follow than its converse, especially if it is the case that human beings are more united in what they dislike than in what they like. On the other hand, he also said (VI,28): 'To apply one's own wishes and desires as a yardstick by which to judge one's behaviour toward others is the true way of jen.'

The roots of *jen*, he affirmed, were piety (*hsiao*) and obedience (*ti*). These were the qualities that characterised the ideal man, or **chun-tzu**, literally 'duke's son', one whose nobility of title is reflected in his behaviour. The piety called for is the veneration of parents by children, and the obedience that of the younger brother to the older, whether within a family or in the community generally; thus respect for the old became a central feature of the Chinese cultural tradition. This does not always mean yielding to them whatever the issue, but treating them in the way to which, by their years, they have become entitled. Confucius (IV,18) was typically practical:

> In serving his father and mother a man may gently remonstrate with them. But if he sees that he has failed to change their opinion, he should resume an attitude of deference and not thwart them. He may feel discouraged, but not resentful.

Mencius, Confucius's natural heir, later (*Mencius* IV,19) linked respect for parents with self-respect:

> Which is the greatest service? The service of parents is the greatest. Which is the greatest of charges? The charge of oneself is the greatest. I have heard of keeping oneself, and thus being able to serve one's parents. But I have not heard of failing to keep oneself, and yet being able to serve one's parents.

The expression of *jen* in relationships is an ideal that Confucius shared with, or in which he was to be joined by, representatives and leaders of most of the major world religions. The second of the two pivots of Confucian ethics is, however, more idiosyncratically K'ung Tzu's emphasis. *Li* is normally translated as 'propriety'; it was originally (that is, in pre-Confucian times) related to the correct conduct of rites and ceremonies, that everything should be done, in St Paul's words, 'decently and in order'. It was extended to embrace the customs and traditions of the community, with the implication that these should be faith-fully preserved. Master K'ung went a step further and applied it to inter-human relationships, giving a structure to the ideal of *jen*. Just as mercy without justice is likely to encourage crime, so *jen* without *li*, he suggested, could easily degenerate into a simplistic expression of mawkish sentimentality. K'ung Tzu could no more have joined the Beatles in singing 'All you need is love' (the idea is in fact hilarious) than he could have deliberately deceived a neighbour over a commercial transaction. The combination of *li* and *jen* makes it possible to win an argument without losing a friend; to accept one's superiority over another without making him or her feel belittled (and inferiority without feeling humiliated); or—quint-essentially Chinese—allowing a defeated opponent to 'save face'. The emphasis of *li* is that some arguments must be won, some people are superior to others, and some opponents have to be defeated.

Master K'ung indicates the significance of *li* with great clarity in the Analects (VIII,2, Wilhelm translation):

> Deference ['courtesy', in Waley's translation] that lacks propriety (form, li) becomes servility ['tiresome'], caution without propriety becomes timidity, courage without propriety becomes rebelliousness, honesty without propriety beomes rudeness [or 'inflexibility becomes harshness' in Waley].

The distinction here is subtle, and an insensitive person may well be incapable of appreciating it. In order to learn what *li* means in practice, any person will need to acquire **chih**, or wisdom, the ability to discriminate between the nicely differing modes of behaviour that are in tune with the forces of *yin* and *yang*. To express propriety in one's dealing with others, therefore, means that nothing is done in excess, whether in words or in actions. In the harmony of *yin* and *yang*, one is never too strident, never too muted; happy doing ordinary things well rather than constantly attempting the extraordinary or the impossible; living well, but living well within oneself. 'Nothing in excess' could be a Confucian catchword, reminiscent of the ideal of the mean as taught by Aristotle, with whom Master K'ung is sometimes compared.

A key element in the practice of *li* is the fulfilling of one's duty, for which the Chinese word is *i*. This quality can be translated as righteousness, honesty, uprightness; people who observe *i* observe the require-ments demanded of them by their roles and stations in life, and the care shown in making this observance must inevitably give direction to any expression of *jen* toward others. This may sound a bland statement, but in fact it is highly pertinent. Master K'ung considered that loving kindness can manifest itself only in ever-widening circles, with the inevitable consequence that the *jen* that is expressed abates in its intensity as the circle widens: this, for K'ung, was a natural state of affairs, an unalterable condition of humanity. An individual's first duty is filial piety, **xiao**, followed by duty to his clan; and although, as we shall see, K'ung laid great significance on the subject's duty to the state, he viewed this as secondary to the primary duties. He would probably have agreed with E.M. Forster, who remarked that, given a choice between betraying a friend or betraying his country, 'I hope I should have the courage to betray my country.'

This concept of circles of relationships is in direct conflict with a philosophy that was to be expressed a century later by the founder of the Mohist School, Mo Tzu, or Mo Ti (Master Mo, *c.* 468–376 BCE). He taught that loving kindness (*jen*) should be shown to others without distinction or favouritism: the needs of distant strangers or local enemies should rank as highly in any person's consciousness as those of his family or clan. Mo was in fact expressing an early form of utilitarianism as was to be taught in the nineteenth century by John Stuart Mill, whose argument was that any moral decision should have as its end the increase in human happiness. With that K'ung would have agreed; where they would have parted company was in Mill's assertion that, when decisions are required about how best to achieve this end in any given circumstance, 'everyone [is] to count as one, nobody to count as more than one'.

To Confucius, and even more to his successor, Mencius, this aim would have seemed both unnatural and against the ground rules of propriety. Each of them had more than his share of common sense, based on calm observation of people. From this they concluded that most people find it difficult enough expressing goodwill to those around them without multiplying the problem by introducing the whole of the human race into the equation. On the other hand, they were also aware that some people find it is easier to express love for people they are never likely to meet than for those with whom they share the frustrations of daily living.

K'ung therefore had no truck either with the ideal of loving one's enemies, which was to receive superb expression in the New Testament, or with the utilitarian ideal of having neither favourites nor 'also-rans' in one's relationships. If love were to be shown as much to one's enemies as to one's friends, what advantage lay in being a friend? And what wife could cheerfully accept that, while her husband loved her no less than all the other women in the world, he loved her no more than them? What was needed, according to Confucius, was the quality of conscientiousness to others (**zhong**); this means that, while one may make a diligent effort to practise *jen*, one is not called upon to repay evil with good.

Master K'ung taught that there are five relationships (**wu-lun**), which together form the basis of human interaction (*wu-ch'ang,* or 'five constants'). The constants are *jen, li, i, chih* (wisdom or insight) and *hsin* (trust); by observing *wu-lun* meticulously (that is, by living according to the implications of the relationships) people may achieve order in their personal lives and, by extension, the community as a whole may c–xist harmoniously. In each of the *wu-lun,* the first named should have the dominant, *yang* role, and the second the submissive *yin.* The five are:

- father and son;
- husband and wife;
- older brother and younger brother;
- (older) friend and (younger) friend;
- ruler and subject.

Thus a man can expect to show both *yin* and *yang* qualities in his relationships. A father, for example, will be *yang* in relation to his wife or his children, and *yin* in relation to the ruler (or older friend). A son will be *yin* in relation to his father and *yang* in relation to any younger brother or friend. K'ung does not discuss the problems that may arise in a family if number two son (to use a Chinese phrase) has more innately dominant qualities than his older brother; nor—and this is a considerably larger sticking-point—does he allow women anything but a *yin* position *vis-à-vis* any male. The *Analects* hint that he was married, with a son and a daughter, but there are no domestic details. We may conclude that, like two other pioneer visionaries of the ideal society, Plato and St Paul, there is a lacuna at this point in his thinking, so that effectively he has nothing to teach us on the subject. K'ung himself seems to have been aware of this omission, suggested by his comment in the *Analects* (XVII,25):

> Women and people of low birth are very hard to deal with. If you are friendly with them, they get out of hand, and if you keep your distance, they resent it.

Some interpreters soften the saying by making it apply to 'maids and valets'.

Master K'ung's main public concern was with the selection of rulers, and the style in which they should govern. His view was that a 'trickle-down effect' operated between ruler and subjects, whereby if he showed virtue in his dealings, they would follow his example. To one ruler he said (XII,19):

> If you desire what is good, the people will be good. The character of a ruler is like wind and that of the people is like grass. In whatever direction the wind blows, the grass always bends.

He accepted in general that rulers reached their position 'with the mandate of heaven', but he argued that this situation was not irreversible. If ever, by despotism or greed, they betrayed the trust thus conferred upon them, it was right that they should be overthrown and replaced. Where this occurred, the qualities to look for were integrity and strength of character, fostered by a love of education. These qualities would enable them to overcome the pettiness that leads to the mistreatment of subjects, causing them in their turn to become rebellious. Mencius was later to give unambiguous expression to this admonition:

> If a ruler regards his ministers as his hands and feet, then his ministers will regard him as their heart and mind. If a ruler regards his ministers as dogs and horses, his ministers will regard him as any other man. If a ruler regards his ministers as dirt and grass, his ministers will regard him as a bandit and an enemy.
>
> (IV,B,3)

A particular concern of Kung Tzu's was what he termed 'the rectification of names', meaning that there should be a correspondence between a person's title and his behaviour. 'Let the ruler *be* a ruler,' he said

(XII,11), 'the minister *be* a minister, the father *be* a father, and the son *be* a son.' A ruler who is too lazy to tackle the problems in his region, a minister who is too greedy to serve others, a father who ignores his paternal obligations and a son who is indifferent to his filial responsibilities: all are, in their different ways, catalysts of disorder and dissension. Get the names right, suggested K'ung, and there arises the possibility of justice and order in the land; ignore the names, and the door is open to contention, disharmony and strife. Every name contains qualities that correspond to the essence of whatever or wh–ver is referred to by that name. If ruler, minister, father or son follows the *Tao* of his role by living up to the ideal that the name indicates, there will be harmony between the name and the expression of it in practice. 'A noble person [*chun-tzu*] will not tolerate disorder in his words. That is what matters', he said (*Analects* XIII,3).

The School of Names was later to become an autonomous school, but without Master K'ung's wise, non-obsessional and, above all, comprehensively human perspective it came to represent a somewhat narrow, even pedantic, form of what Western philosophy might describe as linguistic analysis.

We may summarise Confucius's views on government in the following statements:

1. The purpose of government is to provide for the welfare and happiness of all its people.
2. The right to govern is not sustained by heavenly decree, but by the ability to make its people happy and secure, with equal justice before the law.
3. In the selection of leaders, no role should be played by wealth or breeding, but by integrity and virtue, arising from a love of education.
4. Excessive taxation, barbarous punishments and aggression towards people within the state and beyond should be outlawed.
5. The best government is that which governs least, dedicating itself to the development of the character and culture of the people.

This last statement is a reflection of Taoist thought, especially about *wu-wei*. I quoted on page 93 Confucius's commendation of the legendary ruler, Shun, who seems to have been content to let things be and not to intervene in his subjects' affairs (XV,4):

> To have taken no [unnatural] action [*wu-wei*] and yet have the empire well gov-erned, Shun was the man.

Confucius constantly emphasised education as the key to happy and successful living, 'to go on learning so that you do not notice yourself growing old', as he stated in the *Analects*, and this emphasis puts him among the foremost of the world's humanists. He was one of the first people in history, and certainly the first in China, to take up teaching as a full-time occupation, and to suggest that the educational process was life-long. He thus stands among the protagonists of *educere,* rather than *educare,* as the essence of education: to go on growing, humbly aware that, however learned one is, there is infinitely more to know, rather than viewing education simply as the gateway to a qualification that offers economic opportunities to its owner. L.C. Wu closes his study of Confucius (*op. cit.,* p. 31) with these words:

> Confucius's ethic is a rational approach to human happiness and good society
> without any supernatural grounding. Confucius taught the Chinese that happiness
> and virtue are correlatives which are complementary to each other ... This spirit of
> happiness can be readily found among the Chinese regardless of their educational
> level, social or financial status. This is Confucius's contribution. It is the noblest of
> human achievements.

This may explain why it is that, after some years of neglect, Master K'ung has returned as a compulsory subject of study in Chinese schools. Even Mao Tse-tung acknowledged that he ranked worthy to be studied alongside Marx, Engels and Lenin. How far he would have been happy in their company is, however, a matter of some speculation. Independently of their political views, one suspects that, like any other claimants to possession of the 'truth', their self-assuredness, a corruption of self-assurance, would have made it difficult for him to relate to them at any more than a surface level. To be a *chun-tzu* (gentleman), he knew, a key virtue was the humility to accept that one may be wrong on any issue, however firmly that belief be held.

Mencius (Meng-Tzu)

Second only to K'ung Tzu in the Confucian hierarchy is Mencius (*c.* 372–289 BCE). In many respects both his life and his teachings were remarkably similar to those of his mentor. He was born in the same province, followed in his earlier years the same profession, experienced similar frustrations because of the political and moral chaos brought about primarily through selfish and ineffectual government, eventually became a roaming teacher and counsellor, offering advice to rulers, and disputing with those whom he believed to be the authors of 'perverse doctrines'; and, like Confucius, he felt at the end of his life a sense of disappointment and failure.

The philosophy of Mencius is often described as 'idealistic Confucianism', an expression based partly on his optimistic view of human nature, partly on his greater emphasis on the spiritual dimension in following the Confucian virtues. If Confucius was China's Aristotle, Mencius was more akin to its Plato, of whom he was a contemporary, and with whom he is often compared. He was also a contemporary of Chuang Tzu, but there is no record of their ever having met each other—an encounter that would surely have been beneficial not only to both of them but also to all whose lives have been enriched by their teaching.

Like the Analects, the book *Mencius* was probably edited by disciples, although under closer supervision by their mentor than was the earlier book. It is structured more carefully than the Analects, and from it we can infer that Mencius was a sharp debater, uncompromising in his views, and not so ready as Confucius to admit that he might be wrong on any matter. He seems to have spent considerable time in arguing his case with rival philosophers, who were more numerous in his time than two centuries earlier.

Mencius accepted Confucius's emphasis on the twin virtues of *jen* and *li*: how they embrace *chung* and *shu*, express themselves in *xiao* (*hsiao*) and *chun-tzu*, and are directed by a sense of righteousness, or *i*. So far as guidelines for successful living are concerned, therefore, Mencius offered no radical departures from the Confucianist canon. Where he differed was on a matter that has been the subject of continual debate over the millennia, to which he offered an unambiguous standpoint: human nature, and his view, for which he remains one of the key historical protagonists, that it is inherently good.

Confucius had held the belief that human nature cannot be characterised as inherently either 'good' or 'bad' (the reason for putting those words in quotations will emerge later). In a sense, he took an existentialist view, arguing that each person's nature (what Sartre called 'essence') developed as a direct consequence of the path they followed through life: the choices they made, the priorities they established, the extent to which they observed the five relationships, and so on. Above all, he held that the most certain route to goodness lay along the path of education. The broadening of the mind that this would ensure would enable a person more comprehensively to show loving kindness, observe the proprieties and express righteousness in his or her dealings. In other words, goodness was a product of the *educere* process (see page 125), and, while many were prevented from following this way because of factors beyond their control, nobody was inherently incapable of achieving it. Confucius could, therefore, well have been the first to declare, 'Existence precedes essence.'

Mencius disagreed with this neutral position. His view was that people were born with their natures intact, and that the natural human instinct is towards goodness. 'Which of you,' he asked his audience during one debate on the subject, 'seeing a child playing on the edge of a well and stumbling, would not instinctively spring to its aid, lest it fall to its death?' To Mencius, this—what we should today call reflex—reaction proved that people are predisposed to be altruistic. He observed the generations of people throughout history who had willingly accepted personal inconvenience, sacrifice, suffering and even death for the sake of others: was this to be described as unnatural behaviour? This seemed to him to be necessarily the case if the opposite position were taken.

There is a close similarity here between Mencius's view and that of Plato and, two millennia later, Jean-Jacques Rousseau, although without the Platonic concept of reincarnation after a period in heaven, the world of forms, or ideals, which was an integral feature of their philosophy. Mencius did not discuss *why* people were altruistic from birth; he simply affirmed that this was the case, based on empirical evidence.

His critics wanted to know why, in that case, many people in a host of situations—as observation would continually confirm—behaved selfishly, showing indifference towards others' needs, and even going to the extent of causing them deliberate harm. Mencius's reply was that evil was the result of unnatural behaviour. Because of circumstances, people's natural goodness could be distorted or suppressed; what was needed, therefore, was a community that allowed free rein to their natural constituents: loving kindness, righteousness, respect for others, piety. In a famous passage, he compared human nature to the way water behaves:

> Man's nature is naturally good just as water naturally flows downward. There is no man without this good nature; neither is there water that does not flow downward. Now, you can splash water and cause it to splash upward over your forehead; and by damming it and leading it, you can force it uphill. Is this the nature of water? It is the forced circumstance that makes it so. Man can be made to do evil, for his nature can be treated in the same way.
>
> (VI,1,6)

Mencius lived, of course, 2,000 years before Newton's discovery of gravity, otherwise he would at the very least have needed to find a different analogy. More important philosophically is the question, which relates to Plato's and Rousseau's theories also, of how, if all people are born with perfect natures, imperfections arise at all. Logically it seems the case that, if they are naturally altruistic individually, they will be so collectively; the only escape-route from this logic would be to assert that the natural life is one of isolation, so that all social intercourse is unnatural: which would leave a question mark over the need for altruism in any case.

The fact is that Mencius's whole position is tautological, since by the word 'good' he means whatever is fully in tune with human nature, and by human nature he means whatever may be described as 'good'. This is a circular argument: if, on the one hand, whatever is inborn is defined as human nature, and, on the other, human nature is characterised as 'good', then Mercius's conclusion that 'bad' behaviour must be characterised as 'unnatural', may follow, but only by a monumental process of question-begging. It is as if a person were to argue that Christians live good lives and, on being told of a practising Christian who treats others shabbily, replies, 'In that case I would not describe him as a Christian at all.' (We leave unexplored the vexed questions of how far 'goodness' and 'badness' are absolute terms, and whether the words have any definable meaning at all. Mencius lived not only before Newton, but before the age of postmodernist relativism cf. p.100.)

Independently of these considerations, Mencius made the following statements, which encapsulate the logical consequences of accepting his basic proposition:

1. The ability possessed by men without their having to acquire it is innate ability, and the knowledge possessed by them without deliberation is innate knowledge . . . These feelings are universal in the world.

    (VII,A,15)

2. He who exerts his mind to the uttermost knows his nature. He who knows his nature knows Heaven. To preserve one's mind and to nourish one's nature is the way to serve Heaven.

(VII,A,1)

3. When there is repeated disturbance, the restorative influence of the night will not be sufficient to preserve [the proper goodness of the mind] . . . People see that he acts like an animal, and think that he never had the original endowment [for goodness].

(VI,A,8)

4. Pity the man who abandons the path and does not follow it, and has lost his heart and does not know how to recover it.

(VI,A,11)

5. Confucius said, 'Hold it fast and you preserve it. Let it go and you lose it.' He was talking about the human mind . . . *The way of learning is none other than finding the lost mind.*

(VI,A,11,8)

Those italicised words perfectly express the humanist approach to education, and they are reflected in Pope's famous couplet in his *Essay on Man*:

> Men must be taught as if you taught them not,
> And things unknown proposed as things forgot.

One practical expression of Mencius's idealism was his proposal for the 'well-field system' in agriculture. Each square (*li*) of land (about one-third of a mile squared) is divided into nine equal squares in the shape of a noughts-and-crosses chart. Eight farmers each own one of the outside squares, leaving the central square to be farmed by all of them on a rota basis. Each keeps the proceeds from his own patch, but the proceeds from the central square provide the taxes for all eight of them. (This square can of course be expanded or contracted according to the rate of taxation.) Mencius proposed this as a middle way between totally individualised and completely communalised farming; he believed that it would leave the way open for people both to cooperate with one another and to have the personal satisfaction of reaping the fruits of their own labour.

It is interesting to speculate whether this system would work in practice. Would each farmer work as hard on the central square as he did on his own patch? It would need only one backslider to upset both the system as a whole, and the feelings of the other seven at the same time. One wonders how many of them would find themselves feeling unwell on the eighth day when it was their turn in the middle. Who would be held to blame if the tax authorities felt underpaid? The resolution of this conundrum depends on whether one is an idealist or a cynic: it would certainly be a test of Mencius's theory.

One Confucianist who would have scorned the well-field system on the grounds that it would lead to controversy brought about by self-interest was **Hsun Tzu** (*c.* 298–238 BCE), generally revered as the 'third sage' in the Confucian hierarchy. While in essential aspects he agreed with Confucian teaching, he disagreed with Mencius about human nature. In fact, if Mencius was the Rousseau of Confucianism, Hsun Tzu was its Hobbes. Two of his disciples became leading figures in the Legalistic School, and he has (wrongly, according to many modern sinologists), been characterised as the midway figure between it and Confucianism. The *Hsun-Tzu* consists of thirty-two chapters, which are effectively a series of essays on a range of subjects. They indicate that, if on some issues he was more legalistic than Confucius, in others, such as his view of *T'ien* (Heaven), he was more Taoist. His writings are not included among the Chinese classics, but his critical and analytical approach to philosophy makes him a particularly attractive subject of study in modern China.

Chapter 23 of the *Hsun-Tzu*, probably the best-known essay in the book, is entitled, 'The Nature of Man is Evil'. Its first two paragraphs give the gist of his beliefs on the subject, and because of their simplicity of expression they need no further elucidation:

> The nature of man is evil; whatever is good in him is the result of acquired training. Men are born with the love of gain; if this natural tendency is followed they are contentious and greedy, utterly lacking in courtesy and consideration for others. They are filled from birth with envy and hatred of others; if these passions are given rein they are violent and villainous, wholly devoid of integrity and good faith. At birth man is endowed with the desires of the ear and the eye, the love of sound and colour; if he acts as they dictate he is licentious and disorderly, and has no desire for *li* or justice or moderation.
>
> Clearly, then, to accord with man's original nature and act as instinct dictates must lead to contention, rapacity, and disorder, and cause humanity to revert to a state of violence. For this reason it is essential that men be transformed by teachers and laws, and guided by *li* and justice; only then will they be courteous and cooperative, only then is good order possible. In the light of these facts it is clear that man's original nature is evil, and that he becomes good only through acquired training.

Hsun Tzu's theory is in some respects a reflection of Aristotle's contention, expressed a century earlier, that the law exists to spur people on in the pursuit of 'the good'.

One other emphasis in Mencius's teaching distinguishes him from Confucius and links him somewhat more closely with the Taoist and *Yin–Yang* schools. This is his philosophical mysticism, in accordance with which he speaks not only of cultivating order in the community, but also of achieving order within oneself by cultivating **ch'i**: vital breath, or energy. We have seen earlier (page 91) how important is the concept of *ch'i* in Taoism, both as a focal point of meditation and as a means of achieving physical harmony, both within oneself and in relation to the universe as a whole. *T'ai-ch'i* is the term used for the supreme ultimate, and

T'ai-Ch'i Ch'uan, as we saw on page 106, is a form of physical exercise designed to create a sense of personal harmony with it.

Mencius wrote (II,A,2 and VII,A,1,1):

> When I cultivate this great *ch'i* within me, all things are then complete within me . . . [therefore] he who completely knows his nature, knows Heaven.

By 'Heaven', he was referring to the cosmic order, which for him was a moral one: his view was that moral principles both reflect and devolve from the metaphysical principles of the universe (there is a nuance of Kantianism in this perception). All people are at the same time citizens of society and of Heaven. With this emphasis he went further in the direction of mysticism than had Confucius. The Master had certainly introduced the concept of Heaven into his teaching, but more as an indication of the source of the values he taught than as a goal for people to attain. Mencius stressed that, in the process of cultivating the great *ch'i*, we need not only human principles such as duty and righteousness, which Confucius had unambiguously outlined, but also both an understanding of, and sense of harmony with, the *Tao*.

Mencius thus combines two of the disciplines of Hinduism: Jnana Yoga, or spiritual understanding, and Karma Yoga, the discipline of action and work. This balance gives his teaching the completeness found in the harmony of *yin* and *yang*, which may well be seen as the aim of all religious philosophies and their practitioners (see Chapter 18).

Neo-Confucianism

During the centuries immediately following Mencius's death, the mystical element in his teaching was given little prominence among students of Confucianism, who preferred to concentrate on the school's practical emphases. Advocates of other philosophical schools and perspectives were viewed, on the whole, as rivals rather than exponents of alternative facets of the truth they were all seeking. There were in fact numerous disputations, not all of them harmonious, between adherents of the different philosophies.

Between the third and eighth centuries CE, however, a process of synthesis took place that brought about a modification of the Confucianism taught by the Master. The main schools that were involved in this process were the two which, alongside Confucianism, still constitute the main streams in Chinese philosophy/religion: Taoism and Buddhism. Through the influence of these two schools, Confucian thought underwent a transformation, with the result that it began to acknowledge more directly the role of the mystical when interpreting both the universe in general and human life in particular. It was during this period that the *I Ching* gained its significance as a guide to a spiritual interpretation of the world; and the concept of the *Tao* as the primordial principle of the universe was seen to connect with the practical guidelines of Confucius, so that (for instance) the five relationships taught by the Master could be described as 'the *Tao* of relationships'. This synthesising process is known as Neo-Confucianism and has great significance for any modern discussion of the subject. It was during this period that the so-called Four Books, which were, as mentioned earlier (page 119) used in Chinese Civil Service examinations, assumed their authority.

The most important contribution of Neo-Confucianism, however, was its extension of Mencius's view of the metaphysical rationale for traditional ethics. The person most closely associated with this teaching, and generally regarded as the greatest of the Neo-Confucians, was the twelfth-century philosopher **Chu Hsi** (1130–1200), a prolific writer, and lecturer at the Confucian College of Bai Lu Dong (White Deer Grotto) near Shanghai. In his earlier years he was a student of Buddhism but turned from this philosophy because of its teaching of *anatta*; Chu Hsi held that there is a basic self, and his philosophy is built around this belief.

The two fundamental components of his teaching are *li* and *ch'i*. We have met both these words already, but his interpretation of them, particularly his combination of them, is distinctive. In traditional Confucian teaching, *li* means propriety; but Chu Hsi used it in its second (although not secondary) sense of the absolute, the cosmic order: in fact, as he interprets the word, it becomes highly reminiscent of the *Tao. Li* is the principle, the formal aspect of a thing (the thing-in-itself); *ch'i*, as used by Chu Hsi, is its material representation in any specific instance. *Ch'i* cannot exist without *li*, and *li* cannot be known without *ch'i*. Things are thus the instruments by which *li* finds expression; everything has its *li*, which alone establishes that thing's nature. Furthermore, the *li* of a thing pre-exists the actual coming into being of that thing (as opposed to Confucius's more existentialist perspective): the essence of anyone or anything precedes their actual coming into existence. One is reminded of Plato's theory of forms in this teaching, although the emphasis in Chu Hsi is on what Christians would term 'realised eschatology', described by Dietrich Bonh–ffer as 'the beyond in the midst'. For Plato, the forms remain in Heaven, either dimly remembered by the philosophers who have escaped from the shadows of the cave, or encountered in moments of revelation by those who 'can suddenly perceive a nature of wondrous beauty' (*Symposium*, 211).

For Chu Hsi, the form of a thing (or person), and its actual expression in a particular instance, are potentially one, and he summarised this idea with the words, 'Everything has an ultimate *ch'i*, which is the ultimate *li*' (*Recorded Sayings*, chapter 94). In the same passage, however, he added words that link his teaching more closely with *tao-chia* and, although not quite so directly, with the Hindu idea of *brahman* and the ground of being:

> That which unites and embraces the *li* of heaven, earth, and all things is the Supreme Ultimate [*T'ai-Ch'i*].

In the *Complete Works of the Master Chu*, chapter 49, he adds:

> The Supreme Ultimate is what is highest of all, beyond which nothing can be. It is
> the most high, most mystical, and most abstruse, surpassing everything.

Thus *T'ai-Ch'i* is, as Chu expresses it (p.244), 'the *li* of all *li*, the *li* of the universe as a whole'. Every individual therefore has not only his or her own *li* within his or her *ch'i*, but also partakes of the ultimate *li*. Chu Hsi states:

> This one Supreme Ultimate is received by each individual in its entirety and undi-
> vided. It is like the moon shining in the heavens, of which, though it is reflected
> in rivers and lakes and thus is everywhere visible, we would not therefore say that
> it is divided.
>
> (*Recorded Sayings*, chapter 94)

If we accept the findings, such as they are, of Chapter 2, this must be judged to be a highly religious statement. Chu Hsi adds to this perspective a cosmological consideration. He taught that the universe's existence is a consequence of the continually alternating phases of *ch'i*, which he held to oscillate between rest and motion. It is at rest in *yin* and in movement in *yang*, and from the oscillation arise *wu-hsing*, the five elements of earth, fire, metal, wood and water (discussed on pages 116–7), which, by their infinite combinations, give rise to the material world, There are some reflections here of the alternating appearance and disappearance of the universe (evolution and involution) taught in the Hindu school of Sankya Yoga (see page 26).

Laurence Wu comments on this teaching with these words (*op. cit.* p.245):

> All creation was an evolutionary process from simple to complex life, through a
> continuous succession of birth, decay, death, and re-creation. In view of the role
> played by *li* and *ch'i* in the production of things, Joseph Needham's translation of
> *li* as 'principle of organisation' and *ch'i* as 'matter–energy' in *Science and Civilisation
> in China* are quite apt.

Whether religious or otherwise, these ideas have played a formative part in creating one feature of the Chinese mind.

In the final chapters of this book, we shall consider the similarities and differences between the various Eastern schools on which we have reflected, together with their Western counterparts. The *modus operandi* will be by a process of extrapolation of the key issues, as they seem to the writer, raised in the foregoing chapters.

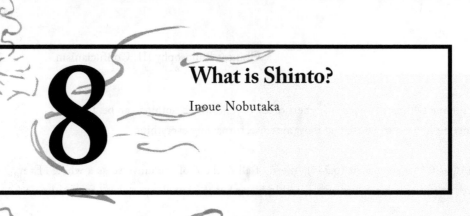

8

What is Shinto?

Inoue Nobutaka

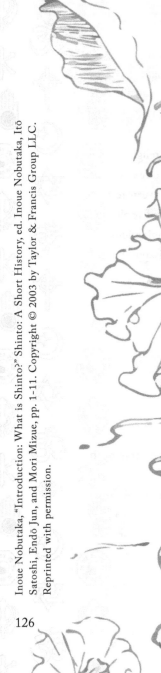

Shinto as a Religious System

The term 'Shinto' is notoriously vague and difficult to define. A brief look at the term's history confuses more than it enlightens. Its first occurrence is in the *Nihon shoki* (720), which writes of Emperor Yōmei (r. 585–7) that he 'had faith in the Buddhist Dharma and revered Shinto.' Here, as in most early usages of the word, it seems to serve as a synonym for Japan's native deities, in Japanese called kami, in contrast to the new 'foreign kami' that entered Japan with the introduction of Buddhism in the sixth century. Only during the medieval and early modern periods was the term applied to specific theological and ritual systems. In modern scholarship, the term is often used with reference to kami worship and related theologies, rituals and practices. In these contexts, 'Shinto' takes on the meaning of 'Japan's traditional religion', as opposed to foreign religions such as Christianity, Buddhism, Islam and so forth.

A central element in a practical definition of Shinto will have to be systems of kami worship and shrine ritual that date back to classical times. Few will doubt that the kami and their cults form the core of what we call Shinto. However, when we try to pin down more specifically what teachings, rituals, or beliefs have constituted Shinto through the centuries, we soon run into difficulty. Some scholars have attempted to categorise Shinto into 'shrine Shinto', 'sect Shinto', and 'folk Shinto', and others have added 'imperial Shinto' (referring to imperial rituals focusing on kami), 'state Shinto' and 'Shinto-derived new religions'. However, many questions remain both as to the legitimacy of these categorisations, and as to their relationship to each other. In particular, it is well-nigh impossible to separate 'shrine Shinto' from 'folk Shinto'. In extreme cases, some have even resorted to labelling all religious folk traditions in Japan 'Shinto'.

In the field of Religious Studies, Shinto is usually described as an 'indigenous religion'. By this term is meant a religion that emerged naturally within the historical development of an indigenous culture, in contrast to 'founded religions', which are based on the teachings of historical founders. These latter are often described as 'world religions', because they spread across national boundaries to assume a global role. In contrast, Shinto as an 'indigenous religion' is inextricably linked with a single nation, Japan.

Shinto also displays many features of what we may call 'folk religion'. This term is here used as a generic term for popular beliefs and practices that are not directly controlled by a shrine, temple or church, or led by a religious professional such as a priest, a monk or a minister. As such beliefs and practices in Japan, we may mention the worship of various deity tablets (*ofuda*), the tabooing of certain dates or directions, belief in different kinds of spirits (such as spirits of the dead, or 'revengeful spirits', *onryō*), worship of natural objects such as trees and mountains, and worship of the kami of fields and mountains (*ta no kami* and *yama no kami*). Most of what is commonly called religious folklore, local customs, or superstition belongs in this category.

Not only Shinto, but also Buddhism and the new religions of Japan are closely connected with folk religion. Even Christianity, both in Japan and elsewhere, contains many folk influences. In the case of Shinto, however, such elements are so prominent that it is impossible to draw a line between folk religion and some fictional 'pure Shinto'. This is a direct result of Shinto's history, which is rooted in a long tradition of kami worship that developed in close relation with the rhythms of everyday life, both cultural and economic.

There is another reason why it is difficult to follow Shinto through history as a distinct religious tradition: the fact that Shinto has been profoundly influenced by other religious traditions. The influence of the religions of China has been prominent since ancient times, and among them, the religion that left the most profound impact was Chinese Buddhism. Even if we were to use the term 'Early Shinto' to refer to some archaic prototype of Shinto, we would find that such a distant ancestor of Shinto would already have been transformed in important ways by Chinese forms of Buddhism. In addition, other continental traditions such as Confucianism, Taoism, and theories about Yin and Yang and the Five Phases of matter (wood, fire, earth, metal and water) left their imprint in ideas about, and practices around, the kami from an early date. These facts further complicate our question, which appears so simple at first sight: what is Shinto? One is reminded of the onion of Peer Gynt: will there really be a 'core' to be found after we have peeled off layer after layer of foreign accretions?

These are the sort of fundamental problems one is faced with when trying to define Shinto. Looking for Shinto's 'core' or 'true essence' will not take us very far in resolving the issue. In this volume, we have chosen a different approach. Here, we will introduce the concept of a 'religious system' as a new angle on Shinto and its historical development.

The concept of a 'religious system' is here proposed as a tool to explore the historical development of religion in its intimate relation with the structural characteristics and changes of society as a whole. Traditionally, religious history has occupied itself with the histories of individual religions, schools or sects. We have histories of Christianity, Islam, Buddhism and Shinto, histories of the Methodist church and of Pure Land Buddhism, and histories of Tenrikyō and Sōka Gakkai. While this is a valuable approach to the history of religion, it tends to ignore the fact that the concept of religion itself can vary widely from period to period, or from religious group to religious group. It is obvious, for example, that the Catholic Church in Korea and its counterpart in Japan differ in many respects, in spite of the fact that both are grounded in the same religion. Similarly, Buddhism in classical Japan was fundamentally distinct in character from modern Japanese Buddhism. Conversely, we find that different religious groups display similar characteristics when developing in a common social and cultural environment. The new religious movements of modern Japan, which are collectively known as the 'new religions', are a good example of this: behind the multitude of sect names we find many similarities in actual teaching and practice. If we were to compare, for example, the modern Risshō Kōseikai and Myōchikai (both Buddhist-derived new religions), we would find that they are much more similar to one another than, say, the Buddhism of the Nara period (710–94) and the Edo period (1600–1867).

If we think of a religion in terms of written doctrine, individual religions or sects display a great deal of continuity over the centuries, but when we consider the roles these same religions or sects have played in actual society in different historical periods or in different cultural areas, we notice radical differences. If we regard individual religions as part of a wider religious 'ecosystem', it becomes clear that traditional histories of religion need to be reconsidered in various ways. It is to tackle these issues that the concept of a 'religious system' is useful. This concept allows us to treat clusters of religious groups that display typological similarities as one religious system. When studying such clusters as a religious system we relate their development to changes within society as a whole. This makes it possible to consider, say, the Sōtō Zen sect and the Jōdo Pure Land sect of the Edo period as two members of the same religious system: early modern Japanese Buddhism. Conversely, the Shingon school in the Heian period (794–1192) can be studied as belonging to a different religious system from its Edo period counterpart.

To study religion from this angle is to exchange the metaphor of religion as an organism for that of religion as an ecosystem. The boundaries of different religious systems are regarded as fluid, both with regard to individual religious movements, and with regard to different historical periods.

When we isolate a particular religious system and try to make out its characteristics, it is necessary to approach it from three angles: the system's *constituents*, its *network*, and its *substance*. The *constituents* of a religious system are the people who carry and maintain it. In most cases, we can distinguish between two groups: the 'makers' and the 'users' of the religion. The first include the founders of religious groups and their successors: monks, shrine priests, ministers, missionaries, and so forth. These are the people who work actively to sustain a particular religious tradition. This category also includes those who carry out the administrative tasks of religious institutions. The 'users' of a religious system are the believers, followers and church-goers who participate in religious activities. It is important to note that not all 'users' are necessarily 'believers'; those who do not necessarily have 'faith' but are active in the periphery of religious groups must also be included in this category. This is because they are important to religious groups as possible future believers, and as targets for missionary education or conversion. The category of 'users', then, can be defined as those who already are, and those who may become, believers of a religion.

This takes us to the term *network*. We use this term to refer to the various elements that are related to the organisational upkeep of the religious system: the channels the religious system uses to ensure its future existence. Here, we can distinguish between 'hard' and 'soft' aspects: the sacred sites, shrine buildings, temples, churches and headquarters of religious groups constitute the first, while the latter includes institutional hierarchies, pilgrimage routes, etc.

The third and last key aspect of religious systems is termed *substance*. This refers to the message that a religion tries to convey to its users through its teachings, practices and rituals. A religion's teachings include both the doctrines laid down in its scriptures, and the contents of the sermons of its preachers—two aspects of teaching that are not always identical or even consistent. Practices and rituals range widely from secret, esoteric rites to public ceremonies.

Religious groups which display a clear similarity in structure or type can fruitfully be studied as components of a single religious system. A new religious system emerges when the three elements of *constituents*, *network* and *substance* come together in some new way. Changes in religious systems occur when one of these three elements is transformed to such a degree that it affects the other two.

If religious systems are formed and transformed in close interaction with the society in which they partake, it follows that Shinto cannot be considered as a single religious system that existed from the ancient to the modern period. Nonetheless, it is also true that the religious system that emerged with the systematisation of kami worship in ancient Japan is connected with modern shrine Shinto through a long string of gradual transformations. The method we will take in this volume is to follow this long history of transformations. As our point of departure, we will choose kami worship as the characteristic that distinguishes Shinto from other religious traditions and gives it continuity through the ages. It will become clear, however, that the concrete beliefs and practices of kami worship changed considerably from period to period, and took on a great variety of disparate forms.

The classical system of kami worship clearly possessed all the elements of a fully fledged religious system. Its origin is difficult to date, but it was completed as a system after the establishment of a central imperial state governed by an adapted version of Chinese law (J. *ritsuryō*). Shrines from all over the country were included in a system of 'official shrines' (*kansha*). This network of official shrines formed the *network* of kami worship as a religious system. Also, the *constituents* of kami rituals were clearly identified, and their message (the system's *substance*) was transmitted to society through ritual prayers (*norito*) and imperial decrees (*senmyō*). It is not possible to identify a religious system that might be described as 'Shinto' before the systematisation of kami worship by the new imperial state during the classical period, because the constituents, network, and substance of kami cults during this early period were too ill-defined.

Together with the decline of the rule of *ritsuryō* law, the classical system of kami worship gradually lost its character as a distinct religious system. The system's network was lost, and as kami cults amalgamated with Buddhism, its substance was radically transformed. During the medieval period, warrior groups became important carriers of kami cults, leading to a partial shift of the religion's constituents. The spread of private estates (*shōen*) and the popular practice of 'inviting' spirits of the deity Hachiman to such estates encouraged the formation of a new network which partly replaced the classical 'network' of official shrines.

Simultaneously, the amalgamation of kami cults and Buddhism that had begun already in early classical times penetrated into all nooks and crannies of kami worship in the course of the medieval period, and in the process not only transformed the classical system of kami worship but also encouraged the founding of new religious systems, such as that of Shugendo. This amalgamation generated changes in the substance of kami cults, because it placed kami cults under the strong influence of Buddhist doctrine. On the other hand, the process of amalgamation also encouraged the development of theological kami thought in opposition to Buddhism. During medieval times, Shinto as a religious system was all but absorbed by the much more powerful system of Buddhism, but nevertheless survived. Developments in the early modern and modern periods proved that medieval Shinto, though largely subsumed in Buddhism, still remained sufficiently autonomous as a religious system to move once more into a direction of its own.

Elements of the classical system of kami worship survived through the middle ages into the early modern period. This period saw the emergence of a new form of Shinto thought in the form of National Learning (*koku-gaku*) and Restoration (*fukko*) Shinto. This form of Shinto can be regarded as a new religious system in its own right, and also proved essential in the later formation of sect Shinto in modern times. On the level of substance, we see that the multitude of medieval kami theories of the medieval period were rearranged into a new, close-knit discourse through the labours of successive thinkers of the National Learning movement. This was an important step in the formation of a new religious system. With regard to the network of Shinto, the early modern period saw the formation of a range of religious 'confraternities' (*kō*), whose existence was an important factor in the development of the Shinto sects of the modern period.

The Buddhist and Confucian forms of Shinto that were prominent during the medieval and early modern periods were incomplete as a religious system, because they did not provide for a network of their own, or only a fragmentary one. On the other hand, they prepared the ground both for the modern system of kami worship and for the formation of sect Shinto and Shinto-derived new religions. Therefore, it is not impossible to regard them at least as a religious system *in nascendo*.

Shugendo, finally, developed in the power field between kami cults and Esoteric Buddhism, and gradually matured into a religious system of its own. Shugendo will not be discussed in detail in this volume, but it was a factor of great importance in the historical development of Shinto.

The East-Asian Sphere of Religious Culture and Shinto

Traditionally, there has been a tendency to stress the 'uniquely Japanese' character of Shinto, and little effort has been made to compare kami worship in Japan with the indigenous religions and folk beliefs of other East-Asian countries. It is only recently that researchers have focused on the similarities between kami cults and Taoism, and on the profound influence of Chinese folk religion and Chinese theories of Yin and Yang and the Five Phases of matter on Japanese kami cults.[1]

Worship of spirits, spirit possession, divination, oracles and polytheism are all features that Japanese kami cults share with East-Asian folk religion. Also, the amalgamation of kami cults with Buddhism in Japan has parallels in the amalgamation of Taoism and Buddhism in China, and of Confucianism and Buddhism in Korea.

The influence of Chinese religion in East Asia is so prominent that the whole region may well be regarded as a single 'Chinese religio-cultural sphere'. Until recently, scholars who have wished to identify the characteristics of Japanese religion did so by comparing Japanese religious traditions with the monotheistic religions of the West. As a result of such comparisons, syncretism, polytheism and animism have frequently been highlighted as typical of Japanese religion as a whole. However, even a superficial glance at the religions of Japan's closest neighbours reveals that these are all features shared by the large majority of religions in the Chinese religio-cultural sphere.

Shinto worships an untold multitude of different kami deities. While this represents an important difference with monotheistic religions such as Judaism, Christianity and Islam, it is a feature that Shinto shares with many other religions across the world, and that constitutes the norm in East Asia. Buddhism incorporated many Hindu deities in India, and once again expanded its pantheon in China with a host of Taoist deities. These countless regional deities play an especially important role on the level of popular religion.

Moreover, popular beliefs and practices revere not only deities but also a multitude of other kinds of spirits and supernatural creatures. Japanese religion recognises many deities and, to some extent, attributes different functions to different deities. The dividing line between deities and human beings is vague, and extraordinary humans are frequently worshipped as 'living kami' (*ikigami*) or as 'emanations of a Buddha' (*keshin*). These features of Japanese religion, too, are widely shared by other religious traditions within the Chinese cultural sphere.

It goes without saying that polytheistic and animistic forms of religion can be found across the globe, and constitute one of the basic types of religion. In East Asia, these features are especially common. Moreover,

East-Asian versions of polytheistic and animistic religions can perhaps be further defined as a special sub-species of this form of religion. Here, the role of Mahāyāna Buddhism and ancient Chinese deity worship, ancestor worship, and beliefs in demons must be emphasised.

The universal religion of East Asia has been Mahāyāna Buddhism, a religion of an exceptionally accommodative character. In the Chinese cultural sphere, Mahāyāna Buddhism absorbed multifarious forms of ancestor worship and deity worship, and through its flexible attitude and its tendency to transform differences and oppositions into expressions of a single religious truth, it contributed to the multifaceted and yet closely interconnected character of East-Asian religion as a whole.

An important issue in all religious traditions is the question of how contact with deities, or with God, can be established and maintained. Christianity and Islam describe how God 'appears' to human beings to convey messages to them (a phenomenon termed theophany); in East Asia, we find a corresponding phenomenon in the various forms of shamanism that are common throughout this region. Shamans can be defined as those who deploy some well-developed technique of interacting with deities or spirits. In contrast to those who encounter a theophany in Christianity or Islam, shamans actively establish contact with deities or spirits and, on occasion, control and use them for their own aims.

Shamanism is often mentioned as a constituent of Shinto. Oracles have formed part of kami cults since the ancient period, and spirit possession is a common element of folk religion to this day. It is perhaps questionable whether all of these phenomena should be termed shamanism, but there is no doubt that they have functioned as important means of communication between kami and their worshippers throughout history. The question remains how exactly kami possession in Shinto relates to shamanic practices current in modern Korea, Taiwan or Mongolia; the least we can say is that all these practices are religious techniques to fathom the will of deities or spirits. Practices of this nature can be found throughout East Asia, and Japan is no exception. In Japan, shamanic features are especially apparent in the activities of different types of spirit ritualists, which are known variously as *ogamiya*, *reinōsha*, *kitōshi*, or, in specific regions of Japan, *yuta* (Okinawa), *kamisan*, *itako*, and *gomiso* (Northern Honshu). The former of these are occupied mainly with healing practices, and the latter specialise first and foremost in contacting the dead and conveying messages from them, and in making predictions for the future.

Another common method to fathom the will of the gods is divination (*uranai*). Techniques to interpret utterances, natural events, or the movements of special contrivances as the will of supernatural beings have been common in most religions since ancient times. In modern Shinto, the drawing of *omikuji* lots springs to mind; older are the reading of cracks in burnt tortoise shells (a technique of Chinese origin), and 'hot-water ordeals' (*kugatachi*), in which a priest sprinkles hot water over the worshippers in the kami's presence. A large variety of annual divinatory rites and ceremonies to predict the prosperity of the coming year are practised at different localities throughout Japan. There are also forms of divination which include an element of spirit possession, such as *yudate*, a ritual closely related to *kugatachi* in which a *miko* priestess sprinkles hot water over herself and the worshippers to become possessed by the kami. Most forms of divination in Japan have been heavily influenced by Chinese folk religion, by Chinese theories of Yin and Yang and the Five Phases of matter, and by the Book of Changes (*Yijing*). In fact, the very idea that good and bad fortune alternate, and the notion that we can read the 'will of Heaven', have their roots in China.

Even more important in the history of kami cults was their interblending with Buddhism. Throughout most of the historical period, kami have been worshipped together with buddhas or bodhisattvas, as a primarily Buddhist set. This not only assimilated the characters of different kami with those of buddhas and bodhisattvas, but also resulted in a situation in which the same individuals or communities followed different religious traditions parallel to each other. Both of these phenomena are commonly termed syncretism.

Syncretism develops naturally in a society where different non-exclusionistic, open-ended religions exist side by side. In Japan, Shinto amalgamated not only with Buddhism but also with Confucianism. Also, most modern new religions are rooted in more than one established religious tradition. In China, Confucianism, Taoism and Buddhism have produced a variety of combinatory cults and theologies, and Korea saw the partial amalgamation of Confucianism with Taoism. In Korea one can even find cults that combine Christian with shamanic elements. It is no exaggeration to argue that syncretism is characteristic of East-Asian religion as a whole.

In addition to this traditional syncretism, we can observe a new trend of forming new religious systems by selecting and combining the 'best points' of more than one religion. This tendency is distinguished from traditional syncretism as 'neo-syncretism'. Neo-syncretism is particularly prominent in modern Shinto-derived new religions, but can also be encountered in some of the new religions of modern Taiwan, Korea and other East-Asian countries.

Another prominent aspect of East-Asian religion is ancestor worship. In Japan, memorial services for ancestors are largely the domain of Buddhist sects, and ancestor worship is often regarded as an element of popular Buddhism; nevertheless, ancestors also play an important role in popular kami practices. In East Asia, ancestor worship has often been tied in with Confucianism, and has played a prominent role in people's religious life. Ancestral genealogies have usually followed the paternal line and are, in China and Korea, linked with specific places of origin. In some modern Japanese Buddhist-derived sects (notably Reiyūkai and sects split off from it), there is a tendency to include maternal ancestors as well. In general, it can be said that the concept of ancestors in Japan is more inclusive than in China or Korea, and the practice of paying reverence to ancestors has consistently occupied a larger proportion of religious activity than in other parts of East Asia. The fact remains, however, that the notion of a shared ancestry has played an important role in the formation of group identities in most societies throughout East Asia.

Ancestor worship mostly takes the form of ritual practice by kin groups or clans, and continues to perform the function of promoting group solidarity, often in secularised ways. Originally, such rituals were strongly religious in character. The ancestors were connected to living individuals or groups not only genealogically, but also as active ancestral spirits that protect their descendants in the present. In Japan, ancestor spirits were not necessarily related to their protégés in a strictly genealogical sense, and could therefore play an important role in community (rather than kin group) rituals. Moreover, ancestor worship has been central to modern ideologies that identify the whole of the state of Japan as an extended family, with the emperor at its head.

As will be clear already from this brief inventory of shared East-Asian features, research into Shinto as a member of the family of East-Asian religions is a promising and necessary avenue to a better understanding of this religious tradition, which has all too often been described as 'uniquely Japanese'.

Notes

1. Examples are Fukunaga Mitsuji, *Dōkyō to Nihon bunka* (Jinbun Shoin 1982), and Yoshino Hiroko, *In'yō gogyōsetsu kara mita Nihon no matsuri* (Kōbundō 1978).

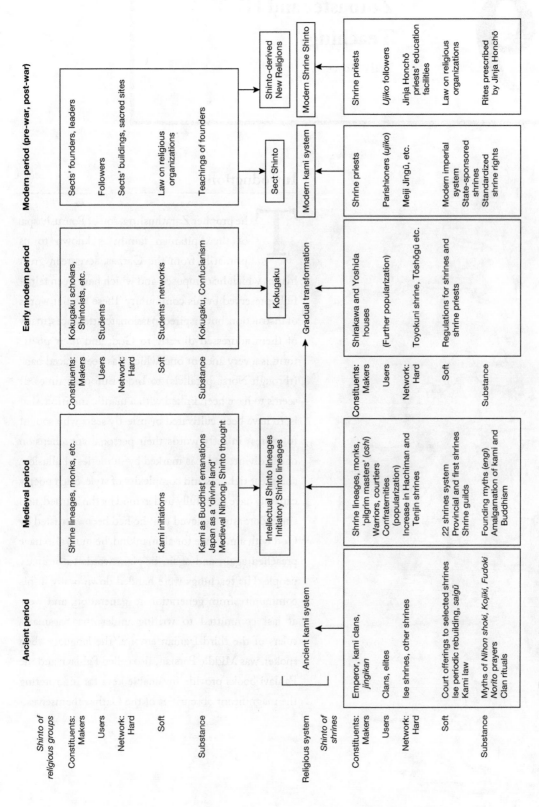

Figure 8.1 An overview of Shinto history

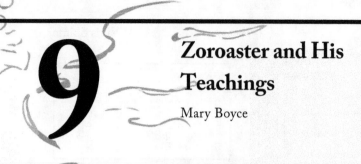

9 Zoroaster and His Teachings

Mary Boyce

Introduction

The prophet Zarathushtra, son of Pourushaspa, of the Spitaman family, is known to us primarily from the Gathas, seventeen great hymns which he composed and which have been faithfully preserved by his community. These are not works of instruction, but inspired, passionate utterances, many of them addressed directly to God; and their poetic form is a very ancient one, which has been traced back (through Norse parallels) to Indo-European times. It seems to have been linked with a mantic tradition, that is, to have been cultivated by priestly seers who sought to express in lofty words their personal apprehension of the divine; and it is marked by subtleties of allusion, and great richness and complexity of style. Such poetry can only have been fully understood by the learned; and since Zoroaster believed that he had been entrusted by God with a message for all mankind, he must also have preached again and again in plain words to ordinary people. His teachings were handed down orally in his community from generation to generation, and were at last committed to writing under the Sasanians, rulers of the third Iranian empire. The language then spoken was Middle Persian, also called Pahlavi; and the Pahlavi books provide invaluable keys for interpreting the magnificent obscurities of the Gathas themselves.

Much valuable matter is preserved also in the 'Younger Avesta'. The dialect which Zoroaster himself spoke is known only from the Gathas and a few other ancient texts. (This linguistic isolation increases the difficulties of interpreting his hymns, since these are full of otherwise unknown words.) The rest of the surviving Avesta consists of liturgical texts preserved in various later stages of the same language (but not in exactly the same dialect). To his followers all these works embodied different aspects of Zoroaster's revelation, and were to be reverenced accordingly. Although Western scholars distinguish the post-Gathic texts collectively as the 'Younger Avesta', some of them contain matter which is very old. This is particularly true of certain of the yashts, hymns addressed to individual divinities.

Zoroaster and His Mission

Zoroaster's date cannot be established with any precision, since he lived in what for his people were pre-historic times. The language of the Gathas is archaic, and close to that of the Rigveda (whose composition has been assigned to about 1700 B.C. onwards); and the picture of the world to be gained from them is correspondingly ancient, that of a Stone Age society. Some allowance may have to be made for literary conservatism; and it is also possible that the 'Avestan' people (as Zoroaster's own tribe is called for want of a better name) were poor or isolated, and so not rapidly influenced by the developments of the Bronze Age. It is only possible therefore to hazard a reasoned conjecture that Zoroaster lived some time between 1700 and 1500 B.C.

In the Gathas he refers to himself as a 'zaotar', that is, a fully qualified priest; and he is the only founder of a credal religion who was both priest and prophet. (In the Younger Avesta he is spoken of by the general word for priest, 'athaurvan'.) He also calls himself a 'manthran', that is, one able to compose 'manthra' (Sanskrit 'mantra'), inspired utterances of power. Training for the priesthood began early among the Indo-Iranians, probably at about the age of seven, and was carried out orally, for they had no knowledge of writing. It must have consisted, basically, of learning both rituals and doctrines, as well as acquiring skill in extemporizing verses in invocation and praise of the gods, and learning by heart great manthras composed by earlier sages. The Iranians held that maturity was reached at fifteen, and it was presumably at that age that Zoroaster was made priest. His own Gathas suggest that he must thereafter have sought all the higher knowledge which he could gain from various teachers; and he further describes himself there as a 'vaedemna' or 'one who knows', an initiate possessed of divinely inspired wisdom. According to Zoroastrian tradition (preserved in the Pahlavi books), he spent years in a wandering quest for truth; and his hymns suggest that he must then have witnessed acts of violence, with war-bands, worshippers of the Daevas, descending on peaceful communities to pillage, slaughter and carry off cattle. Conscious himself of being powerless physically, he became filled with a deep longing for justice, for the moral law of the Ahuras to be established for strong and weak alike, so that order and tranquillity could prevail, and all be able to pursue the good life in peace.

According to tradition Zoroaster was thirty, the time of ripe wisdom, when revelation finally came to him. This great happening is alluded to in one of the Gathas (Y 43), and is tersely described in a Pahlavi work (Zadspram XX-XXI). Here it is said that Zoroaster, being at a gathering met to celebrate a spring festival, went at dawn to a river to fetch water for the haoma-ceremony. He waded in to draw it from midstream; and when he returned to the bank—himself in a state of ritual purity, emerging from the pure element, water, in the freshness of a spring dawn—he had a vision. He saw on the bank a shining Being, who revealed himself as Vohu Manah 'Good Purpose'; and this Being led Zoroaster into the presence of Ahura Mazda and five other radiant figures, before whom 'he did not see his own shadow upon the earth, owing to their great light'. And it was then, from this great heptad, that he received his revelation.

Ahura Mazda and His Adversary

This was the first of a number of times that Zoroaster saw Ahura Mazda in vision, or felt conscious of his presence, or heard his words calling him to his service, a summons which he whole-heartedly obeyed. 'For this' (he declares) 'I was set apart as yours from the beginning' (Y 44.11). 'While I have power and strength, I shall teach men to seek the right (asha)' (Y 28.4). It was as the master of asha (order, righteousness and justice) that he venerated Ahura Mazda. This was in accordance with tradition, since Mazda had been worshipped of old as the greatest of the three Ahuras, the guardians of asha; but Zoroaster went much further, and in a startling departure from accepted beliefs proclaimed Ahura Mazda to be the one uncreated God, existing eternally, and Creator of all else that is good, including all other beneficent divinities.

One cannot hope to retrace with any certainty the processes of thought which led Zoroaster to this exalted belief; but it seems probable that he came to it through meditating on the daily act of worship which he as priest performed, and on the cosmogonic theories connected with this. Scholar-priests, as we have seen, had evolved a doctrine of the genesis of the world in seven stages, with the seven creations all being represented at the yasna; and they had postulated primal unity in the physical sphere, with all life stemming from one original plant, animal and man. From this, it would seem, Zoroaster was inspired to apprehend a similar original uniqueness in the divine sphere also, with, in the beginning, only one beneficent Being existing in the universe, Ahura Mazda, the all-wise, and also the wholly just and good, from whom all other beneficent divine beings emanated.

Harsh experience had evidently convinced the prophet that wisdom, justice and goodness were utterly separate by nature from wickedness and cruelty; and in vision he beheld, co-existing with Ahura Mazda, an Adversary, the 'Hostile Spirit', Angra Mainyu, equally uncreated, but ignorant and wholly malign. These two great Beings Zoroaster beheld with prophetic eye at their original, far-off encountering: 'Truly there are two primal Spirits, twins, renowned to be in conflict. In thought and word and act they are two, the good and the bad. . . . And when these two Spirits first encountered, they created life and not-life, and that at the end the worst existence shall be for the followers of falsehood (drug), but the best dwelling for those who possess righteousness (asha). Of the two Spirits, the one who follows falsehood chose doing the worst things, the Holiest Spirit, who is clad in the hardest stone [i.e. the sky] chose righteousness, and (so shall they all) who will satisfy Ahura Mazda continually with just actions' (Y 30.3-5).

An essential element in this revelation is that the two primal Beings each made a deliberate choice (although each, it seems, according to his own proper nature) between good and evil, an act which prefigures the identical choice which every man must make for himself in this life. The exercise of choice changed the inherent antagonism between the two Spirits into an active one, which expressed itself, at a decision taken by Ahura Mazda, in creation and counter-creation, or, as the prophet put it, in the making of 'life' and 'not-life' (that is, death); for Ahura Mazda knew in his wisdom that if he became Creator and fashioned this world, then the Hostile Spirit would attack it, because it was good, and it would become a battleground for their two forces, and in the end he, God, would win the great struggle there and be able to destroy evil, and so achieve a universe which would be wholly good forever.

The Heptad and the Seven Creations

These teachings were fundamentally new; but it was the old cosmogony which provided the basis for Zoroaster's thought. So the first act which he conceived Ahura Mazda as performing was the evocation, through his Holy Spirit, Spenta Mainyu, of six lesser divinities, the radiant Beings of Zoroaster's earliest vision. These divinities formed a heptad with Ahura Mazda himself, and they proceeded with him to fashion the seven creations which make up the world. The evocation of the six is variously described in Zoroastrian works, but always in ways which suggest the essential unity of beneficent divinity. Thus Ahura Mazda is said either to be their 'father', or to have 'mingled' himself with them, and in one Pahlavi text his creation of them is compared with the lighting of torches from a torch.

The six great Beings then in their turn, Zoroaster taught, evoked other beneficent divinities, who are in fact the beneficent gods of the pagan Iranian pantheon. (He himself invokes a number of them in the Gathas, notably the 'other Ahuras', that is, Mithra and Apąm Napat; Sraosha, Ashi and Geush Urvan.) All these divine beings, who are, according to his doctrines, either directly or indirectly the emanations of Ahura Mazda, strive under him, according to their various appointed tasks, to further good and to defeat evil. Collectively they are known in Zoroastrianism as Yazatas, 'Beings worthy of worship', or Amesha Spentas, 'Holy Immortals'. Although the latter term does not occur in the Gathas, it was most probably coined by Zoroaster himself to distinguish those beings revealed to him as beneficent from the generality of pagan gods, who are invoked as 'All the Immortals' in the Vedas; for Zoroaster rejected with the utmost courage and firmness the worship of the warlike, amoral Daevas—that is, Indra and his companions—whom he regarded as being 'of the race of evil purpose' (Y 32.3). 'The Daevas chose not rightly, because the Deceiver came upon them as they consulted, so that they chose the worst purpose. Then together they betook themselves to Wrath, through whom they afflicted the life of man' (Y 30.6). To Zoroaster the Daevas were thus both wicked by nature and wicked by choice, like Angra Mainyu himself—false gods who were not to be worshipped because they stood for conflict among men, luring them through their greed for offerings to bloodshed and destructive strife.

The crucial word 'spenta', used by Zoroaster of Ahura Mazda and all his creation, is one of the most important terms in his revelation. Basically, it seems, it meant 'possessing power', and when used of beneficent divinities, 'possessing power to aid', hence 'furthering, supporting, benefiting'. Through constant religious use spenta acquired overtones of meaning, like the word 'holy', which similarly meant originally 'mighty, strong'. 'Holy' is therefore a close rendering for it; but to avoid suggesting concepts alien to Zoroastrianism, some scholars have preferred 'bounteous' as a standard translation. This, however, has the weakness that it has no religious associations in English, and so does not convey the sense of reverence implicit in Zoroastrian spenta. The rendering 'holy' has therefore been generally preferred in this book.

Although the title Amesha Spenta may be used of any of the divinities of Ahura Mazda's creation, it is applied especially to the great six of the prophet's own vision, the other lesser divinities being referred to as the Yazatas. The doctrine of the six Holy Immortals is fundamental to Zoroaster's teachings, and has far-reaching spiritual and ethical consequences, since these Beings hypostatize qualities or attributes of Ahura Mazda himself, and can in their turn (if rightly sought and venerated) bestow these upon men. For every individual, as for the prophet himself, the Immortal who leads the way to all the rest is Vohu Manah, 'Good Purpose'; and his closest confederate is Asha Vahishta, 'Best Righteousness'—the divinity personifying the mighty principle of asha, whom Zoroaster names in the Gathas more often than any other of the six. Then there is Spenta Armaiti, 'Holy Devotion', embodying the dedication to what is good and just; and Khshathra Vairya, 'Desirable Dominion', who represents both the power which each person should properly exert for righteousness in this life, and also the power and the kingdom of God. The final pair are Haurvatat and Ameretat, 'Health' and 'Long Life', who not only enhance this mortal existence but confer that eternal well-being and life, which may be obtained by the righteous in the presence of Ahura Mazda.

That divine attributes should be isolated, and then invoked and worshipped as independent beings, was a characteristic of the pagan Iranian religion, as we have seen in the case of Mithra, surrounded as he is by Friendship, Obedience, Justice, Courage and Divine Grace. So the mould was already old in which Zoroaster cast his new doctrines. Fie saw the great six as remaining similarly close to the supreme Lord; and it is said of them in the Younger Avesta (Yt 19.16–18) that they are 'of one mind, one voice, one act. . . . Of them one beholds the soul of the other, thinking upon good thoughts, good words, good deeds . . . they who are the creators and fashioners and makers and observers and guardians of the creations of Ahura Mazda.' The tendency also existed in the old Iranian religion to link 'abstract' divinities with physical phenomena, so closely that (as in the case of Mithra and Apąm Napat) the phenomena could be regarded as representing the divinities themselves; and already in the Gathas the association of the seven Amesha Spentas with the seven creations was of this kind. The nature of the link in each case appears to have been understood by the prophet through his meditations upon the yasna, the daily act of worship by which the seven creations were sustained and blessed. In pondering on its rituals he came, it seems, to apprehend that within each of the things which he as priest saw or handled was an immaterial presence, a hidden divinity, so that through these rites, performed primarily for the sake of the physical world, priest and worshippers could at the same time seek a moral and spiritual good, honouring and striving to unite themselves with the great invisible Amesha Spentas. A new dimension was thus added to the age-old observance.

The link of each divinity with his creation is a reasonable one, for Zoroastrianism, once its intuitively held—or divinely revealed—premises are granted, is essentially a rational faith. So Khshathra Vairya, Desirable Dominion, is lord of the hard sky of stone, which arches protectively over the earth. Lowly earth itself belongs to Spenta Armaiti, Holy Devotion. Water is the creation of Haurvatat, Health, and plants belong to Ameretat, Long Life or Immortality. Vohu Manah, Good Purpose, is lord of the mild beneficent cow, who for the nomad Iranians was a powerful symbol of creative goodness, of that which sustains and nourishes. Fire, which pervades the other creations, and, through the sun, controls the seasons, is under the protection of Asha Vahishta, the Order which should pervade and regulate the world. Finally man himself, with his intelligence and power of choice, belongs especially to Ahura Mazda, the Lord Wisdom, who made the first choice of all. These associations, subtly alluded to in the Gathas, are plainly set out in the later literature.

The order of the great heptad of divinities often does not correspond with the chronological sequence of the seven creations. This was because it was natural to name them usually according to spiritual dignity and worth, with Ahura Mazda in his rightful place at their head. Any of the great seven may be entreated by any individual worshipper—indeed he should invoke them all, if he is to become a perfect man; but two among them had particular links with two groups of society. Armaiti, as guardian of the enduring, fertile earth, mother of all things, was the natural protectress of women. In the words of an ancient text: 'This earth then we worship, her who bears us, together with women' (y.38.1). Her great partner, Khshathra, lord of the lofty, protective sky, and so of stone everywhere, was as fittingly the guardian of just men, who had the duty to use their weapons—their flint-tipped arrows and spears, their slingstones and heavy maces—to protect the poor and weak, and not to despoil or harm them. The priests, who were the learned class, trained in religious lore, evidently felt themselves especially under the protection of Ahura Mazda, the Lord Wisdom, whose creation, mankind, they represented at the yasna; but the supreme Lord's power is so all-encompassing that this link is not made so much of in the tradition.

Being the creation of Ahura Mazda, every man has the duty not only to cherish the six lesser creations, but also to watch over his own physical and moral well-being, and to care for his fellow-men, since each of them is likewise the special creature of God. The particular ethical code which Zoroaster gave his followers to live by demanded of them good thoughts, good words and good deeds—an admirable moral law which seems a generalization of the threefold demand made of the Iranian priest, who to perform an act of worship effectively needed good intention, right words and correct rituals.

The doctrine of the seven Amesha Spentas and the seven creations thus inspired a comprehensive morality, and inculcated in man a deep sense of responsibility for the world around him. He is the chief of the creations, but he is bound to the other six by the link of a shared purpose, for all spenta creation is striving for a common goal, man consciously, the rest by instinct or nature, for all were brought into existence for this one end, namely the utter defeat of evil.

Creation and the Three Times

Another aspect of the relationship between tangible and intangible was embodied in Zoroaster's teaching (best known to us from the Pahlavi books) that Ahura Mazda accomplished the act of creation in two stages. First he brought all things into being in a disembodied state, called in Pahlavi 'menog', that is, 'spiritual, immaterial'. Then he gave it 'material' or 'getig', existence. The getig existence is better than the previous menog one, for in it Ahura Mazda's perfect creation received the added good of solid and sentient form. Together, the fashioning of these two states constituted the act of Creation, called in Pahlavi 'Bundahishn'. The achievement of the getig state set the field for the battle with evil, for unlike the menog one it was vulnerable to assault; and Angra Mainyu straightway attacked. According to the myth as set out in the Pahlavi books, he broke in violently through the lower bowl of the stone sky, thus marring its perfection. Then he plunged upwards through the water, turning much of it salt, and attacked the earth, creating deserts. Next he withered the plant, and slew the Uniquely-created Bull and the First Man. Finally he fell upon the seventh creation, fire, and sullied it with smoke, so that he had physically blighted all the good creation.

The divine beings then rallied their forces. Ameretat took thé plant, pounded it up (as haoma is pounded in the yasna-ritual), and scattered its essence over the world by cloud and rain, to grow up as more plants everywhere. The seed of the Bull and Man were purified in the moon and sun, and more cattle and men sprang from them. So in the Zoroastrian version of the ancient myth the beneficent sacrifice attributed originally to the pagan gods was assigned as an evil act to Angra Mainyu, for it was he who brought decay and death into the perfect, static world of Ahura Mazda. The Amesha Spentas were able, however, through their holy power to turn his malicious acts to benefit; and such must be the constant endeavour of all the good creation.

'Creation' was the first of the three times into which the drama of cosmic history is divided. Angra Mainyu's attack inaugurated the second time, that of 'Mixture' (Pahlavi 'Gumezisn'), during which this world is no longer wholly good, but is a blend of good and evil; for the cycle of being having been set in motion, Angra Mainyu continues to attack with the Daevas and all the other legions of darkness which he had brought into existence to oppose the Yazatas, and together they inflict not only physical ills but every moral and spiritual evil from which man suffers. To withstand their assaults man needs to venerate Ahura

Mazda and the six Amesha Spentas, and to bring them so fully into his own heart and being that there is no room there for vice or weakness. He should also worship all the beneficent Yazatas, some of whom, like the two lesser Ahuras (twice invoked by Zoroaster himself in the Gathas) will also help him in his moral struggles, while others, such as Sun and Moon, will play their part in keeping the physical world strong and in accordance with asha.

According to Zoroaster's new revelation, mankind thus shared with the spenta divinities the great common purpose of gradually overcoming evil and restoring the world to its original perfect state. The glorious moment when this will be achieved is called 'Frasho-kereti' (Pahlavi Frashegird'), a term which probably means 'Healing' or 'Renovation'. Therewith history will cease, for the third time, that of 'Separation' (Pahlavi 'Wizarishn') will be ushered in. This is the time when good will be separated again from evil; and since evil will then be utterly destroyed, the period of Separation is eternal, and in it Ahura Mazda and all the Yazatas and men and women will live together for ever in perfect, untroubled goodness and peace.

In thus postulating not only a beginning but also an end to human history, Zoroaster made a profound break with earlier ideas, according to which the process of life, once started, was expected to continue forever, if men and gods both bore their part. The old concept of co-operation between divinity and worshipper, as necessary in order to maintain the world according to asha, persists in his teachings; but he gave this co-operation new significance by seeing it, not as directed simply to preserving the world as it is, but to reaching an ultimate goal of restored perfection. Moreover, his revelation lent man new dignity, for according to it he was created to be God's ally, working with him to achieve the victory over evil which is longed for by both.

The doctrine of the Three Times—Creation, Mixture, Separation—makes history in a sense cyclical, with the getig world restored in the third time to the perfection it possessed in the first one. Meanwhile all the sorrows and strivings of the present time of Mixture are part of the battle against Angra Mainyu. Zoroaster thus not only saw a noble purpose for humanity, but also offered men a reasoned explanation for what they have to endure in this life, seeing this as affliction brought on them by the Hostile Spirit, and not imputing to the will of an all-powerful Creator the sufferings of his creatures here below.

Death and the Hereafter

The most general human affliction is death; and death forces individual souls, throughout the time of Mixture, to leave the getig world and return for a while to the deficient menog state. As each spirit departs, according to Zoroaster, it is judged on what it has done in this life to aid the cause of goodness. He taught that women as well as men, servants as well as masters, may hope to attain Paradise, for the physical barrier of pagan days, the 'Bridge of the Separator', becomes in his revelation a place of moral judgment, where each soul must depend, not on power or wealth of offerings in the life it has left behind, but on its own ethical achievements. Here Mithra presides over the tribunal, flanked by Sraosha and by Rashnu, who holds the scales of justice. In these are weighed the soul's thoughts, words and deeds, the good on one side, the bad on the other. If the good are heavier, the soul is judged worthy of Paradise; and it is led by a beautiful maiden, the personification of its own conscience ('daena') across the broad bridge and up on high. If the scales sink on the bad side, the bridge contracts to the width of a blade-edge, and a horrid hag, meeting the soul as it tries to cross, seizes it in her arms and plunges with it down to hell, 'the dwelling-place of Worst Purpose' (Y 32.13), where the wicked endure a 'long age of misery, of darkness, ill food and the crying of woe' (Y 31.20). The concept of hell, a place of torment presided over by Angra Mainyu, seems to be Zoroaster's own, shaped by his deep sense of the need for justice. Those few souls 'whose false (things) and what are just balance' (Y 33.1) go to the 'Place of the Mixed Ones', Misvan Gatu, where, as in the old underworld kingdom of the dead, they lead a grey existence, lacking both joy and sorrow.

Even for souls in Paradise bliss is not perfect during this time of Mixture, for complete happiness can come again only at Frashegird. The pagan Iranians had presumably held, like the Vedic Indians, that soon after each blessed soul reached Paradise it was reunited with its resurrected body, to live again a happy life of full sensation; but Zoroaster taught that the blessed must wait for this culmination till Frashegird and the 'future body' (Pahlavi 'tan i pasen'), when the earth will give up the bones of the dead (Y 30.7). This general resurrection will be followed by the Last Judgment, which will divide all the righteous from the wicked, both those who have lived until that time and those who have been judged already. Airyaman, the Yazata of friendship and healing, together with Atar, Fire, will melt all the metal in the mountains, and this will flow in a glowing river over the earth. All mankind must pass through this river, and, as it is said in a Pahlavi text, 'for him who is righteous it will seem like warm milk, and for him who is wicked, it will seem as if he is walking in the flesh through molten metaP (GBd XXXIV. 18–19). In this great apocalyptic vision Zoroaster perhaps fused, unconsciously, tales of volcanic eruptions and streams of burning lava with his own experience of Iranian ordeals by molten metal; and according to his stern original teaching, strict justice will prevail then, as at each individual judgment on earth by a fiery ordeal. So at this last ordeal of all the wicked will suffer a second death, and will perish off the face of the earth. The Daevas and legions of darkness will already have been annihilated in a last great battle with the Yazatas; and the river of metal will flow down into hell, slaying Angra Mainyu and burning up the last vestige of wickedness in the universe.

Ahura Mazda and the six Amesha Spentas will then solemnize a last, spiritual yasna, offering up the last sacrifice (after which death will be no more), and making a preparation of the mystical 'white haoma', which will confer immortality on the resurrected bodies of all the blessed, who will partake of it. Thereafter men will become like the Immortals themselves, of one thought, word and deed, unaging, free from sickness, without corruption, forever joyful in the kingdom of God upon earth. For it is in this familiar and beloved world, restored to its original perfection, that, according to Zoroaster, eternity will be passed in bliss, and not in a remote insubstantial Paradise. So the time of Separation is a renewal of the time of Creation, except that no return is prophesied to the original uniqueness of living things. Mountain and valley will give place once more to level plain; but whereas in the beginning there was one plant, one animal, one man, the rich variety and number that have since issued from these will remain forever. Similarly the many divinities who were brought into being by Ahura Mazda will continue to have their separate existences. There is no prophecy of their re-absorption into the Godhead. As a Pahlavi text puts it, after Frashegird 'Ohrmazd and the Amahraspands and all Yazads and men will be together. . . ; every place will resemble a garden in spring, in which there are all kinds of trees and flowers . . . and it will be entirely the creation of Ohrmazd' (Pahl. Riv.Dd. XLVIII, 99, 100, 107).

Zoroaster was thus the first to teach the doctrines of an individual judgment, Heaven and Hell, the future resurrection of the body, the general Last Judgment, and life everlasting for the reunited soul and body. These doctrines were to become familiar articles of faith to much of mankind, through borrowings by Judaism, Christianity and Islam; yet it is in Zoroastrianism itself that they have their fullest logical coherence, since Zoroaster insisted both on the goodness of the material creation, and hence of the physical body, and on the unwavering impartiality of divine justice. According to him, salvation for the individual depended on the sum of his thoughts, words and deeds, and there could be no intervention, whether compassionate or capricious, by any divine Being to alter this. With such a doctrine, belief in the Day of Judgment had its full awful significance, with each man having to bear the responsibility for the fate of his own soul, as well as sharing in responsibility for the fate of the world. Zoroaster's gospel was thus a noble and strenuous one, which called for both courage and resolution on the part of those willing to receive it.

10 Reform, Orthodox, and Conservative Judaisms, Zionism

Jacob Neusner

The urgent question that was deemed by many Jews to require an answer shifted in modern times, the eighteenth century to the present. The question "Why is Israel subordinated to the gentiles?" had found its answer in Israel's sanctification and God's judgment for Israel's failures. With the political changes represented by the emancipation of the Jews and their gaining citizenship, a new urgent question arose: How is it possible to be both an Israelite and something else—a French, German, British, or American citizen, for example?

Reform Judaism responded and fixed the pattern of all modern Judaism. It redefined "Israel" to stand for a religious community with a universal mission. It affirmed changes in the way of life and worldview of the received, rabbinic system. These were meant to affirm that the Israelite could integrate and be in addition loyal to France, Britain, Germany, or the U.S.A. Practices that separated the Israelite from the rest of humanity—dietary laws, for example—were to be dropped. Responding to the advent of Reform Judaism, Orthodox Judaism in Germany and the other Western countries rejected the changes Reform made. But Orthodoxy in its integrationist model held that while Judaism endured unchanging, the Israelite should combine study of the Torah with study of secular sciences. So one could both practice Judaism and integrate one's life within the national culture. Conservative Judaism mediated between the two positions, affirming that tradition could change, but only in accord with the historical processes of Judaism over the centuries.

A political, not a religious system, Zionism did not trust the promise of emancipation. It rejected the hope that the Jews could ever be secure in the gentile nations and proposed the creation of a Jewish state in Palestine, where Jews in security could be Jewish and nothing else, for example, speaking Hebrew as their everyday language.

Competition in Defining Judaism in Modern Times

Basic to Judaism from the nineteenth century to the present day has been the division, into distinct movements, of the received Rabbinic Judaism. Of these in the English-speaking world, in the U.S.A., Canada, Britain, and elsewhere, three sizable denominations or movements predominate: Orthodox, Reform, and Conservative Judaism. In North America, approximately half of all Jews affiliated with synagogues identify as Reform, about a third are Conservative, and most of the rest are Orthodox.

To the same circle of new versions of Scripture and tradition belongs Zionism, a political movement aimed at restoring the Jewish people to the Land of Israel, founding the Jewish state, and realizing the nationalism of the Jewish people. Zionism came to fruition in the middle of the twentieth century in the creation of the State of Israel in 1948. These four systems—three religious and Judaic, one political and Jewish—competed productively and continue to thrive. All form mass movements, not just celebrations of particular theologians and their doctrines. All have endured for more than a century.

Why Did the Rabbinic System Meet Competition?

In the late eighteenth and nineteenth centuries, sweeping changes made urgent political issues that formerly had drawn slight attention. The Jews had formerly constituted a distinct group. They segregated themselves in culture and ethnic identity and in politics as well. Now in the West they were expected—and aspired—to integrate and form part of an undifferentiated mass of citizens, all of them equal before the law. Jews wanted civil rights and accepted civil obligations of citizenship.

The received Judaism did not address that circumstance. It fostered the self-segregation of the Jews as Holy Israel, their separation from the gentiles in politics and culture, not only in religion. The received system rested on the political premise that God's law formed God's people and governed the Jews. And that sufficed to identify what was meant by "Israel," "a people that dwells apart," in the language of Scripture. The received system did not answer the question, "How can Jews both practice Judaism and also participate in secular society and culture?" None aspired to a dual role. The two political premises—the one of the nation-state, the other of the Torah—scarcely permitted reconciliation.

The consequent Judaic systems, Reform Judaism, a Westernized Orthodoxy that is called integrationist Orthodox Judaism, positive Historical Judaism (in the U.S.A. "Conservative Judaism"), each addressed issues of politics and culture that were regarded as acute and not merely chronic. Reform favored total integration of the Jews into Western culture. Integrationist Orthodoxy concurred but reaffirmed the separateness of Israel, the Holy People, in religious matters. Positive Historical Judaism / Conservative Judaism took the middle position.

The three systems met the political challenge and mediated the cultural ones. All repudiated Judaic self-segregation. Each maintained that Jews could both practice Judaism and serve as good citizens of the nation and participants in the culture of the countries where they found themselves. All alleged that they formed the natural next step in the unfolding of "the tradition," meaning the Judaic system of the dual Torah. Where politics precipitated a new problem, the Judaic systems that emerged responded. In the Russian Empire before Communism (1917), in Russian Poland, White Russia, and Ukraine, Reform, integrationist Orthodox, and Conservative Judaism never registered; the received system continued to answer the urgent questions of the age. No political revolution required change.

Reform Judaism

Reform Judaism (a.k.a. liberal or progressive Judaism) responded to the new questions Jews faced in political emancipation. These changes, particularly in western Europe and the U.S.A., accorded to Jews the status of citizens like other citizens of the nations in which they lived. But they denied the Jews the status of a separate, holy people, living under its own laws and awaiting the Messiah to lead it back to the Holy Land at the end of history. Rather, Reform Judaism looked forward to a messianic age, when the social order would be perfected in justice and humanity, and defined for its "Israel" a mission to hasten the coming of the messianic age. Meanwhile Jews would integrate themselves into the common cultures of the nations where they lived.

Reform Judaism insisted that change in the religion, Judaism, in response to new challenges represented a valid continuation of that religion's long-term capacity to evolve. Reform Judaism denied that any version of the Torah enjoyed eternal validity. All responded to the changes that history brought. Accordingly, Jews should adopt the politics and culture of the countries where they lived, preserving differences of only a religious character, with religion narrowly construed.

Changes in Synagogue Worship

Reform Judaism finds its beginnings to the nineteenth century in changes, called reforms and regarded as the antecedents of Reform, in trivial aspects of public worship in the synagogue (Petuchowski 1971). The motive for these changes derived from the simple fact that many Jews rejected the received theological system and its liturgical expression. People were defecting from the synagogue. Since it was then taken for granted that there was no secular option, giving up the faith meant surrendering all ties to the group. (Secular Jewish systems, Jewish but not religious, typified by Zionism, emerged only at the beginning of the twentieth century.) The beginning of change addressed two issues at one time: (1) Making the synagogue more attractive so that (2) defectors would return, and others would not leave. The reform of Judaism in its manifestation in synagogue worship—the cutting edge of the faith—therefore took cognizance of something that had already taken place. And for a sizable sector of Jewry that was the loss for the received system—way of life, worldview, addressed to a defined Israel—of its standing as self-evident truth.

To begin with, the issue involved not politics but merely justification for changing anything at all. The reformers maintained that change was all right because historical precedent proved that change was all right. But change long had defined the constant in the ongoing life of the received Judaism. The normative Judaism endured, never intact but always unimpaired because of its power to absorb and make its own the diverse happenings of culture and society. That fact is established in Chapter 9. Implacable opposition to change represented a change. That was not the real issue. The integration of Israel among the gentiles was.

Reform Judaism affirmed integration and made important changes in the law and theology of Judaism to accommodate it. It did this when the Reform rabbis in the U.S.A. adopted the Pittsburgh Platform of 1885, which stated the Reform system in a clear way (see Box 10.1). The Platform takes up each component of the Reform system in turn. Who is Israel? What is its way of life? How does it account for its existence as a distinct, and distinctive, group?

Israel once was a nation ("during its national life") but today is not a nation. It once had a set of laws that regulate diet, clothing, and the like. These no longer apply, because Israel now is not what it was then. Israel forms an integral part of Western civilization. The reason to persist as a distinctive group was that the group has its work to do, a mission—to serve as a light to the nations. That meant, namely, to realize the messianic hope for the establishment of a kingdom of truth, justice, and peace. For that purpose Israel no longer constitutes a nation. It now forms a religious community.

What that means is that individual Jews do live as citizens in other nations. Difference is acceptable at the level of religion, not nationality, a position that accords fully with the definition of citizenship of the Western democracies. The Reform worldview then lays heavy emphasis on an as-yet-unrealized, but coming, perfect age. Its way of life admits to no important traits that distinguish Jews from others, since morality, in the nature of things, forms a universal category, applicable in the same way to everyone. The theory of Israel then forms the heart of matters, and what we learn is that Israel constitutes a "we," that is, that the Jews

BOX 10.1 THE PITTSBURGH PLATFORM OF REFORM JUDAISM

For Reform Judaism in the nineteenth century, the full and authoritative statement of the system—its worldview, with profound implications on its way of life, and its theory of who is Israel—came to expression in America, in an assembly in Pittsburgh in 1885 of Reform rabbis. At that meeting of the Central Conference of American Rabbis, the Reform Judaism of the age, by now nearly a century old, took up the issues that divided the Judaism and made an authoritative statement on them, one that most Reform Jews could accept. What is important is its formulation of the issue of Israel as political circumstances defined it. Critical to normative Judaism was its view of Israel as God's people, a supernatural polity, living out its social existence under God's Torah. The way of life, one of sanctification, and the worldview, one of persistent reference to the Torah for rules of conduct, on the one side, and of the explanation of conduct, on the other, began in the basic conception of who is Israel. Here too we find emphasis on who is Israel, with that doctrine exposing for all to see the foundations of the way of life and worldview that these rabbis had formed for the Israel they conceived:

> We recognize in the Mosaic legislation a system of training the Jewish people for its mission during its national life in Palestine, and today we accept as binding only its moral laws and maintain only such ceremonies as elevate and sanctify our lives, but reject all such as are not adapted to the views and habits of modern civilization . . . We hold that all such Mosaic and rabbinical laws as regular diet, priestly purity, and dress originated in ages and under the influence of ideas entirely foreign to our present mental and spiritual state . . . Their observance in our days is apt rather to obstruct than to further modern spiritual elevation . . . We recognize in the modern era of universal culture of heart and intellect the approaching of the realization of Israel's great messianic hope for the establishment of the kingdom of truth, justice, and peace among all men. We consider ourselves no longer a nation but a religious community and therefore expect neither a return to Palestine nor a sacrificial worship under the sons of Aaron nor the restoration of any of the laws concerning the Jewish state . . .

continue to form a group that, by its own indicators, holds together and constitutes a cogent social entity. All this, in a simple statement of a handful of rabbis, forms a full and encompassing Judaism, one that, to its communicants, presented truth of a self-evident order.

Reform Judaism would evolve beyond the Pittsburgh Platform in the mid-twentieth century, affirming the peoplehood of Israel and renewing received rites. When in 1897 Zionism made its appearance, Reform Judaism rejected it: "Germany is our promised land, and Berlin is our Jerusalem." But by the later 1930s,

Reform Rabbis affirmed Zionism. By the twenty-first century, its principles had defined the norm for all communities of Judaism outside the Orthodox framework. It was and remains the most successful Judaic system of modernity. One cannot help admiring the nineteenth-century framers of Reform Judaism for their optimism and their adaptability, their affirmation of progress and their invention of a mission of Israel to help God perfect creation.

But the hopeful version of Reform Judaism would meet its challenge in the Holocaust, and Reform Judaism from World War II onward parted company from its classical formulation in Pittsburgh. Today, Reform Judaism makes provision for religious practices that differentiate Jews from gentiles. It stresses Jewish peoplehood, the ethnic side to things that the founding generations of Reform Judaism relinquished.

Integrationist Orthodox Judaism

The broad category, Orthodox Judaism, requires definition and differentiation. The point of distinction is attitude toward gentile culture. "Integrationist Orthodoxy" differs from "self-segregationist Orthodox."

By "integrationist Orthodox Judaism" in the context of modernizing Judaic systems is meant a very particular approach. It is one that affirms the divine revelation and eternal authority of the Torah, oral and written, *but* that favors the integration of the Jews ("holy Israel") into the national life of the countries of their birth. In cultural terms, this meant study of the Torah and also study of philosophy. I call it "integrationist" for its cultural policy. It also is known as "modern Orthodoxy" or "Western Orthodoxy" or "neo-Orthodoxy."

Other Orthodox communities of Judaism—and they are diverse and many—in common favor the segregation of the holy Israel from other people in the countries where they live, including the State of Israel. Indicators such as clothing, language, above all, education differentiate integrationist from self-segregationist Judaisms. For example, integrationist Orthodoxy holds that secular studies are legitimate, indeed essential, so that Yeshiva University in the U.S.A. and Bar Ilan University in the State of Israel, both successful institutions of integrationist Orthodoxy, offer full academic programs in all sciences and humanities. In them, Judaic religious sciences take cognizance of the challenges of reason and history.

Self-segregated communities of Judaism bear a variety of names, such as traditional, authentic, Haredi (a Hebrew word referring to those that tremble before the Lord), and the like. Self-segregationist Orthodox centers of learning, called *yeshivot*, teach only the sacred sciences, for instance the Talmud and its commentaries. One indicator of the difference between integrationist- and self-segregationist Orthodox Judaisms is the matter of language. The self-segregationists reject the use of Hebrew and preserve Yiddish as the everyday language of the community. Integrationist Orthodoxy in the State of Israel is Hebrew-speaking, like other Israelis. A wide variety of communities of Orthodox Judaism fall into the category of self-segregation. Some are Hasidic, such as we met in Chapter 9, some reject Hasidism and adhere to the classical tradition in all its depth of reason and rationality. But all self-segregated communities of Judaism concur that Holy Israel is not to mix with the gentiles.

Integrationist Jews kept the law of the Torah, for example as it dictated food choices and use of leisure time (to speak of the Sabbath and festivals in secular terms). They sent their children to secular schools, in addition to or instead of solely Jewish ones, or in Jewish schools, they included in the curriculum subjects outside of the sciences of the Torah. In these ways, they marked themselves as integrationist. For the notion that science or German or Latin or philosophy deserved serious study in the nineteenth century struck as wrong those for whom the received system remained self-evidently right. Those Jews did not send their children to gentile schools, and in Jewish schools did not include in the curriculum other than Torah study.

Exactly where and when did integrationist Orthodox Judaism come into being? It was in Germany, in the middle of the nineteenth century, a generation after Reform got going in the same country. Integrationist Orthodoxy responded to the advent of Reform Judaism, which defined the issues of debate. The issues addressed by all parties concerned change and history. The reformers held that Judaism could legitimately change. Judaism was a product of history. The integrationist Orthodox opponents (not to mention the self-segregationist communities of Judaism) denied that Judaism could change. They insisted that Judaism derived from God's will at Sinai and was eternal and supernatural, not historical and man-made. In these two convictions, of course, the integrationist Orthodox recapitulated the convictions of the received system and no one in the self-segregationist Orthodox world would take exception to this position.

Accordingly, the integrationist Orthodox Judaism dealt with the same urgent questions as did Reform Judaism, questions raised by political emancipation. But it gave different answers to them, even though both Reform and integrationist Orthodoxy set forth equally reasoned, coherent theological answers to questions of history and ambient culture. That Orthodoxy maintained the worldview of the received dual Torah, constantly citing its sayings and adhering with only trivial variations to the bulk of its norms for the everyday life. At the same time, integrationist Orthodoxy held, and today holds, that Jews adhering to the dual Torah may wear clothing similar to that which non-Jews wear. The sole exceptions were religious duties not to mix flax and wool (vegetable and animal products woven into cloth), obligatory by the law of the Torah (Lev. 19:19 and Deut. 22:9–11) and to wear show-fringes. They live within a common economy and do not practice distinctively Jewish professions. Many shave and do not grow beards. They take up a life not readily distinguished in important characteristics from the life lived by ordinary people in general.

So for integrationist Orthodoxy, a portion of an Israelite's life may prove secular. The Torah does not dictate and so sanctify all of life's details under all circumstances. The difference between integrationist Orthodoxy and the normative, received system, such as persisted in self-segregationist Judaic circles, therefore comes to expression in social policy: Integration, however circumscribed, versus the total separation of the Holy People from the nations among whom they lived.

Integrationist Judaism thus faced critics in two directions, inside and outside. But it was Reform that precipitated the organization of the integrationist communities of Judaism. Just as the reformers justified change, the integrationist Orthodox theologians denied that change was ever possible. As Walter Wurzburger wrote, "Orthodoxy looks upon attempts to adjust Judaism to the 'spirit of the time' as utterly incompatible with the entire thrust of normative Judaism which holds that the revealed will of God rather than the values of any given age are the ultimate standard" (Wurzburger 1971). To begin with the issue important to the reformers, the value of what was called "emancipation," meaning, the provision to Jews of civil rights, defined the debate. If the Reform made minor changes in liturgy and its conduct, the Orthodox rejected even those that, under other circumstances, might have found acceptance.

Saying prayers in the vernacular, for example, provoked strong opposition. But everyone knew that some of the prayers were said in Aramaic, the vernacular of the ancient Near East. The Orthodox thought that these changes, not reforms at all, represented only the first step of a process leading Jews out of the Judaic world altogether, so, as Walter Wurzburger says, "The slightest tampering with tradition was condemned."

Conservative Judaism

We treat the German Historical School and Canadian and U.S. Conservative Judaism as a single Judaism, because they share a single viewpoint: Moderation in making change, accommodation between "the tradition" and the requirements of modern life, above all, adaptation to circumstance—all validated by historical research and precedent. The emphasis on historical research in settling theological debates clearly explains the name of the group of German professors who organized the system.

Arguing that its positions represent matters of historical fact rather than theological conviction, the Historical School and Conservative Judaism maintained an essentially secular position. It was that "positive historical scholarship" would prove capable, on the basis of historical facts, of purifying and clarifying the faith, joined to far stricter observance of the law than the reformers required. Questions of theology found their answers in history. Representing in practice a middle position, between integrationist Orthodoxy and Reform, it was in fact an extreme proposition, since it abdicated the throne of theology altogether and established a regency of secular learning. Reform Judaism appealed in the end to systematic religious thinking, while Conservative Judaism accorded an at-best-perfunctory hearing to theological argument and system-building.

The fundamental premise of the Conservatives' emphasis on history rested on the conviction that history and verifiable fact demonstrated the truth or falsity of theological propositions. We should look in vain in all of the prior writings of Judaic systems for precedent for that insistence on critical fact, self-evident to the nineteenth- and twentieth-century system-builders. The appeal to historical facts was meant to lay upon firm, factual foundations whatever change was to take place. In finding precedent for change, the Conservatives sought reassurance that some change—if not a great deal of change—would not endanger the enduring faith they wished to preserve. But there was a second factor. The laws and lessons of history would then settle questions of public policy near at hand.

Both in Germany in the middle of the nineteenth century and in America at the end of the nineteenth century, the emphasis throughout lay on "knowledge and practice of historical Judaism as ordained in the law of Moses expounded by the prophets and sages in Israel in Biblical and Talmudic writings," so the articles of Incorporation of the Jewish Theological Seminary of America Association stated in 1887. Calling themselves "traditionalists" rather than "Orthodox," the conservative adherents accepted for most Judaic subjects the principles of modern critical scholarship. Conservative Judaism therefore exhibited traits that linked it to Reform but also to Orthodoxy, a movement very much in the middle. Precisely how the Historical School related to the other systems of its day—the mid- and later nineteenth century requires attention to that scholarship that, apologists insisted, marked the Historical School off from Orthodoxy.

Not surprisingly, Conservative Judaism derived from professors and relied for its institutions upon academic authority. In the U.S.A., the head of the organization of Conservative Judaism is the academic chancellor of the Jewish Theological Seminary of America. Maintaining the law and theology of the received Judaism alongside integrationist Orthodoxy, the Historical School, a group of nineteenth-century German scholars, and Conservative Judaism, a twentieth-century mass movement of Judaism in America and Canada, like Reform Judaism, affirmed through secular historical fact the religious legitimacy of change.

The Historical School began among German Jewish theologians who advocated change but found Reform extreme. They parted company with Reform on some specific issues of practice and doctrine, observance of the dietary laws and belief in the coming of the Messiah for example. But they also found the ambient Orthodoxy immobile. Conservative Judaism in America in the twentieth century carried forward this same centrist position and turned a viewpoint of intellectuals into a way of life, worldview, addressed to an Israel. The Historical School, accordingly, shaped the worldview, and Conservative Judaism later on brought that view into full realization as a way of life characteristic of a large group of Jews, nearly half of all American Jews in the middle of the twentieth century, but only a third of American Jewry by the early twenty-first century.

The Historical School in Germany and Conservative Judaism in America affirmed a far broader part of the received way of life than Reform, while rejecting a much larger part than did Orthodoxy of the worldview of the received system. The Historical School concurred with the reformers concerning the norm-setting power of history (Hertzberg 1971). That meant that questions of theology and law could be referred to historians, who would settle matters by appeal to historical precedent. Thus, for example, if one could show that a given law was not practiced prior to a specified period of time, that law could be set aside or modified. If it could be shown, by contrast, that that law goes "way back," then it was treated as sacrosanct. The reformers had held that change was permissible and claimed that historical scholarship would show what change was acceptable and what was not. Concurring in principle, the proponents of the Historical School differed in matters of detail.

Toward the end of the nineteenth century, rabbis of this same centrist persuasion in the U.S.A. organized the Jewish Theological Seminary of America, in 1886–7, and from that rabbinical school, the Conservative Movement developed. The order of the formation of the several Judaisms of the nineteenth century therefore is, first, Reform, then Orthodoxy, finally, Conservatism—the two extremes, then the middle. Reform defined the tasks of the next two Judaisms to come into being. Orthodoxy framed the clearer of the two positions in reaction to Reform, but, in intellectual terms, the Historical School in Germany met the issues of Reform in a more direct way.

The stress of the Historical School in Europe and Conservative Judaism in America lay on two matters. First, critical scholarship, such as yielded the secular account of the history of Judaism given in Chapter 8, was assigned the task of discovering those facts of which the faith would be composed. Second, Conservative Judaism emphasized the practical observance of the rules of the received Judaism. A fissure opened, then, between scholarship and belief and practice. A professedly free approach to the study of the Torah, specifically through what was called "critical scholarship," would yield an accurate account of the essentials of the faith. But what if that did not emerge? Then the scholars and lay people alike would keep and practice nearly the whole of the tradition just as the Orthodox did.

The ambivalence of Conservative Judaism, speaking in part for intellectuals deeply loyal to the received way of life, but profoundly dubious of the inherited worldview, came to full expression in the odd slogan of its intellectuals and scholars: "Eat kosher and think *traif*." "Traif" refers to meat that is not acceptable under Judaic law, and the slogan announced a religion of orthopraxy: Do the right thing and it doesn't matter what you believe. That statement meant people should keep the rules of the holy way of life but ignore the convictions that made sense of them. Orthopraxy is the word that refers to correct action and unfettered belief, as against Orthodoxy, right action, and right doctrine. Some would then classify Conservative Judaism in America as an orthoprax Judaism defined through works, not doctrine. Some of its leading voices even denied Judaism set forth doctrine at all; this is called "the dogma of dogmaless Judaism."

What separated Conservative Judaism from Reform was the matter of observance. Fundamental loyalty to the received way of life in the nineteenth and earlier twentieth centuries distinguished the Historical School in Germany and Conservative Judaism in America from Reform Judaism in both countries. When considering the continued validity of a traditional religious practice, the Reform asked "Why?", the Conservatives, "Why not?" The Orthodox, of course, would ask no questions to begin with. The fundamental principle, that the worldview of the Judaism under construction would rest upon (mere) historical facts, came from Reform Judaism. Orthodoxy could never have concurred. The contrast to the powerful faith despite the world, exhibited by integrationist Orthodoxy's stress on the utter facticity of the Torah, presents in a clear light the positivism of the Conservatives, who, indeed, adopted the name "the *positive* Historical School."

But orthopraxy did not yield a stable social order. In America, a pattern developed in which essentially nonobservant congregations of Jews called upon rabbis whom they expected to be observant of the rules of the religion. As a result, many of the intellectual problems that occupied public debate concerned rabbis more than lay people, since the rabbis bore responsibility—so the community maintained—for not only teaching the faith but, on their own, embodying it. An observer described this Judaism as "Orthodox rabbis serving Conservative synagogues made up of Reform Jews."

How do the Reform, integrationist Orthodox, and Conservative systems then compare? Reform identified its Judaism as the linear and incremental next step in the unfolding of the Torah. The Historical School and Conservative Judaism later on regarded its Judaism as the reversion to the authentic Judaism that in time had been lost. Change was legitimate, as the Reform said, but only that kind of change that restored things to the condition of the original and correct Judaism. That position formed a powerful apologetic, because it addressed the Orthodox view that Orthodoxy constituted the linear and incremental outgrowth of "the Torah" or "the tradition," hence, the sole legitimate Judaism. It also addressed the Reform view that change was all right. Conservative Judaism established a firm criterion for what change was all right: The kind that was, really, no change at all. For the premise of the Conservative position was that things should become the way they had always been.

Here we revert to the strikingly secular character of the Reform and Conservative systems: Their insistence that religious belief could be established upon a foundation of historical fact. The category of faith, belief in transcendent things, matters not seen or tangible but nonetheless deeply felt and vigorously affirmed—these traits of religiosity hardly played a role. Rather, fact, ascertained by secular media of learning, would define truth. And truth corresponded to here-and-now reality: How things were. Scholarship would tell how things had always been and dictate those changes that would restore the correct way of life, the true worldview, for the Israel composed of pretty much all the Jews—the center. Historical research therefore provided a powerful apologetic against both sides. Like Orthodoxy, Conservative Judaism defined itself as Judaism, pure and simple. But it did claim to mark the natural next step in the slow evolution of "the tradition," an evolution within the lines and rules set forth by "the tradition" itself.

Zionism

Another response to the question of political emancipation, Zionism, founded in Basel, Switzerland, in 1897, constituted the Jews' nationalist movement. Its "Israel" was a nation ("the Jewish people") in quest of a state. It was a secular political movement utilizing the story of Scripture concerning the restoration of Israel, defined as "a People, One People," to the Land of Israel in the end of days. It achieved its goal in the creation of the State of Israel in 1948.

Zionism dismissed the questions answered by Reform and integrationist Orthodox and Conservative Judaisms. Reform Judaism had begun in the premise that the Jews could find a place for themselves in the European nation-states, if they adapted themselves to the duties of shared humanity and a common politics. Integrationist Orthodoxy addressed the same issue. But political anti-Semitism at the end of the nineteenth century—the organization of political parties on a platform of exclusion and repression of the Jews in the European nations—called into question the premises of the Reform and integrationist Orthodox theologians.

It became clear that the Jews, now resident in Europe for more than fifteen centuries, could not hope for the integration they had anticipated at the beginning of the century and for which they had prepared themselves. The urgent question became, "What is to be done to solve what the gentile Europeans called 'the Jewish question'?" Foreseeing exterminationist anti-Semitism, Zionism thus responded to a political crisis, the failure, by the end of the nineteenth century, of emancipation, meaning the promises of political improvement in the Jews' status and condition.

Once more, history defined the arena of contention. To formulate its worldview, Zionism, like Reform Judaism, invented a usable past. Zionism, furthermore, called to the Jews to emancipate themselves by facing the fact that gentiles hated Jews. As to its way of life, Zionism defined itself as the political movement aimed at founding a Jewish state where Jews could free themselves of anti-Semitism and build their own destiny. Activities to secure political support and also persuade the Jewish communities of the need to found a Jewish state formed the way of life.

The Zionist system corresponds in its components to those of Reform and integrationist Orthodoxy: A definition of Israel, a worldview, a way of life (see Box 10.2). Let us therefore turn to the analysis of Zionism viewed within the categories we have used to describe any Judaic system.

For one thing, Zionism enunciated a powerful and original doctrine of Israel. Jews form a people, one people, and should build a nation-state. Given Jews' secular diversity, people could more easily concede the supernatural reading of Judaic existence than the national construction given to it. For, scattered across the European countries as well as in the Muslim world, Jews did not speak a common language, follow a single way of life, or adhere in common to a single code of belief and behavior. What made them a people, one people, and further validated their claim and right to a state, a nation, of their own, constituted the central theme

BOX 10.2 ZIONISM AND JUDAISM: COMPETING WORLDVIEWS

The Zionist worldview explicitly competed with the religious one. The formidable statement of Jacob Klatzkin (1882–1948) provides the solid basis for comparison:

In the past there have been two criteria of Judaism: The criterion of religion, according to which Judaism is a system of positive and negative commandments, and the criterion of the spirit, which saw Judaism as a complex of ideas, like monotheism, Messianism, absolute justice, etc. According to both these criteria, therefore, Judaism rests on a subjective basis, on the acceptance of a creed . . . a religious denomination . . . or a community of individuals who share in a *Weltanschauung* . . . In opposition to these two criteria, which make of Judaism a matter of creed, a third has now arisen, the criterion of a consistent nationalism. According to it, Judaism rests on an objective basis: To be a Jew means the acceptance of neither a religious nor an ethical creed. We are neither a denomination nor a school of thought, but members of one family, bearers of a common history . . . The national definition too requires an act of will. It defines our nationalism by two criteria: Partnership in the past and the conscious desire to continue such partnership in the future. There are, therefore, two bases for Jewish nationalism—the compulsion of history and a will expressed in that history.

(Hertzberg 1971)

of the Zionist worldview. No facts of perceived society validated that view. In no way, except for a common fate, did Jews form a people, one people. True, in Judaic systems they commonly did. But the received system and its continuators in Reform and integrationist Orthodox Judaisms imputed to Israel, the Jewish people, a supernatural status, a mission, a calling, a purpose. Zionism did not: A people, one people—that is all.

What about its worldview? Zionist theory sought roots for its principal ideas in the documents of the received Judaism, Scripture for example. Zionist theory had the task of explaining how the Jews formed a people, one people, and in the study of "Jewish history," read as a single, continuous and unitary story, Zionist theory solved that problem. The Jews all came from some one place, traveled together, and were going back to that same one place: One people. Zionist theory therefore derived strength from the study of history, much as had Reform Judaism in its quest to validate change, and in time generated a great renaissance of Judaic studies as the scholarly community of the nascent Jewish state took up the task at hand.

The sort of history that emerged took the form of factual and descriptive narrative. But its selection of facts, its recognition of problems requiring explanation, its choice of what mattered and what did not—all of these definitive questions found answers in the larger program of nationalist ideology. The form was secular and descriptive, but the substance ideological.

At the same time, Zionist theory explicitly rejected the precedent formed by the Torah, selecting as its history not the history of the faith, of the Torah, but the history of the nation, Israel construed as a secular entity. So we find a distinctive worldview that explains a very particular way of life and defines for itself that Israel to which it wishes to speak.

Like Reform Judaism, Zionism found more interesting the written component of the Torah than the Oral; Scripture outweighed the Talmud. And in its search for a usable past, it turned to documents formerly neglected or treated as not authoritative—for instance, the book of Maccabees, a Jewish dynasty that exhibited military prowess. Zionism went in search of heroes unlike those of the present, warriors, political figures, and others who might provide a model for the movement's future, and for the projected state beyond. So instead of rabbis or sages, Zionism chose figures such as David or Judah Maccabee or Samson—David the warrior king; Judah Maccabee, who had led the revolt against the Syrian Hellenists; Samson the powerful fighter.

These provided the appropriate heroes for a political Zionism. The secular system thus proposed to redefine Jewish consciousness, to turn storekeepers into soldiers, lawyers into farmers, corner grocers into builders and administrators of great institutions of state and government. The Rabbinic Judaism had treated David as a rabbi. The Zionist system saw David as a hero in a more worldly sense: A courageous nation-builder.

In its eagerness to appropriate a usable past, Zionism and Israeli nationalism, its successor, dug in the sand to find a deed to the Land. That stress in archaeology on Jewish links to the past extended to even proofs for the biblical record to which, in claiming the Land of Israel, Zionism pointed. So in pre-state times and after the creation of the State of Israel in 1948, Zionist scholars and institutions devoted great effort to digging up the ancient monuments of the Land of Israel, finding in archaeological work the link to the past that the people, one people, so desperately sought.

Archaeology uncovered the Jews' roots in the Land of Israel and became a principal instrument of national expression. Zionism was not alone, for contemporary believers in Scripture archaeology would prove the truths of the biblical narrative. It was not surprising, therefore, that in the Israeli War of Independence, 1948–9, and in later times as well, Israeli generals explained to the world that by following the biblical record of the nation in times past, they had found hidden roads, appropriate strategies—in all, the key to victory.

Why did Zionism succeed where nineteenth-century Reform Judaism gave way? Its advocates claimed that history validated its worldview, way of life, and definition of Israel. From the end of the nineteenth century, Zionism faced political reality and explained it and offered a program, inclusive of a worldview and a way of life, that worked. At the end of World War II, with millions murdered, as Zionism had predicted they would be, Zionism offered Jewry the sole meaningful explanation of how to endure. Zionism had led at least some Zionists to realize as early as 1940 what Hitler's Germany was going to do. At a meeting in December 1940, Berl Katznelson, an architect of Socialist Zionism in the Jewish community of Palestine before the creation of the State of Israel, announced that European Jewry was finished:

> The essence of Zionist awareness must be that what existed in Vienna will never return, what existed in Berlin will never return, nor in Prague, and what we had in Warsaw and Lodz is finished, and we must realize this! Why don't we understand that what Hitler has done, and this war is a kind of Rubicon, an outer limit, and what existed before will never exist again … And I declare that the fate of European Jewry is sealed.
>
> (Shapira 1974).

Zionism, in the person of Katznelson, even before the systematic mass murder got fully underway, grasped that, after World War II, Jews would not return to Europe, certainly not to those places in which they had flourished for 1,000 years, and Zionism offered the alternative: The building, outside of Europe, of the Jewish state. So Zionism took a position of prophecy and found its prophecy fulfilled. Its fundamental dogma about the character of the diaspora as exile found verification in the destruction of European Jewry. And Zionism's further claim to point the way forward proved to be Israel's salvation in the formation of the State of Israel on the other side of the Holocaust. So Katznelson maintained: "If Zionism wanted to be the future force of the Jewish people, it must prepare to solve the Jewish question in all its scope" (Shapira 1974: 290).

The secret of the power of Zionism lay in its power to make sense of the world and to propose a program to solve the problems of the age. That same power animated Reform, integrationist Orthodox, and Conservative Judaisms.

11

Christianity and the Divine

James Adair

In [God] we live and move and have our being.

(Epimenides, quoted in Acts 17:28)

In This Chapter

This chapter begins by discussing the contrast between the sacred and the profane in religion in general and in Christianity in particular. The sacred (or holy) plays a major role in Christianity, and the role of the sacred in several aspects of the Christian experience is surveyed.

Main Topics Covered

- Definition and distinction between the sacred and the profane
- Sacred time
- Sacred space
- Sacred symbols and artefacts
- Sacred interactions (i.e. interactions between God and humans)
- Sacred personages
- Sacred metatime (the time beyond time)

Sacred and Profane

Like most other world religions, Christianity recognizes a distinction between the world of ordinary experience and the divine realm. This difference is illustrated by a variety of word-pairs that are frequently employed: physical and metaphysical, human and divine, temporal and eternal, natural and supernatural, finite and infinite, imminent and transcendent, normal and paranormal, profane and sacred. At the root of this fundamental distinction, for Christians at least, is the belief in God. Almost all Christians would affirm their belief in God, but the Christian understanding of God varies considerably, depending on the individual person or group.

For many Christians, God is a discrete being of immense power (omnipotence) and knowledge (omniscience). In this view, God stands outside of creation and is separate from it. For some, God is intimately involved in the day to day operation of the universe. For others, God has set up the universe with physical laws (e.g. the laws of motion, the four fundamental forces, general and special relativity, quantum mechanics) and with a set of universal constants (e.g. Planck's constant, the mass of a resting electron or quark, the speed of light), which God has designed to bring about the world as we know it. In this view, God has designed the universe so well that intervention is rarely required. (While some Christians insist on continuing to use traditional masculine titles (e.g. Father, King, Lord) and pronouns when referring to God, most acknowledge that this practice is conventional rather than an accurate description of God as a male being. In this book, outside of direct quotations, references to God will avoid male pronouns such as "he," "him," "himself," etc. Instead, words such as "God" or even "Godself" will be used.)

Other Christians see God not as *a being* but as *being itself*, or as theologian Paul Tillich put it, *the Ground of being*. God is the source of all matter, life, and thought, but is not composed of these materials. God is not so much separate from creation as beneath it; the acts of creating and sustaining are essentially the same. One common way of describing God that is consistent with this approach is as *Wholly Other*.

The distinction between the sacred and the profane is discussed at length by Rudolf Otto, in *The Idea of the Holy*. Otto describes the Holy (or Sacred) as that mysterious something which makes rational humans tremble in fear when they encounter it. Paradoxically, not only does the Holy make rational humans tremble, and thus strive to avoid contact, it also fascinates and attracts them to itself. Otto describes the Holy as non-rational, or perhaps supra-rational, using human rationality as a standard of comparison. This description is interesting in the light of classical portraits of God, drawing on Greek philosophical traditions, as ultimate Reason (*logos*).

Christian scripture and tradition identify the sacred, present to a greater or lesser extent, in many different areas of human experience. Over the remainder of this chapter we will discuss the concepts of sacred time, sacred space, sacred symbols, sacred interactions, and sacred personages. We will conclude with a section on sacred meta-times, unique events that are beyond ordinary human history.

Sacred Time

The apostle Paul wrote, "Some judge one day to be better than another, while others judge all days to be alike" (Rom 14:5). Already in the first decades after Jesus, Christians debated the holiness of certain days of the week or year. Some early Christians apparently followed the Jewish custom of fasting on Monday and Thursday, but soon Wednesday and Friday became the days designated each week as days set aside for fasting.

Most of the earliest Christians were Jews, and they observed the Sabbath (sundown Friday to sundown Saturday) as a day of rest and worship. By the beginning of the second century, however, when Christianity had become largely Gentile, Sunday was the more common day of worship, in commemoration of Jesus' resurrection "on the first day of the week" (Matt 28:1).

The idea of a Christian liturgical year developed gradually, perhaps influenced in part by a similar practice in Judaism. The first event to be commemorated annually by many Christians was the Feast of the Resurrection, or Easter. Although Sunday was celebrated on a weekly basis in memorial of the resurrection, a larger, more elaborate annual celebration had developed by the second century. After the emperor Constantine legalized Christianity in 313 c.e., he called the first ecumenical council at Nicaea in 325, and one of the items on the agenda was a discussion of the proper day to celebrate Easter: some celebrated it always on Sunday, while others observed Easter on whatever day of the week the anniversary of Christ's resurrection happened to fall. Like the Jewish feast of Passover, whose celebration coincided with the crucifixion and resurrection, the date of Easter was based on a lunar calendar, so its exact date (on the solar calendar) varied considerably from year to year. The Christians meeting at Nicaea decided that Easter should always be celebrated on Sunday, so to the present day Easter is celebrated on the Sunday following the first full moon after the vernal equinox, which corresponds to the first month in the traditional Jewish calendar. Western (Roman Catholic and Protestant) and Eastern Christians have slightly different methods of calculating the date of Easter, so it is common for Catholic/Protestant Easter to fall on a different date than Orthodox Easter.

Other important events in the life of Jesus came to be celebrated on certain days of the year as well. No one knew the date of Jesus' birth, but the church eventually chose December 25 as the date to celebrate the birth of Christ (Christmas), probably because of that date's association with the Roman feast of Saturnalia, the birth of the new year. Jesus' baptism and the visit of the Magi came to be celebrated on January 6, popularly called Epiphany. Other important events on the Christian Calendar (or Liturgical

Calendar) include Pentecost (50 days after Easter), a celebration of the gift of the Holy Spirit as described in Acts 2, and the seasons of Advent (the four weeks prior to Christmas) and Lent (the seven weeks prior to Easter).

3–24 December 2006	Season of Advent
25 December 2006	Christmas Day
25 December 2006–5 January 2007	Season of Christmas
6 January 2007	Epiphany
6 January–20 February 2007	Season of Epiphany
21 February 2007	Ash Wednesday
21 February–7 April 2007	Season of Lent
8 April 2007	Easter
8 April–26 May 2007	Season of Easter
27 May 2007	Pentecost
27 May–1 December 2007	Season after Pentecost

Not all Christians observe the Liturgical Calendar, and Catholics, Protestants, and Orthodox who do follow it do so with some variations in tradition. For those who do observe it, the following table shows a typical year in the church. Note that the Christian Calendar begins with the season of Advent, which anticipates the coming of Christ.

Many other days are recognized on the Christian Calendar, such as Good Friday, Ascension Sunday, Trinity Sunday, and the Reign of Christ, also known as Christ the King Sunday. In some Christian traditions various days on the calendar are associated with Christian saints (e.g. Mary the Mother of God, St. Francis of Assisi, or St. Catherine of Siena), are set aside for special observances (e.g. rogation days), or are associated with local events or personalities of importance (e.g. the Virgin of Guadalupe in Mexico and elsewhere).

Special days on the calendar often call for special worship services, at which particular prayers may be cited or scriptures read. The Season of Lent, which commemorates the suffering and death of Jesus, is often observed with fasting or voluntary abstinence from certain foods or activities for the duration of Lent. Even Christian groups that do not follow the Liturgical Calendar usually observe at least Christmas and Easter to a greater or lesser extent. All Christians who celebrate such holidays, whether many or only a few, see them as "holy-days," times not just for rest from labor but for celebration, introspection, and spiritual renewal.

Sacred Space

The Lord is in his holy temple;

 let all the earth keep silence before him! (Hab 2:20)

For many Christians, particular locations, whether geographical or relative, have great spiritual meaning. Jerusalem is often referred to as the Holy City by Christians, and the land that today falls within the nation of Israel and the Palestinian territories is called the Holy Land. These places, as well as specific sites within them, such as the Church of the Holy Sepulcher in Jerusalem or the Cave of the Nativity in Bethlehem, are considered sacred by many Christians, because of their association with the earthly life and death of Jesus, and they are popular travel destinations for many Christians from around the world. Despite the importance that they attach to these sacred sites, Christians do not see a visit to the city of Jerusalem in the same way that Muslims might see a visit to the city of Mecca, as a sacred obligation. It is rather a place where events of great spiritual importance occurred, and many Christians hope that a visit to such a sacred site might impart a meaningful spiritual experience.

In the Middle Ages, the symbolic importance of the city of Jerusalem was evident not only in the numerous campaigns (the Crusades) that were fought to "liberate" it from its Muslim conquerors, but also in a series of maps that were drawn called Mappae Mundi (maps of the world). These maps were not drawn with correct proportions or accurate representations of land masses or water in mind. They were rather ideological representations of the world known to Europeans. Many of these maps, such as the Mappa Mundi in Hereford Cathedral in England, locate Jerusalem in the very center of the map, where it represents the center of the world, the source of divine guidance and blessing.

Relatively early in the history of Christianity other sites of special religious significance, or associated with Christian saints and especially martyrs, became destinations of pilgrimage for many Christians (the word *martyr* comes from a Greek word meaning "witness"). Chaucer's *Canterbury Tales* is set against the backdrop of a pilgrimage to Canterbury Cathedral undertaken by various travelers, who tell stories along the way to keep themselves entertained. Other great European churches were also frequented by Christian travelers on pilgrimages: Chartres Cathedral in France, St. Peter's Basilica in Rome, and Cologne Cathedral in Germany, to name a few. In modern times many Christians continue to flock to sites associated with apparitions of the Virgin Mary, including the Virgin of Guadalupe in Mexico City, Our Lady of Fatima in Portugal, and the Virgin of Medjugorje in Bosnia. Many Christians report receiving special blessings associated with these sites.

When travel to the holy lands became too dangerous during the Middle Ages, Christian leaders in various cathedrals laid out a "virtual" pilgrimage trail, or labyrinth. The most famous labyrinth was at the cathedral in Chartres. Pilgrims walked the intricate maze, laid out in a circle divided into four quadrants, praying or meditating. If the purpose of their visit to the labyrinth was repentance, they often traversed it on their knees. The center of the labyrinth represented the goal of their journey and was sometimes equated with Jerusalem.

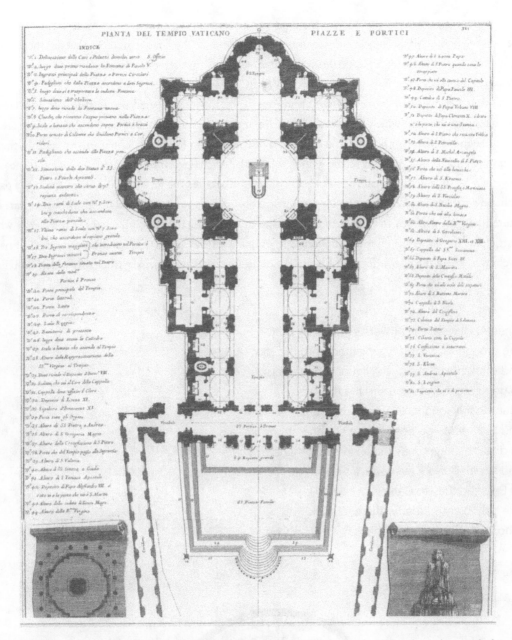

Figure 11.1 The floor plan for St. Peter's Basilica in Rome is typical of many churches, although on a larger scale than most. The central aisle (vertical) and the transept (horizontal) form the shape of a cross.

Church architecture itself is often designed with the concept of sacred space in mind. The high ceilings and tall towers of many church buildings symbolize the vertical relationship that Christians have with God—vaulted ceilings are a way of capturing a little bit of the sky, which is associated with the holy realm of heaven. Some cathedral ceilings are even painted to resemble the starry night sky, as was the ceiling of the

Sistine Chapel, before Michelangelo was commissioned to produce the famous frescoes that are there now. Other churches are built with high, vertically oriented windows that serve the dual purpose of admitting light and making the sky seem part of the sanctuary itself.

Many churches, particularly among more liturgical denominations, are laid out in the form of a cross, reminiscent of the cross on which Jesus was crucified, and the interior of the sanctuary is divided into areas of varying holiness. Many of the medieval cathedrals of Europe also follow the cruciform pattern. In these churches, the long, central portion of the church where the congregation stands or sits is called the nave. The nave may be surrounded by one or more pairs of aisles. Together, the nave and the aisles are in the part of the building that corresponds to the longer, vertical portion of the cross. The transept is in that part of the church that corresponds to the horizontal portion of the cross, and it is intended for the clergy who will participate in the service. Beyond the transept, in line with the nave, is the sanctuary, the holiest part of the church, where the altar is located. Located underneath the altar in many, particularly older, churches

When April with his showers sweet with fruit
The drought of March has pierced unto the root
And bathed each vein with liquor that has power
To generate therein and sire the flower; . . .
Then do folk long to go on pilgrimage,
And palmers to go seeking out strange strands,
To distant shrines well known in sundry lands.
And specially from every shire's end
Of England they to Canterbury wend,
The holy blessed martyr there to seek
Who helped them when they lay so ill and weak.

(Chaucer, Canterbury Tales, Prologue)

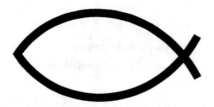

Figure 11.2 The fish is an ancient symbol used by Christians. It may have been chosen because several of Jesus' earliest followers were fishermen or because the letters of the Greek word for fish are an acronym for "Jesus Christ, God's Son, Savior."

is a crypt; many early churches were built on top of Christian holy sites, especially the graves of saints and martyrs. Twentieth-century excavations under the altar of St. Peter's Basilica in Rome confirmed ancient legends that the earliest church built on that spot (the present structure was built between the sixteenth and seventeenth centuries) was constructed on top of the grave of the apostle Simon Peter, one of Jesus' original disciples. In most Protestant churches the place of honor which is accorded to the altar in Roman Catholic and Orthodox traditions is assigned instead to the pulpit, the lectern or cabinet from which the sermon (from a Latin word meaning "word" of God) is proclaimed.

Sacred Symbols and Artefacts

From almost the beginning of the Christian movement, followers of Jesus made use of symbols to represent who they were and what they believed. Although the most widely recognized symbol in use today by Christians is the cross, the earliest Christian symbol was probably not the cross, but rather the fish. The fish may seem an unusual symbol for the religious movement that became Christianity, but early Christians recognized a number of significant parallels between the simple fish symbol and the origins of their faith. Several of Jesus' earliest disciples, including Simon Peter, had been fishermen. Stories that related how Jesus called his first disciples said that he called them from being fishermen to being "fishers of men." Several of the narratives that circulated in the early church involved fishing: Jesus' miracle of the loaves and fishes, the miraculous catch of fish, Peter's catching of a fish with a coin in its mouth, and others. Finally, the Greek word for fish, *ichthys* (ιχθυς), was used as an acronym that expressed the essence of the Christian proclamation about Jesus. The five Greek letters are the first letters of the words "Jesus Christ, God's Son, Savior." The fish symbol is attested from the last decades of the first century and may be even earlier. In settings where the observance of the Christian religion was prohibited, Christians may have identified themselves to one another by means of the simple, dual-arc fish: one Christian would draw an arc in the dirt, and if the other person was a Christian, he or she would draw the second arc and complete the diagram. The fish symbol fell out of widespread use among Christians for centuries but has been revived in recent decades—usually in the form of the simple dual-arc fish, also known as the Jesus fish—so that it is once again a popular Christian symbol.

Jesus' sayings were passed down orally among the earliest Christians, decades before the current gospels were composed. One group of sayings, many of which are recorded in the Gospel of John, are the so-called "I am" sayings, in which Jesus compares himself metaphorically to a number of things. "I am the door." "I am the light of the world." "I am the way, the truth, and the life." Perhaps the most popular "I am" statement, at least as reflected in early Christian art, was "I am the Good Shepherd." Images of Jesus as the Good Shepherd are frequently found on or near early Christian graves, which were often placed in underground burial grounds (catacombs).

Figure 11.3 In ancient Egypt, the *ankh*, a looped cross, was a symbol for life, and this meaning, together with its resemblance to other types of crosses, led to its adoption as a symbol used by Egyptian Christians. The Greek cross, with its vertical and horizontal pieces of equal length, is the version of the Christian symbol that came to be favored by the Eastern Church. The Latin cross, whose vertical segment is longer than its horizontal piece, was favored by the Western Church.

Without a doubt the most important Christian symbol throughout time has been the cross. The cross symbolizes the instrument of Jesus' death, but it also alludes to the redemptive value that Christians see in Jesus' death, and to Jesus' resurrection from the dead. Although the cross on which Jesus was crucified likely took the shape of a capital T, the shape that came to predominate in Christian symbolism more closely resembles a simple, lowercase t (Roman cross), or even a plus sign (equilateral cross), though variants abound. For example, an Egyptian variant of the cross has a loop at the top; Egyptian Christians apparently borrowed the hieroglyphic symbol for life (*ankh*) for this cross. One form of the cross used frequently by Orthodox Churches resembles a large plus sign, with smaller equilateral crosses in the four quadrants of the larger cross. Another variant of the cross, commonly associated with Roman Catholicism, is the crucifix, a Roman cross on which is placed the body of the crucified Jesus.

Other Christian symbols in general use today include the steeple, a vertical spire on church buildings pointing to the heavens, the communion cup, the fleur-de-lis (also a symbol of the Virgin Mary), and the Greek letters Alpha (A) and Omega (Ω). Many symbols are associated with particular sacred times of the Christian year, such as the following.

Christmas/Epiphany:	Star
	Creche
	Angel
	Holly
	Pomegranate
	Dove

Lent/Easter:	Crown of thorns
	INRI (Latin acronym for Jesus of Nazareth, King of the Jews)
	Lamb
	Palm branches
	Spear
Pentecost:	Fire
	Clover or shamrock
	Dove

Whereas symbols are abstract representations of particular aspects of the Christian faith that can be replicated at will, sacred artefacts—often called relics—are concrete objects that many Christians associate with a manifestation of the divine. Such artefacts are usually associated with a Christian saint, particularly a martyr, and they may be divided into two groups: body parts and other items (e.g, articles of clothing). As already noted, graves of Christian martyrs became places of pilgrimage in the early history of Christianity, and shrines and churches were frequently built over the tombs. Other churches acquired relics of the martyrs—locks of hair, fragments of bone, or teeth—and became pilgrimage destinations as well. A church's desire to attain such relics was based both on the miracles frequently attributed to the relics by the faithful and on the economic benefits that pilgrimage destinations enjoyed.

One of the most famous examples of the quest for relics was the search undertaken by Helen, the mother of the first Christian emperor Constantine, for the true cross of Jesus. After her son became emperor, she traveled to the Holy Land in search of the cross upon which Jesus was crucified. Legend says that she located three crosses in Jerusalem and identified the true cross by its healing power. Pieces of the true cross, along with nails from that cross, are alleged to exist in a number of different places.

The sacred artefact that has most occupied the imagination of Christians for the past several hundred years, primarily through fictionalized accounts of its quest in literature and film, is the Holy Grail, or the cup (or dish) from which Jesus drank at the Last Supper on the night before his crucifixion. Despite the popularity of the legend, it is apparently quite late; the first reference to the Grail is found in the medieval story of Percival, one of King Arthur's knights, written by Crétien de Troyes in the late twelfth century. Another artefact, real but apparently late medieval in origin, is the Shroud of Turin, which some identify as the burial cloth of Jesus.

Although many Christians continue to view sacred artefacts as containing some sort of spiritual power, deriving from their association with Christian saints or martyrs, other Christians see the attention paid to sacred objects as misguided, even if they are authentic relics, or even idolatrous. Another approach to such artefacts, prevalent especially among Orthodox Christians, but not limited to the Orthodox, sees them as legitimate objects of veneration, alongside works of art such as icons.

Orthodox worship often includes the veneration of icons, or sacred images. Icons are painted depictions of Jesus, Mary, the saints, or angels, usually painted in accordance with certain stylistic conventions. The difference between an icon and a painting that is a work of art is largely a matter of intent. Icons are generally produced to be used in worship, whereas typical paintings, even of religious scenes, are not. Although Christian critics of the veneration of icons often refer to the practice as worship of the images, the Orthodox make a distinction between worship, which is properly directed toward God, and veneration, which uses an icon as an aid to worship or honor the figure represented in the icon. The veneration of images, including statues of Jesus, Mary, and the saints, is also practiced in the Roman Catholic Church, though it is not as prevalent as in the Orthodox Church, particularly since the Second Vatican Council (1962–1965). However, the veneration of images continues to be popular among Catholics in many countries.

Sacred Interactions

For Christians, the primary way in which humanity encounters God is through worship. Although Christians believe that God is omnipresent (present everywhere), they believe that people come into contact with God in an especially profound way through worship. Thus, it is preferable to speak of sacred interactions between God and humans than of sacred human acts, as though humans could conjure up the divine of their own volition. Sacred acts, properly speaking, are the exclusive domain of God.

According to Matthew's gospel, Jesus told his disciples, "Wherever two or three of you are gathered together in my name, there I am in the midst of you" (Matt 18:20). While the original context of this saying indicates that it was mainly intended as a statement concerning ecclesiastical authority, the idea of Jesus' presence with Christians when they gathered for worship was generally acknowledged. Specific acts of worship such as prayer, singing, and confession of sins are directed toward God and are seen as part of the divine–human interaction that occurs in worship, especially corporate worship. The exposition of God's word, called the sermon or homily, is considered a divine–human interaction that flows in the opposite direction, from God, through the messenger, to the people of God.

For many Christians, the divine–human interaction is crystallized in a series of symbolic acts called sacraments in some traditions, ordinances in others. As the name implies, those who consider these acts sacraments (Catholics and Orthodox) see a more direct contact with the divine than do those who view them as ordinances (most Protestants). For Catholics and Orthodox, the sacraments are means through which divine grace is transmitted in a mystical way to worshipers.

The initial sacrament/ordinance which Christians receive is usually baptism, an initiation into the body of Christ. Baptism is performed only on adults and older children in some traditions and on infants in other traditions. It may consist of the sprinkling of water on the head, pouring water over the head, or total immersion. Baptism represents the new birth into the Christian life, the washing away of sins, and the believer's identity with the death, burial, and resurrection of Jesus.

The most frequently practiced sacrament/ordinance is variously called Holy Communion, the Eucharist (from a Greek word meaning "thanksgiving"), or the Lord's Supper. It consists of a symbolic meal of bread and wine, representing the body and blood of Jesus and commemorating Jesus' final meal with his disciples prior to his crucifixion. Some churches substitute wafers or another starchy food for bread, and others use non-alcoholic alternatives to wine. While most Christians who regularly attend public worship receive communion once a week, others receive it daily, while members of other traditions receive it only monthly or less frequently. In the sacramental traditions, the Eucharist is believed to impart divine grace to the recipient. The early second century bishop Ignatius of Antioch referred to it as "the medicine of immortality" (Ignatius *Eph.* 20). The Eucharist is a meal that believers in Christ share with one another and with God. For many Christians, however, it is not only a meal but also a reenactment of Jesus' sacrifice on the cross. For Roman Catholics, the bread and wine are literally transformed into the body and blood of Christ, hence their healing power. For other Christians, particularly many Protestants, the Eucharist is a memorial meal that symbolizes communion with God.

While baptism and communion are the two most commonly observed sacraments or ordinances, some Christians recognize others as well. Marriage is considered a sacrament in the Roman Catholic and Orthodox traditions, as are Holy Orders (the commitment to full-time Christian ministry), Penance/Confession, Confirmation/Chrismation, and Anointing of the Sick. Whether these sacred interactions are considered to impart grace directly, as in the sacramental traditions, or are seen as symbols of spiritual truths or mysteries, all Christians see great value in observing them.

Sacred Personages

According to the New Testament, Jesus' disciples commonly addressed him as *Lord*. Since they spoke Aramaic, the word they would have used was probably *Mar*, which is equivalent to the Hebrew *Adon*, "lord" or "master." Although God is often referred to in the Hebrew Bible as *Adon*, the word most commonly rendered "Lord" in English translations (often printed in small capitals as Lord) is the proper name for God, *YHWH*, often rendered "Yahweh" in modern discussions. However, Greek translations of the Old Testament regularly rendered both *YHWH* and *Adon* as *kyrios*, "Lord," and this word is used as well in the New Testament as an appellation for Jesus (and occasionally for other people as well). Regardless of whether the practice of using the Greek *kyrios* to render both Hebrew words originated with Jews or Christians (scholars debate this

Figure 11.4 Detail from Michelangelo's *Pietà* located in St. Peter's Basilica in Rome, which represents two of Christianity's most sacred personages, Jesus and the Virgin Mary.

point), it is clear that the early church referred to both God and Jesus as Lord, an indication that Jesus was considered to have a special relationship with God—at the very least—from the beginning.

Paul's letter to the Christians of Galatia, one of the earliest preserved Christian documents, refers to Jesus as the *Son of God*, and this appellation undoubtedly goes back to the earliest days of Christianity, although Jesus apparently did not use the term of himself (he called himself *Son of Man*, an Aramaic phrase meaning "human being," though some scholars posit a more nuanced meaning). The term Son of God could properly be applied to anyone in covenant relationship with God (e.g. Gal 3:26; John 1:12); however, referring to Jesus as *the* Son of God quickly became popular in early Christianity (cf. Mark 1:1; 15:39), and it is clear that Jesus was seen by early Christians as God's son in a unique way. In the Hebrew Bible, the term *Son of God* is often used to refer to the Davidic king (e.g. Ps 2:7), and it was used in reference to the messiah in the Second Temple period, including by the Qumran community. For Paul, the title Son of God presented Jesus' claim to be the Jewish messiah, which is equivalent to the Greek word *Christ*, another title associated with Jesus. It did not directly imply Jesus' divinity. However, other Pauline language, including his application of Old Testament references to Yahweh as applying to Jesus (e.g. Rom 10:13; Phil 2:10–11), show that Paul understood Jesus to be intimately and uniquely associated with God. If the letter to the Colossians was written by Paul (scholars

Saints in Christian tradition

The list of people considered saints is long, and differences of opinion exist among the various Christian traditions that recognize saints. All would consider Mary, the 11 disciples (minus Judas Iscariot), the Apostle Paul, and James and Jude the "brothers" of Jesus as saints. There is general agreement about many other people as well, but Catholics recognize many people not recognized by the Orthodox, and vice versa. Anglicans mostly follow the Catholics in their recognition of saints, at least those who were recognized prior to the Reformation. Some of the more interesting figures who are recognized as saints by one or more traditions are the angels Gabriel (Orthodox, Catholic) and Michael (Anglican, Orthodox, Catholic), Czar Nicholas II (Orthodox), King Charles I of England (Anglican), and Pope Pius X (Catholic), the most recent Roman Catholic Pontiff to be canonized. One Oriental Orthodox communion, the Ethiopian Orthodox Church, recognizes Pontius Pilate, the Roman governor who sentenced Jesus to death, as a saint, based on a local tradition that Pilate later converted and was martyred for his faith.

debate this point), then the comment in Col 2:9, that in Christ the whole fullness of deity dwells in bodily form, supports Paul's view of Jesus' unique relationship with God (Hurtado 2003: 101–8).

As Christianity developed in the Gentile world as the first century drew to a close, terms like *Son of God* and *Lord* lost the more nuanced meanings that they usually have in the New Testament writings themselves and became understood as direct claims of divinity. Son of God meant God, and Lord also meant God. The most explicit statements in the New Testament itself concerning the equation Jesus = God are found in the Gospel of John, the latest canonical gospel, probably written at the very end of the century. John 1:1–18 contains a hymn celebrating Jesus as the *Word* (*Logos*) of God, a Greek philosophical term that can also be rendered the *Reason* of God. The very first verse of this passage equates the Word with God. Near the end of the same gospel, the apostle Thomas, upon seeing the resurrected Jesus, cries out, "My Lord and my God!" (John 20:28). This statement is the most explicit statement in the New Testament concerning Jesus' divinity, but the idea that Jesus was somehow equal to, or part of, God was quickly established as the dominant Christian view. Although for centuries after this the church debated the exact nature of the relationship between the Son of God and God the Father, Jesus' status as a divine figure was firmly established as the official position of Christianity from this time.

If Jesus is the most important divine personage in Christian thinking and worship, the second most important figure for many Christians through the ages has been his mother Mary. The gospels of Matthew and Luke present Mary as a virgin, God's chosen vessel who gave birth to Jesus. Although the New Testament doesn't make any claims about Mary's Perpetual Virginity, the tradition that she remained a chaste virgin throughout her life was popular by the second century (Jesus' brothers and sisters, referred to in the New Testament, were assigned to Joseph and a previous wife, who died prior to his betrothal to Mary, or else they were considered cousins rather than siblings). Other traditions about Mary, including her immaculate conception (i.e. her sinlessness from the point of her own conception) and her bodily assumption into heaven, arose relatively early in the history of Christianity and are commonly accepted by many Christians today, especially Roman Catholics. The Orthodox often refer to Mary as *Theotokos*, a Greek term meaning "God bearer," roughly equivalent to "Mother of God," a term used by Catholics. Protestants, though assigning great honor to Mary as the mother of Jesus, generally reject the doctrines of Mary's perpetual virginity, immaculate conception, and bodily assumption as being unscriptural, since they arose in Christian tradition after the close of the New Testament.

In addition to Jesus and Mary, many others who lived lives of great piety, who were martyred for their faith, or who are believed to have performed miracles are identified as saints by many Christians. Saints may be defined as ordinary people who lived extraordinary lives or had extraordinary faith in God. In Catholic and Orthodox traditions, they are often treated as intercessors on behalf of living Christians, passing the requests of the faithful on to God. Although they certainly recognize the superior lives of certain believers throughout history, most Protestants do not recognize the special status of any deceased believers as saints. To be more precise, they believe that all Christians are saints, by virtue of God's grace and their relationship with God through faith in Christ. Anglicans and Lutherans, however, join Catholics and Orthodox in recognizing specific people as saints.

In addition to human men and women, Christians traditionally recognize as sacred personages the class of semi-divine beings known collectively as angels and demons. Earlier parts of the Old Testament sometimes refer to beings called "the sons of God" (Ps 29:1; Job 1:6) or even "the gods" (Pss 82:1; 138:1), among whom is "the Satan," (i.e. the Accuser; Job 1:6). By the late Second Temple period, Jewish thought had developed to the extent where leading heavenly beings allied with God (angels) were sometimes given names—Gabriel, Michael, Raphael, Uriel—as were leading evil beings (demons)—Satan, Asmodeus, Beelzebub. Gabriel, Michael, and Satan are all mentioned in the New Testament, which also includes numerous references to unnamed angels and demons, as well as other spiritual powers (see, e.g. 1 Cor 15:24; Eph 1:21). Christian art and literature is full of references to angels and demons, and many Christians today from all traditions continue to accept these beings as playing a part in life on this planet, albeit usually behind the scenes. Other Christians see these beings as mythological expressions of supernatural power, good and evil.

Sacred Metatime

Abandon all hope, you who enter here.

(Words over the gate to hell in Dante's *Inferno*)

Our earlier discussion of sacred time focused on recurring days of special significance throughout the week (Sunday) or within the Christian year (e.g. Advent, Christmas, Easter). These sacred times are based on the cycle of the seasons and the rhythm of the earth as it journeys around the sun once a year. Despite recognizing these cyclical events, however, Christianity has a profoundly linear view of history, with a distinct beginning and end. These events are, strictly speaking, considered to be outside of time, so they may be referred to as sacred metatime.

The Christian doctrine of the beginning of the earth and/or universe is often called *cosmogony*, from Greek words that mean "beginning of the world." Both the Old and the New Testaments refer to the beginning as a unique act of God, but it is the first chapter of Genesis that most fully describes the events of creation. Though many Christians take this passage in a more or less literal sense, most Christians recognize the mythological character of the language. The creation of the universe, and specifically of the earth and its inhabitants, is described as taking place over six days. The basic structures of the universe, as seen from the perspective of earth, are described: heaven and earth; sun, moon, and stars; waters above the vault of the sky (i.e. the source of rain) and waters below (i.e. rivers, seas, etc.). The immovable boundaries of the earth are similarly detailed: light and dark; dry land and sea; individual species of animals. A modern, scientific understanding of the origins of the universe and of life on earth does not match a literal reading of the first chapter of Genesis, but they present no difficulty to a mythological reading. From this perspective, the God who is responsible for the creation of the world and its inhabitants is the same God who called Abraham out of Ur, spoke to Moses in the burning bush, and was the Father of Jesus Christ. Creation is not self-sufficient or self-organizing. It owes its very existence to God.

Just as the beginning of the universe falls outside the scope of normal time, so too does the end of the world. The Christian doctrine of the end of the world, or *eschatology* ("the study of last things"), is described in the New Testament in various ways: kingdom of God, end of the age, Parousia (Second Coming of Christ), new heaven and new earth. At some point in history, God will intervene in the natural course of events and bring them to an end. This intervention is not the result of the natural development of history, so it cannot be predicted by futurologists. Though some Christians believe that they recognize in certain current events signs that the end of the world is coming soon, most understand that Christians throughout history have thought the same thing, so the eschaton is completely unpredictable. As is the case with biblical descriptions of the beginning of the world, so biblical descriptions of the end of the world are couched in mythological language. The book of Revelation is the classic example of the use of complex imagery and figurative language to describe the events leading to the end of the age. Other parts of the New Testament that describe the end include 1 Thes 5:1–11; Mark 13 (and parallels in Matthew and Luke); and 2 Pet 3:8–10. Events leading up to the end of the world include war, earthquakes, and unusual meteorological phenomena, though at other times the end is projected to come suddenly, "like a thief in the night." The end itself is described as including the total destruction of the earth by fire, the resurrection of the dead, a final judgment, the physical return of Jesus, and the creation of a new heaven and a new earth. That these descriptions are not totally consistent with one another is a reminder that the biblical writers used conventional, sometimes mythological, language to describe the expected end of history.

In addition to creation and the eschaton, another type of sacred metatime involves the disposition of the souls of the dead in the interim between the present and the end of the age. The predominant view in the Hebrew Bible concerning the state of the departed was that they occupied a place called *Sheol*, a place of darkness and lack of knowledge, isolated from God, similar to the Greek concept of Hades. At some point in the Second Temple period, however, the idea of a differentiated judgment arose. The dead would ultimately be raised and judged according to their deeds, with the good taken to be with God and the wicked forever separated from God (see Dan 12:1–2). By New Testament times, the predominant Jewish position was that the righteous dead would eventually be raised to eternal life in *heaven* with God, while the wicked would be cast into a place of eternal torment, *hell*, along with Satan and his demons. This, at least, was the view of the Pharisees, as well as of Jesus and his disciples. Since the Pharisaic party formed the basis for Rabbinic Judaism, which survived the fall of Jerusalem (70 C.E.) and two Jewish rebellions against Rome (66–73 C.E. and 132–135 C.E.), a common belief in heaven and hell as the destination of the dead was shared by Jews and Christians. Some Christians believed that departed believers entered a state of unconsciousness, or sleep, until they were awakened for the final judgment. Others believed that souls were sent immediately to either heaven or hell, and the final judgment was merely a confirmation of their reward or punishment.

As Christianity developed in the second and subsequent centuries, the concept of *soul-sleep* was set aside by the vast majority of Christians, who believed that the dead went immediately to their place of reward or punishment, according to their faith and their deeds. By the beginning of the third century, many Christian scholars posited a third possible destination for the souls of the dead: *purgatory*. The word purgatory comes from a Latin word meaning "cleansing," and purgatory came to be seen as the destination of the majority of Christians, those who died with unconfessed venial (minor) sins or who had not experienced the full punishment for their sins while on earth. Those Christians who accepted the doctrine of purgatory believed that the wicked went directly to hell, the saints directly to heaven, and the vast majority of Christians to purgatory for a varying period of time, where they would suffer punishment in accordance with their sins, before eventually being allowed to enter heaven. In the early fourteenth century, Dante Alighieri, a native of Florence, wrote an imaginative description of hell, purgatory, and heaven that has shaped the view of many people since that time: *The Divine Comedy*. Today the doctrine of purgatory is accepted primarily by Roman Catholics. It is rejected by Orthodox and Protestant Christians. The doctrine of soul-sleep has been revived in relatively modern times by some groups of Anabaptists and by Seventh-day Adventists. Some Christians subscribe to the idea of *annihilationism*, in which the righteous dead live forever in heaven, while the souls of the unrighteous are destroyed, rather than condemned to an eternity of torture in hell. Still others are *universalists*, who believe that all people, regardless of their deeds while on earth, will eventually be reunited with God. In regard to the exact nature of existence in the afterlife, Christians are divided between those who look for a resurrection of the physical body (the traditional view) and those who do not.

Key points you need to know

- Christian perspectives on God vary from seeing God as a supernatural being to seeing God as the ground of being.

- Rudolf Otto described the Holy (or Sacred) as something that is at the same time terrifying and fascinating, a description that fits well with Christians' views of God.

- Most Christians recognize different seasons of the Christian year, beginning with Advent (in late autumn) and proceeding through seasons such as Christmas, Epiphany, Lent, and Eastertide. Other Christians only recognize Sunday, or in some cases Saturday, as a day that is special.

- Many Christians consider places such as sites associated with Jesus (e.g. the Cave of the Nativity in Bethlehem or the Church of the Holy Sepulcher in Jerusalem) as sacred. Others consider some of the great cathedrals around the world to be sacred. Church buildings themselves, or parts of the buildings such as the altar, are often considered sacred as well.

- Although the most important symbol of Christianity throughout history has been the cross, the earliest sacred symbol was probably the fish.

- Relics of the saints, icons, and other objects like the Shroud of Turin are considered sacred by many Christians.

- Although Christians believe that God is everywhere, they most frequently experience encounters with God in worship, especially corporate worship. In many Christian traditions, sacred rituals knows as sacraments or mysteries are important ways in which Christians may encounter the divine.

- For Christians, the most important and universally acknowledged sacred personage is Jesus Christ. Many Christians also acknowledge the holiness of specific saints, particularly Mary the mother of Jesus, and of angels.

- Christians have a linear view of time, so they believe it has a definite beginning (the act of creation) and end (the eschaton). Beyond these boundaries is eternity, which encompasses heaven, hell, and, for Roman Catholics, purgatory. Some Christians, however, deny the existence of hell as a place of permanent torment for the wicked.

Discussion Questions

1. Why is the distinction between sacred and profane necessary in Christianity?
2. What makes a place sacred? Can sacred places be moved elsewhere and retain their holiness (e.g. moving a cathedral stone by stone or moving the ground upon which an important event occurred)?
3. What is the difference between veneration and worship of an object?
4. Why is the sacrament of communion so important for many Christians?
5. How does the concept of sacred metatime fit into the scientific worldview, which proposes both a Big Bang at the beginning of the universe and an eventual dissipation of the universe's energy as the stars burn out?

Further Reading

Bradner, John 1977. *Symbols of Church Seasons and Days*. Harrisburg, PA: Morehouse.

Bruyneel, Sally and Alan G. Padgett 2003. *Introducing Christianity*. Maryknoll, NY: Orbis.

Eliade, Mircea 1959. *The Sacred and the Profane: The Nature of Religion*. Translated by Willard R. Trask. New York: Harcourt, Brace & World.

Hurtado, Larry W. 2003. *Lord Jesus Christ: Devotion to Jesus in Earliest Christianity*. Grand Rapids, MI: Eerdmans.

Otto, Rudolf 1958. *The Idea of the Holy*. Translated by John W. Harvey. New York: Oxford University Press.

Figure Credits

12 Islam and God

Oliver Leaman

The Qur'an

Proofs of the existence of God are frequently to be found in Islam, starting with the Qur'an itself. The Qur'an sees itself as a rational and not a poetic work, although the language is often remarkably beautiful, inviting its readers or hearers to think, reflect and ponder. The most significant of these of course is that there is a God who created the world, and we can come to accept this by looking at that world in the right sort of way. The argument here is not demanding, and invites us to look at nature and then consider how it came about, and the answer is that God made it. We can call these arguments informal, and they have proved very popular in the modern Islamic world. What they bring out quite nicely though is that for most Muslims questioning the existence of God is regarded as wildly implausible, since it is so obvious that he exists.

There has arisen a sort of popular Islam which seeks to oppose the secularism of the modern world by producing evocative but weak arguments in favor of the existence of God. While these arguments hark back to the Qur'an, they really do not represent it adequately. Their arguments tend to be rhetorical in the sense that they work from Qur'anic passages and *ahadith* to build up a religious picture of the world, and then compare that with a materialist interpretation of the same state of affairs, which is invariably thinner by contrast, and invite the reader to choose.

There are some definite arguments in the Qur'an for the existence of God and in particular for the existence of just one God. At 21.22 we are told that if there were more than one God, the heavens and earth would be confused, presumably because the different gods would all be doing different and uncoordinated things. It is not obvious why the different deities could not work together. It might even be said that our experience of the world provides more evidence of such variety of governing forces than the reverse. 6.75–8 provides an account of Abraham's thinking when he watches the planets and thinks they are variously in charge of the world, revising his beliefs all the time as their lights wax and wane. Even the sun proves to be insufficient, and Abraham concludes that the cause of the world cannot be in it, it cannot be something that is associated with other physical things but must be some unique being that is behind everything that happens. This leads him to monotheism, and the particular type of monotheism put forward in the Qur'an. Despite the beauty of the passage in which this argument is found, the argument itself is not particularly strong. Once philosophers got working on these issues they tried to present more rigorous approaches to the topic.

Philosophical Arguments for the Existence of God

The most common is some version of the cosmological argument, which all basically stipulate that the existence of the world can be traced back to an ultimate cause, and this series of events cannot proceed indefinitely and must stop at a "first cause," God the creator. Another argument is broadly called ontological, and argues that since we can conceive of a God that is in our minds and is the greatest being that can be conceived of, either it exists only in thought or also in reality, but since the latter is a superior existence or possibility to the former, this "greatest being" must exist in thought and in reality as well as in thought. Then there are arguments broadly from design, which fit in nicely with the Qur'an, where we observe all the wonderful complexity and harmony of creation and conclude that a supremely powerful, kind, and wise creator is behind it all. Finally there are proofs which are based on personal spiritual experience. Some arguments combine a variety of these features.

A problem that the early philosophers had was that while the theological vocabulary of Islam was well developed right from the start, the philosophical vocabulary was not. This had to be created as texts were translated and translators struggled to find Arabic equivalents for the language they were translating out of. One of the most energetic sources of proofs for the existence of God is Ibn Sina (Avicenna) who created a rich ontological vocabulary based very much on the pioneering work of al-Farabi. He discusses two kinds of existence to distinguish between the divine and the mortal, between the necessary and the merely possible, and something which is possible requires something else to bring it into actual existence. If it is only possible

181

then something must happen to move it from just being possible to being actual. Not everything can be possible in the sense of depending on something else to bring it into existence. If everything could, there would be an infinite regress, there has to be something that is more than possible, but actually necessary, to be at the basis of the whole series of existing things and get them moved from possibility to actuality. Whatever it is that makes the possible actual, it itself requires something to bring it into existence, and so we continue until we reach the ultimate cause, the one thing that brings everything into existence and does not itself require anything to bring it into existence, a being which necessitates its own existence and does not require a cause. In any case, if we think of a being with necessary existence we cannot think of it as not existing, since if we could think of it as not existing it cannot be the concept of something necessarily existing.

These fairly brief remarks by Ibn Sina have been built on a great deal in Islamic philosophy, and Tusi distinguishes between three sorts of argument that can be derived from Ibn Sina's remarks in the *Metaphysics* section of his *al-Shifa*, and these are the *kalam* cosmological argument, the proof from motion that derives from Aristotle's *Physics*, and an ontological argument. The last argument has the highest status and Ibn Sina himself calls it the *burhan al-siddiqin*, the proof of the veracious. Mulla Sadra develops the argument into what he calls the way of the veracious (*sabil al-siddiqin*). What he means by *siddiq* is not the same as Ibn Sina and the gap in meaning is a good illustration of the difference in their philosophical method. For Mulla Sadra, the *siddiq* is one who possesses inner religious experience that is achieved through grace and spiritual exercise. In the exegesis of 57.19 on the phrase "those who believe in God and His messengers are the veracious ones and witness before their Lord," he argues that the *siddiq* is characterized by witnessing the truth through inner revelation. It is not just a matter of coming to grasp a theoretical argument but also involves personal feelings and insights. This is more than just an intellectual achievement. It represents the result of inner mystical revelation (*kashf*) and the overcoming of the body and its influence on us, all aspects of having been on a serious and successful Sufi path.

Ibn Sina's argument was insufficient in part because Mulla Sadra disapproved of his prioritizing essence over existence. There was a protracted dispute in Islamic philosophy as to whether existence or essence is the basic ontological concept. Some thinkers argued that we should start by looking at the things which actually exist, and work from there to discuss the concepts we can form of them and of other things also, such as things we can only imagine. Others took the opposite line, and started with concepts, some of which encompass existing things and some which deal with objects in a wider sense. One can see advantages and disadvantages in both approaches. Mulla Sadra saw Ibn Sina as avoiding the concrete reality of being and remaining stuck in the realm of ideas. Existence is a concrete reality that is simple and unique. There is no distinction among its individuals essentially except in terms of degrees of perfection and imperfection and intensity and weakness. Journey III of the *Four Journeys* begins with a discussion of the ways of proving the existence of God. Having noted previous cosmological and ontological proofs, Mulla Sadra expresses his own "method of the veracious" (*manhaj al-siddiqin*). This is based on the reality of existence (*haqiqat al-wujud*), which is simple (*amran basitan*), and so without an essence or a constituent property or a means of being defined. It is identical to the necessary, requiring the most complete perfection that is infinitely intense, because every other degree of existence, which is weaker in intensity, is below the level of the pure reality of existence.

Apart from the necessary being, everything else is lacking since it is deprived, to a degree, of perfection. Its existence is limited.

The argument goes like this:

1. There is existence.
2. Existence in its purest form is a perfection and cannot be refined further as an idea.
3. God is perfection and by definition is also an actualized perfection.
4. Existence is a reality.
5. That reality is graded in intensity in a scale of perfection, so most examples of it are not completely simple.
6. The continuum of existence must have a limit point, a point of greatest intensity and of greatest existence.
7. That extreme point is equivalent to God, who then must exist.

Thus the proof begins with the concept and reality of existence and of God and ends with it. Given Mulla Sadra's enthusiasm for the role of existence, this is entirely appropriate. It seems to be a type of ontological proof, and so tautological. Even Mulla Sadra is not that happy with it, and he argues that the reality of existence is so rich that it eludes human ability to confine it to discourse through description. It is not surprising then that he calls it a *manhaj al-siddiqin* or way to the truth and not strictly speaking a demonstrative proof. This is well understood in contemporary Islamic theology, and Tabataba'i suggests that Mulla Sadra does not provide a demonstration because in effect all proofs for the existence of God begin with his effects and deduce his existence as the cause of those effects. This is because existence is an a priori intuition that all sound intellects possess and, within that intuition, the existence of a Necessary Being is logically necessary in the sense that it is something we cannot deny. Proofs for the existence of God, therefore, are not attempts at producing demonstrations that convince but are mere reminders to what we already know through experience. They merely confirm what information we already possess. This brings out nicely the ways in which many leading Muslim thinkers do not take seriously the prospect of atheism.

Some Arguments from Contingency

In Islamic theology two types of argument proved to be very popular, the argument from particularization (*takhsis*) and through tipping the scales (*tarjih*). Al-Juwayni produces a good example of the former, when he argues that since the world could have been created at any time at all, the fact that it was created at a particular time and in a particular way demonstrates that someone must have made the decision to create it thus. This form of argument is based no doubt on Ibn Sina's notion of contingency, whereby something is always needed to bring the possibly existent into actual existence. This cause must eventually be linked with a necessary existent, something that can bring the line of causes and effects to an end. Ibn Sina himself would not have accepted that the proof shows that the world was created in time, something for which he was attacked later on by al-Ghazali. For Ibn Sina the world could not be created in time since that would presuppose an infinite regress of causes of creation. Al-Ghazali rejected this in favor of the view that since any moment of time before the existence of the world is indistinguishable from any other, there must be an agent who tips the scales (*tarjih*) in favor of a particular time and creates the world then (Leaman 2001: 55–77, Leaman 2009: 24–6). A variation of this theme can be found in Ibn al-'Arabi who uses the Qur'anic notion of the *barzakh* (25.53) or limit to explain how things can be composed of two different sorts of entities which would normally be expected to be incompatible, or destroy each other. Yet they coexist within a particular event, the creation of something, and that can only be possible if someone brings that about, and in that specific way, and that creator is ultimately God. Were it not for God there could be no explanation for how such incompatible things could get together and result in something else.

Ibn Rushd follows what he takes to be Aristotle's approach to the proof for the existence of God, arguing that there must be a first cause to avoid the existence of an infinite regress of causes. Apart from it, every other cause is also an effect in a long and complex series. There must be something at the source of the series to start it off without itself being in the series.

The *Kalam* Cosmological Argument

One form of the cosmological argument has recently been revived in the Anglo-American philosophical sphere by William Lane Craig and called the *kalam* cosmological argument (nicely described in Meister 2009: 76–83). The crucial starting point of the argument is that the world is finite and so requires a cause.

1. Everything that has a beginning of its existence has a cause of its existence.
2. The universe has a beginning of its existence.

Therefore:

3. The universe has a cause of some kind of its existence.
4. If the universe has a cause of its existence then that cause is either God or something impersonal.
5. The cause of the universe is not impersonal

Therefore:

6.   The cause of the universe is a God who exists.

What makes the title of this argument very appropriate is the fact that it does accurately represent the ways in which many of the philosophers in the Islamic world challenged strenuously the Aristotelian thesis that the world has no beginning and so is infinite, which was then the main cosmological view of philosophy. The modern argument is particularly interested in theories of the creation of the universe such as Big Bang which do indeed suggest that the universe had a start at some point, which of course also fits in nicely with the theistic principle embedded in most understandings of the Qur'an. The argument is valid as it stands but the question is whether the premises are true.

One aspect of the argument that has been much examined is the idea that the world has to have a beginning and cannot go into the past forever. We tend to think that an infinite series going back into the past is inconceivable. In any case, there are theories which we accept today such as the second law of thermodynamics according to which energy decreases over time, and so things must have started at some point for them to reach the present level with which we are familiar. In any case, the increasing popularity of the Big Bang theory of the creation of the universe does suggest a start at some point, and this also fits in nicely with the *kalam* cosmological argument. But the important issue is whether we have to posit a personal creator as at the source of such a creation. The idea of the original event occurring all by itself seems mysterious, and solving it with God causing the world to come into existence fits in nicely with Islam. What caused God to do this, though? Nothing, he did it freely and of his own accord, and not in a way that was determined by anything prior to him. Then of course we have an example of an uncaused cause, which is what the argument suggests we cannot have, but perhaps this only works for God, given his uniqueness. This seems to beg the question, though, or at the very least explains the creation of the world by asking us to believe something that is difficult to understand.

Arguments from Design

The teleological/design argument has also been used by a number of classical Muslim thinkers who see it as following the various scriptural passages that point to a purpose that God has in creating the world (21.16). Not only is there a purpose but it can be observed when looking at the world in the right sort of way.

Probably the earliest version of it goes back to al-Kindi who suggested that the orderly and wonderful phenomena of nature could not be purposeless and accidental. Al-Baqillani expressed the argument thus: the world must have a maker and a fashioner (*muhdith wa musawwir*) just as writing must have a writer, a picture must have a painter, and a building a builder. This sort of argument is frequently referred to in both Islamic philosophy and theology. In his short *Decisive Treatise*, Ibn Rushd begins his demonstration of the lawfulness of doing philosophy, for those who are capable of it, by defining philosophy as the discovery of the meaning of the world in terms of how it is organized and who set it in motion. In his *Kashf* he refers to the order of creation as providing evidence of the existence of a creator. It is the order of creation that establishes the need for a creator and so rules out the suggestion it could have come about through natural processes alone. The argument is that the organization of the world is evidence of the existence of a creator who decided it should take that shape, and it is not possible for the world to have come about in any other way. His differences from the theologians are that they tend to argue from the principle that the nature of existence is constructed by someone outside nature, while Ibn Rushd goes further and argues that the more one understands the structure of the natural world, the more certain one can be that it originates with a creator. The philosopher then understands the nature not only of the world but also its links with God better than the theologian who really only establishes a link between the world and a creator, without really understanding the nature of that link, since they do not really understand much about the nature of the order that persists naturally.

He has a point in that the Ash'arites were so concerned to emphasize the power of God over everything that happens that they reinterpret the organization of nature as just what God does, since they regard it as the result of divine action. God does not have to create the world in a particular way, for our benefit for example, or for his. On the contrary, God could have created it in any way he wanted to so for them it is just the fact of creation that points to a creator, as al-Baqillani suggests. Yet Ibn Rushd suggests with some justification that noting the organization of creation, its apparent providence, works as an argument both for the public at large and for those who are able, through their understanding of science, to appreciate the finer details of the nature of creation, i.e. natural science. That is why the pursuit of philosophy is lawful in Islam on his view, it helps us elucidate the nature of the world that logically leads to the idea and explanation of the role of the creation. In fact, he goes further and suggests that philosophy must be used by those capable of employing it since it provides the only clear and certain route to the truth concerning its subject matter.

The Divine Attributes and the Unity Of God

The early theologians in Islam were interested in a number of issues relating to God, in particular the reconciliation of the rather anthropomorphic language sometimes used in the Qur'an and the insistence in Islam on the unity of God and his distinctness from anything material. Yet the Book refers to God sitting on a throne and so on, and this gives rise to the familiar problems in reconciling physical imagery with a non-physical subject. The God of Islam is taken to be perfectly and only one and this is repeated several times a day in the prayers, in the phrase "there is no God except God and Muhammad is his messenger." Although the Arabic term *Allah* has no plurals, the term which it comes from, *al-ilah*, does, referring to deities, and in pre-Islamic Arabia there were many religions that believed in gods, and also some that believed in just one God. In pre-Islamic Mecca the Ka'ba site was the home of both the gods and God himself, as we are told in the Qur'an, and the main and obvious difference between them seems to have been that God was not represented physically while the gods were. The gods were presumably not difficult to describe since they were physically there in front of their worshippers, or their representatives were, but God himself is more mysterious, since he is immaterial. Muslims are constantly warned not to try to define him, but rather to concentrate on understanding him through concentrating on his effects.

One of the approved paths to thinking about God is meditation on his names, of which there are often taken to be 99, although this number is not actually mentioned in the Qur'an, and there are other calculations also. There is a passage at 59.22–4 which mentions around 15 names but some argue that a careful analysis of the Qur'an will yield 99 and yet more names (7.180, 17.110, 20.8). The theology before the time of the Prophet is not easy to describe from what we know now, but perhaps it was taken to be God himself who rules and organizes everything (10.31, 39.38), while the lesser gods did the lighter lifting. Even when polluted by polytheism the Ka'ba was regarded as significant by the Qur'an, and the attack with an elephant of the Ethiopian king Abraha, a Christian ruler, was defeated by divine intervention through flying insects (105.1–2). *Sura*s 105 and 106 speak with some respect of the ceremonies that surrounded the structure, even though they were not at all monotheistic, perhaps recalling the time of the origins of the building at the time of Abraham and Ishmael. This location is taken to be originally used for the purest forms of worship that the Prophet was sent to re-establish. The Qur'an fiercely rejects the idea that the gods are required to act as mediators between humanity and God himself (10.18), an idea which comes to be classified as *shirk* or idolatry, quite appropriately, and to interfere with the transcendence of the one God. On the other hand, there are some fairly approving references in the Qur'an to lesser beings, which may be believed in provided that they are regarded firmly as God's creatures and not independent of him or indeed as providing independent channels to him.

Perhaps one of the innovations that Islam makes is to identify God with the God of Judaism and Christianity, and so linked with Abraham, Moses, and Jesus. This is the God of the Quraysh, Muhammad's tribe and the controllers of the lucrative Mecca pilgrimage business. But the trouble here is that the divine attributes can only really be linked through human understanding and so are limited compared to the perfect way in which they are exemplified in the deity himself. It also means that we might think we know what God is like, and then we think we know who he is, and yet the nature of God is far beyond our understanding. This is nicely captured by the suggestion by many theologians that we just have to accept what we read in the Qur'an without really understanding what it means, *bi la kayfa*, as the Arabic goes. So we are famously told that God sits on a throne, but we have no idea how he could do this, since he has no body. We just have to believe it without understanding what it really means or how it could be done.

The most concise definition of God in Islam is given in the four verses of *sura Ikhlas* which is Chapter 112 of the Qur'an: "Say: 'He is God, one and only. God, the eternal, absolute. He begets not, nor is He begotten. And there is none like Him'" (112.1–4). This is often recited during important ceremonies or at crucial life stages, and it is a particularly fine piece of linguistic expression, economical and yet at the same time suggestive. The principle of *tawhid*, the unity of God, is difficult to make clear since so much of our lives and experience is diverse and out of harmony with the notion of complete unity. The Qur'an accordingly goes into a lot of detail on what divine unity means in various places, and why it is so important. The theme is that this original belief in one God had been corrupted over time until at the time of the Prophet many gods were worshipped in Arabia, and the Arabs in particular tended to associate the one God with other deities. The final message of the Qur'an is designed to replace this new set of beliefs and practices with a revived monotheism. The aim is to get humanity back to where it was in the past and provide the last in the long series of revelations.

We are told: "No vision can grasp Him but his grasp is over all vision: He is above all comprehension, yet is acquainted with all things" (6.103). This is the familiar problem with describing a being in terms we can understand while not allowing those terms to limit him in our conception in unacceptable ways. If we say that we cannot describe him then it looks as though we cannot talk about him, nor his properties, and then it is difficult to know what it means to use the name, or to say that he is one. Yet the Qur'an tells us a lot about God, for instance that he is constantly just: "God is never unjust in the least degree" (4.40), never gets things wrong or forgets: "My Lord never errs or forgets" (20.52), and God has power over all things (2.106; 2.109; 2.284; 3.29; 16.77; and 35.1). "God is the doer of all that He intends" (85.16) expresses this nicely. So we have some ideas about God here which makes him a bit like us, in the sense that like us he knows things and can do things he wants to do, but unlike us he never makes mistakes and there is nothing he cannot do, and this looks like a difference of degree, not kind. Ibn Taymiyya (*al-ʿAqida al-wasitiyya*) argues that what we should believe is that we can appropriately predicate of God what he has predicated of himself or what the Prophet has predicated of him, without changing it in any way (*tahrif*), or draining it of content (*taʿtil*) or saying anything about its modality (*takyif*) or imagining it on the pattern of anything else (*tamthil*). It is not correct to liken his properties to the attributes of his creatures. "There is nothing like him, though he is hearing and seeing" (42.11). There is absolutely nothing like him, either in his essence or in his attributes or in his acts. The interesting question is how it is possible to understand this.

God's Names

We are told:

> And to God belong the most beautiful names, so call on Him by them. And keep apart from those who practice deviation [*ilhad*] concerning his names. They will be recompensed for what they do.

> (7.180)

A plausible meaning of *ilhad* is to incline, to turn aside. It is used in this and other contexts to denote inclining toward some falsehood. This includes giving him inappropriate names, to deny (*taʿtil*) or distort their meanings (*tahrif*, *ta'wil*), or claim they have no meaning (*tafwid*), to consider them to be like human attributes (*tajsim*, *tamthil*, *tashbih*), to name idols or other beings with the names of God or their derivatives from the beautiful names, such as al-'Uzza from al-'Aziz, al-Manat from al-Mannan, and so on.

One way of exploring the unity idea is by criticizing alternatives such as the idea that there could be other deities in existence along with the one God: "If there were, in the heavens and the earth, other gods besides God, there would have been confusion in both!" (21.22). This is the argument that a multiplicity of gods would bring about disharmony in the running of the world. We shall return to it on a number of occasions. It might be said as an objection that our experience of the world is more in line with the existence of many gods, since for many people there is confusion in the heavens and the earth. Terrible things happen for no apparent reason, prayer often seems to have no effect on our future during this world, and the idea that the world is controlled by arbitrary divine forces who are often in conflict with each other seems quite plausible. We could then provide some account of how the gods disagree with each other, pick favorites and have affairs amongst themselves and others which impinge on our lives, rather like the gods in the Greek myths, and use that as the background to explain the activities of the heavens and the earth with which we are familiar.

The Qur'an has no patience with such a view. If there were more than one God, they would have taken away what they created, disagreed among themselves about what to create, leading to confusion (23.91). It is not clear why this is so, since there need not be a survival of the fittest rule among the gods. The more powerful gods could have coexisted with the weaker, that is what happens with the Greek gods. The idea is that what one god did another god could undo, and that is true, and they did according to the myths. Homer in his account of the Trojan campaign and the return of Odysseus to his home afterwards speaks of the ways in which the different gods supported different individuals, right from the start of the conflict which was started by Paris engaging the support of one deity at the expense of hostility from others. The Greek fleet was only allowed to set off when a particularly gruesome sacrifice was made to a god, that of the commander's daughter, and it was the role of the soothsayers to divine the wishes of the gods and try to find ways of assuaging them and bringing them on side. One of the delights of Homer is that he makes this sequence of events very plausible, not in the sense that we necessarily believe that they happened like that, but that they could have, and we can imagine different powerful deities supporting different people and seeing them as playing out a role in their disputes with other gods. In fact, our experience is often of things happening which could accord with this, disasters suddenly occur for no apparent reason, successes also. Perhaps there is some drama going on in heaven which has an effect on this world and is inexplicable to us but needs to be addressed by the carrying out of religious rituals such as sacrifices to particular divine beings whom we hope will support our cause.

The Qur'an rules out such a possibility: "Say: 'Who is it that sustains you from the sky and from the earth? Or who is it that has power over hearing and sight? And who is it that brings the living out from the dead and the dead from the living? And who is it that rules and regulates all affairs?' They will soon say, 'God'. Say, 'Will you not then show piety?'" (10.31). A similar example is repeated in *Sura* Zukhruf: "If you ask them who created them, they will certainly say, 'God': how then are they deluded?" (43.87). The pagan Meccans knew that God was their creator but they were not Muslims because they also worshipped other gods besides God. God categorized them as *kuffar* (disbelievers) and *mushrikun* (idol worshippers and those who associate partners with God) (12.106).

So the argument is that the other candidates for divinity are powerless and there is no point in praying to them. They can do nothing on our behalf.

The two names which are frequently applied to God are *al-rahman* and *al-rahim*, the compassionate, the merciful, and these might be taken to be his outstanding characteristics that control many of the others. At one stage it is likely that the Arabs found the use of the name *al-rahman* confusing, wondering how it connected up with their conception of Allah, since we find in the Qur'an at 17.110 "Pray to Allah or pray to *al-Rahman*, whichever you call upon, to him belong the beautiful names." Muslims frequently invoke the name of God in a formula before initiating action or just in reacting to news and greeting others. Every *sura* except one (9) starts with the phrase: "In the name of God, the merciful, the compassionate."

Some argued that the divine attributes were themselves created by God, so as not to interfere with divine unity, while others that they really coexisted with him. If the Qur'an was created by him then he was its author, while others in what turned out to be the more popular view took the line that it was eternal. This led to a protracted debate on whether God controlled everything in the world, or whether there was some scope for human freedom. The debate also discussed whether God was obliged to do what is good and right, and act in our interests, or whether whatever he does is by definition good and right. No independent principles of morality can be regarded as governing his actions, since this would be to detract from his perfection and omnipotence, the Ash'arites argued. Their view prevailed, as did their suggestion that really God controls everything that happens in the world and the only reason it does not seem to be thus is because we appear to acquire (*kasb*) what he does. This interpretation fits in nicely with the stress in the earlier verses of the Qur'an of divine *rububiyya* (sovereignty) and absolute rule. Divine knowledge extends to every leaf that falls (6.59) and the conception of every woman (35.11). One of the constant themes of the Qur'an is the significance of the afterlife and our punishment and/or reward there, and God's role in distinguishing between who deserve to go where. A range of attributes is mentioned which mean that we must both fear God and hope for his forgiveness, expect to be tested by him and also hope to receive his mercy. As we shall see, there are a variety of ways of interpreting these principles also.

Further reading

Corbin 1993, Craig 1979, 1993, Davidson 1968, 1987, Genequand 1984, al-Ghazali 1997, Leaman 2001, 2009, Mayer 2001, Meister 2009, Morewedge 1979, Mulla Sadra 1981.